A Life of
Magic

HEATHER KRISTIAN STRANG

Lord, make me an instrument of thy peace.
Where there is hatred, let me sow love;
Where there is injury, pardon;
Where there is doubt, faith;
Where there is despair, hope;
Where there is darkness, light;
Where there is sadness, joy.
O Divine Master, grant that I may not so much seek
To be consoled as to console,
To be understood, as to understand,
To be loved as to love;
For it is in giving that we receive;
It is in pardoning that we are pardoned;
It is in dying that we are born to eternal life.
-Prayer of St. Francis

Ask, and it shall be given you; seek, and ye shall find; knock, and it shall be opened unto you: For every one that asketh receiveth; and he that seeketh findeth; and to him that knocketh it shall be opened.
-*Jesus Christ*, Matthew 7:7,8

INTRODUCTION: WHO ARE THE JOGS ANYWAY?

At a workshop in the Spring of 2008, I had a conversation that changed my life forever. There, I was told for the first time about the healer John of God in Brazil.

Instantly, I knew I had to go to Brazil to see him. It was one of the first times I can recount that my intuition took over immediately, and as I would soon learn, it would not be the last.

I had been sick for some time, and despite having surgery via Western medicine for a cystic tumor on my ovary (which they had pronounced as benign) and trying every form of medicine I could get my hands on – from Reiki to acupuncture to naturopathic care to medical intuitives – I was not getting better. In fact, it seemed as though I was getting worse.

And so, even though I had a trip that summer planned for Paris, I scrapped it all to go see John of God in Brazil. I couldn't explain it, but I knew I had to go and I had to go right away. I felt a deep urgency within me that pushed me forward – receiving a psychic surgery from John of God was mandatory for me, I simply knew it.

Almost immediately upon booking the trip, I began having dreams about John of God or JOG (as I began to lovingly refer to him) and I knew with each passing day that I was meant to be in Brazil and in front of John of God.

I had no idea consciously just how paramount this experience would be – and the ripple effect that would carry on throughout the rest of my life.

And how could I have? I had been raised in an extreme fundamentalist religion, which some would classify as a cult, of the Jehovah's Witnesses and my "beliefs" about God were limited to the white-man on a throne variety, along with the fear of the Devil and Spirits. By the time I visited John of God in Brazil I had fully abandoned these ideologies. I had spent several years previously self-studying most of the world's religions and settled uncomfortably on agnosticism – sure that a Higher Power existed but completely unsure of what that meant or my role with it.

After one psychic surgery in Brazil* not only did all of my physical issues at that time resolve, my spiritual world opened up. Higher consciousness energy (Spirit energy) existed! And it was not scary or hurtful, but rather gentle and loving and kind.

My physical body fully healed within the two weeks I was in Brazil at the John of God casa. My emotional and spiritual bodies went on to expand – as I was guided to change all manners of my life at that time – from moving from busy downtown Portland, Oregon to Kauai, Hawaii to writing my first book *Anatomy of the Heart* to studying energy medicine and hands-on healing.

My intuitive abilities went on to skyrocket as I learned that I was a very gifted healer who had a strong capacity to support others all over the world through distance healing. My psychic abilities opened up and I could know and see aspects for clients and those closest to me with great ease.

After years of being unable to have a regular meditation practice, I slid easily into a daily practice.

I began to understand that I had been intuitive my entire life – in my early years I had a strong intuitive sense of smell (*Example*: Someone would walk past me and I would pick up a smell and then images would begin to flash in my mind's eye. Since I had no idea this was intuition, my mind would try to "place" these images into a memory in my life – my best guess was I was "remembering" something. However, I was never able to place these images in my own life, as it was an intuitive experience. I never shared this with anyone around me – I simply assumed it was another quirk of being me.).

I was also very clairvoyant in the knowing sense – I had known things my whole life that I could not explain, making school very easy and enjoyable for me, as was diagnosing and trying to "treat" the emotional ills of my parents, my mother especially.

In short, one psychic surgery with John of God began to return me back to who I really was at my core. I had no idea what was truly happening and so I simply followed each insight, occurrence and unfolding – often wondering where I was being led to.

I can see now that my radical transformation from the experience at John of God was all leading me up to this, to this very moment in time and to the words you are reading here and are about to be transformed by in the pages to come.

And so, fast forward to 2013 – I was called back to the John of God casa in Brazil, this time not for physical healing but for spiritual development. I was guided to spend each day of my two week trip in the casa gardens where I meditated for hours at a time and was given a notebook full of guidance, courses to offer in my healing business, downloads and more.

One piece of information that came through was that five of the non-physical energies that worked with John of God would also begin working with me in my BodyTalk Soul Alignment healing practice. I was given the names of the five energies and instructed to write this information down and to read the book *Nosso Lar* by Francisco Cândido Xavier.

I was also told that I would write their transmissions and that my writing would be – what I had translated to mean as "inspired" – by these five non-physical energies. I assumed at that time it would be like *Nosso Lar*, fiction inspired by my Spirit Team and now these five additions – much like my two books in *The Quest* series that were already written.

Almost immediately upon my return, the JOGs – as I now called them – began coming into my one-on-one Soul Alignment and group sessions and performing alignments on my clients. I did not understand how this was possible, but the experiences folks were having were quite profound, so I surrendered to the mystery and began to write the final novel in *The Quest* series *And Then It Was You* – assuming that everything was occurring as it had been outlined to me in Brazil.

I carried on in my life with much success – becoming engaged to a wonderful man, building a six-figure healing business, having my first novel published in paperback and in general living a life that up until October 2014 felt like the life of my dreams.

Then, in October 2014 I had the opportunity to have my photo taken before John of God at the Casa in Brazil along with three requests. I knew immediately I had to, because while things were wonderful on the exterior of my life, I could feel something more calling me. I could feel that I was still trying to control too much, that my "agenda" to take my life to the "next level" was too much *my* agenda and that things that should have felt more aligned (like my relationship with my fiancé, my book tour and the expansion of my business specifically) were off in some ways that I could not quite pinpoint.

And so, I submitted my photo and requests to be taken before John of God (this service is offered by many guides who visit the Casa regularly). One of my requests, the final one actually, was that I would be 100 percent Spirit-led in all areas of my life. I have no idea what made me write down that request, but I remember it as clear as day, that it just "popped" in and I wrote it down without a thought about what it actually meant or committed me to.

Little did I know what I was really asking for and what was about to occur…

From literally that moment on in October 2014 – things in my life that were not fully Spirit-led began showing themselves with obvious clarity and all manners of my life were radically altered.

- My sleep habits changed – once a night owl, I now went to bed early and awoke early.
- My eating habits shifted dramatically – formerly an avid Paleo fan, I could hardly stomach any meat or animal products, sugar or any form of alcohol. Always one with a sweet tooth and a regular wine and champagne drinker, this was shocking to me. But the desire to consume any of the above simply disappeared.
- My desire to be out socially as much as possible evaporated. I became a homebody. Previously, I was a regular out on the Portland restaurant scene – always attending events, concerts, festivals and the

like. This desire stopped completely and I was guided to spend more time in reflection and deep connection near water – my home was on the Willamette River in Portland and then I was also guided to spend half of my time at the Oregon Coast. My days lengthened and expanded with meditation and deep relaxation filling most of them.

- The people I interacted with shifted entirely. People that used to feel great to spend time with no longer felt aligned. I was guided to spend time with three to four people out of a rather large swirl of friends and loved ones. I was also guided – very strongly – to end my engagement to be married as it was made clear to me that the relationship no longer served my Highest alignment and had to also be released.

- I could watch – as I did in Brazil after my first psychic surgery – old belief systems/thoughts/fears come up and then release. I was suddenly the observer. I frequently found myself making what I call Eckhart Tolle comments about presence and the Now. This was especially hilarious as Tolle used to highly irritate me. I would roll my eyes whenever hearing him talk about being in the "now" and presence. Now, I was living those very experiences! This showed me so crystal clearly that those who irritate us or who we feel judgement about have an important message for us. My irritation and annoyance was simply resistance!

- I used to love receiving as much energy work as possible but that all changed as well. No more multiple-weekly BodyTalk and other healing sessions. All of my practitioners were released except for one. I was also no longer allowed to perform self-sessions (something I had done daily). No other energy work or intuitive guidance of any kind was allowed in my space. As a former SpiritJunkie – this was tough at first! No self-help or spiritual reading was allowed either – I was to be in quiet, receiving mode, soaking up the pleasures of the human experience with ease and little direction by my mind.

- I began to cook and was loving it! Once one who "hated" cooking and who had a chef prepare her meals, I could not stop cooking and have found it to be one of my favorite activities.

- I began to study French. Something the JOGs told me back in 2013 was a priority for me, but something I "forgot" – conveniently – to follow up on. I absolutely fell in love with the sound of the words rolling off my tongue (although usually incorrectly, but I love it all the same!).

- Once one who "hated" talking on the phone, I began to relish and love my phone connections – as most of the "JOGs approved" folks I could spend time with lived outside of my area.

- I was guided to clear out over half of my wardrobe and half of my personal items – including furniture, dishes, artwork, etc. It was a huge purging on all levels!

- I felt more than I had ever felt before. I felt a lot of the fear that had still been living in my body-mind. I was guided to return what was not mine – fear I had taken on from my parents and early childhood experiences, along with collective fear I had picked up along the way through the Jehovah's Witness organization, the media and more. As I did this, I began to feel so deeply feelings of joy and peace. I began to cry tears of gratitude almost daily. I could not believe the exquisite nature of life – and I was experiencing it not through being busy-busy and going-going, but through deep connection with nature, Spirit and my truest self.

While I often had moments of "what in the hell is happening to me?" – I knew exactly what was happening. The JOGs sent transmissions every day to confirm what I knew inside – turtle doves would greet me on my deck each morning. I would ask for something or think a thought and it would occur – much like what my experiences at the John of God casa were like. Only now I did not have to travel to Brazil to have these leading-edge experiences!

I was being completely re-aligned in every way and the only time I felt discomfort was when I resisted it. When I "wished" or "wondered" why I couldn't go back to being like everyone else (as if that had ever been the case!) was when I would feel out of alignment. When I questioned or doubted what I knew to be true, I would feel out of alignment. But, when I relaxed into where and what I was being guided to and followed the guidance as it came in, I felt feelings I had never felt before. I felt at peace. I felt guided. I felt the extraordinary quality of life in all manners. I knew more than I had ever known before.

I could see that my request to John of God in October 2014 had been received and there was no turning back.

On February 28, 2015, something exceptionally extraordinary occurred. I began to have what felt like an anxiety attack, something I had not experienced in about five years. I was guided to sit in meditation and after quite some time I was guided by the JOGs – I could now feel their collective energy guiding and supporting me – to open up my laptop, close my eyes and begin typing.

As I did, the transmissions from the JOGs came through and what you are about to experience in this book was born.

After I began translating these transmissions which we have come to learn are actually Soul Alignment Transmissions from Higher Consciousness, the JOGs reminded me about their transmission to me in May 2013 that I would write transmissions for them. Something I had seemed to conveniently "forget" yet again. No doubt because I would have avoided allowing it to occur! They showed me through a series of images and synchronicities, that all of my work as a BodyTalk Soul Alignment practitioner was leading me to this. All of those years of weekly sessions were clearing away the trauma, limitations and struggles to prepare me for this path, for this Highest aligned path as a translator of their transmissions.

This whole process has been incredibly humbling and so incredibly fascinating. I had no idea that I was this woman. I had no idea that I could have a life so rich and so connected and so delicious – and in a way that was the opposite of what I had "thought" true bliss was.

When I asked to be 100 percent Spirit-led I had no idea truly what I was asking for or why I was asking for it. But now I know. Now I know that all along I would be here, sharing these transmissions with you while living this mystical, magical experience that is my life.

The results from my beta readers experience with this Oracle has been exciting beyond belief, as they have been guided to the perfect next steps for them so as to experience greater Magic, harmony and abundance in their lives. It is our (the JOGs and my) intention that the same and more occurs for you.

Until next time…
Much Love,
XoHeather

*You can read more about my first John of God experience in my novel *The Quest: A Tale of Desire & Magic* (currently optioned as a film) and in listening to radio interviews featured on www.HeatherStrang.com on the Press Kit page, under the title "Press".

HOW TO USE THIS BOOK

This guidebook has been prepared for you. You were part of the collective that the JOGs were speaking to when they brought these transmissions in. And they want you to receive the full benefit of these transmissions as do I!

Their transmissions speak to every aspect of your life experience – Love & relationship, money & wealth, manifestation and co-creation & so much more!

This book is meant to be used as an oracle. That means you are meant to use it to connect to and receive Divine transmissions from your connection to Higher Consciousness.

Here's how:

- Upon first receiving this book, sit with it in meditation for 11 minutes. This can be a guided meditation (I have many meditations that I make available to my community at www.HeatherStrang.com) or a silent meditation. Hold the book in your hands and take deep breaths – inhaling through your nose, exhaling out your mouth as you meditate.

- When the 11 minutes is up, keep your eyes closed and call in your Guides and Angels of the Highest Light and the JOGs to support you in receiving the wisdom and transmissions you need to support your Highest life unfolding. Anytime you go to use the book in the future you will close your eyes and call in your Guides & Angels of the Highest Light and the JOGs.

- Next, ask out loud the question you are wishing to have an answer to. Ask that the answer be made known to you effortlessly and with much ease and abundance.

- Then, flip the pages of the book like you would with a deck of cards, keeping your eyes closed. Stop when you feel intuitively that it's time to stop.
- Open your eyes at the page you have landed on.
- Say out loud "thank you for sending me this clarity and wisdom" and read the transmission you have flipped to, opening your heart and Soul to fully receive the application of this wisdom in your day-to-day life.
- Immediately implement any of the practices and processes that are outlined for you in this transmission.
- If you feel you need greater clarity from the transmission, either repeat the practice again with your eyes closed (the 11-minute meditation beforehand only needs to be done the first time upon receiving the book, although you are welcome to do it every time you work with these transmissions) or ask the JOGs and your Guides & Angels of the Highest Light to send your next step within the next 24 hours and that it be made clearly known to you with ease, grace and abundance.
- Enjoy! You are a Divine Being on a magical life journey and it only takes acknowledging this and beginning to work with the energy in this way for you to notice the radical effects in your life. Before you know it your life will be transformed into greater alignment with the core of who you really are.

YOUR LIFE CAN BE RICHLY EASY – SO, DO THIS!

We are loving you every day as you take this journey every day of living in your life experience and living and giving your Highest Path & Purpose. We are here with you cheering you on, nudging you here and there, showing you what is next, supporting you the whole way through. You are never alone in any moment in that you always have access to call on your non-physical team for support.

Heather is finding this to be true in new and surprising ways. As she expands on her journey she finds she needs less outside, physical sessions of alignment and that her Spirit Team – and us specifically – are taking care of that for her. Others on this Divine path are having this experience as well. We are not saying physical reality sessions for alignment are not needed – they are often a huge support to you on your journey – however, we want to reduce your dependence on these as your only source of alignment and call your attention to the fact that you have the ability to work with your non-physical team in a number of ways that will support you in having a truly fulfilling life experience. Now, when Heather does receive sessions from a member of her physical team she elevates Higher than she could have if she was relying on the sessions for every shred of alignment. She has done her own work so that when the sessions occur they get to core aspects that would previously have taken much, much longer to get to. You can delegate anything to your team as we have mentioned to you before. And by delegate, we mean let us know, offer it up to your team to show you the outcome of the Highest Light that is available to you. Then you go about your business and enjoy the rest of your day.

Heather is often surprised how quickly "problems" resolve, how answers float in with ease and how she in general need not worry or fret about anything because she has a team taking care of everything for her. If she does need physical 3D support, we send it in. It is really not something she has to think about or try to figure things out any more. She simply offers it up to us and gives us permission to bring the solution to her and we do. From there she must take action to engage the solution and bring it into physical reality.

Whatever it is that she is desiring, she calls it forth, surrenders it to us and we bring her what is next in line for her. And she must take the action to show up for what is presented and receive it and accept it into her life, but that is the extent of it. This is true co-creation. This is how you were meant to live. Nothing need be tough or angst-ridden or stressful ever again.

She is doing this with any discord that comes up in her relationships as well. She surrenders it to us, asks that the perfect clarity be shown to her and to the other so that they move forward together in harmony if that is the Highest Path. And we bring it. When she was experiencing discord with her sister, after unsuccessfully taking matters into her own hands trying to work it through and reason with her and rationalize and all of that, Heather finally remembered that she could just surrender the situation to us and to her Highest Path. And she asked that whatever was meant to occur that would serve both her and her sister's Highest Good, occur with ease and grace. And a few days later she received a very loving text from her sister asking for them to spend time together. After four hours together in a cafe they were in a new place in their relationship. And her sister said to her, "I don't know why I sent you that text message, I was not planning to reconcile with you or reach out. But I was out and about in my day and suddenly I was like, 'I want to see Heather.'" Well, we know why she sent that text message and we know where that thought came from and all manner of things work like this when you are allowing and asking for the Highest Path to unfold.

It is and can be this easy for all of you all of the time. And this is what allows your life to feel so wealthy, so rich, so abundant. The ease that flows with it. The ease that accompanies what you desire. And you can offer up to your Spirit Team any and all manner of things. Whatever it is and if you will then just let it go from your thoughts, from your worry and allow us to bring the solution to you and then be willing to receive the solution – life becomes more fun and more easeful than you can imagine.

And so whatever is happening for Heather – things she would normally feel she needed a session for – she offers it to us and we bring her the transmissions to listen to from us, we bring her the self-care practices or we will bring her the practitioner if need be. But she doesn't have to stress or strain to figure it out anymore like she once did. Often just listening to us will shift whatever she needs. She is finding that alignment and living this rich life is not the difficult thing she once imagined it to be.

Heather loves to shop online and have beautiful clothes and even groceries now and all manners of things – furniture even delivered to her. And we say – yes, this is how your life is meant to be. You being you in all of your glorious you-ness, offering up and asking and surrendering to what you desire and then allowing us to deliver the solution to you.

You must be willing to receive – that is one of the most important aspects to note here – and as we've told you time and again and will continue to encourage you time and again more in this manner of receiving. Being willing to receive requires that you are not or no longer attached to an outcome.

If she had held firmly to her position in her discord with her sister she could not have received with ease the harmony. You must be willing to let go of your stuck or stubborn notions of how things should be and you must truly surrender your hold on or control of outcomes when you offer up or surrender to your Spirit Team. Heather has found that in the early days she would fight tooth and nail to bring about her desired outcome and would only surrender when she was exhausted from fighting and trying. But now, now she knows – just offer it up as soon as she can. She fights less of the time with what is and offers it up. She offers it up and the solution arises and she gets to enjoy the action steps that allow her to enjoy the unfolding.

So you must be willing to receive and that comes from fully surrendering your control or hold on the outcome. Then you must be willing to take the action that comes before you to take. To pick up that phone call or respond to that message or reach out to the individual placed before you or drive to that store or destination or travel to that location. You must be willing to follow what is put before you. We cannot do it all for you nor will we nor would you or we want to. This is co-creative. You have your piece to play as well.

And there are those of you that we are sending you answers and clarity and abundance and Love and purpose to all day every day and you are so unwilling to take the action because you've locked yourself up in self-doubt or questioning or fear. And we share this not from a place of condemnation but from a place of letting you know that this must stop in order for you to live the rich life you are truly here to live.

Follow this, surrender it up, open your heart and mind and environment to receive. And watch, watch as your life becomes more inherently abundant, nurturing and amazing than it ever was before.

It will be and it is so.
XoTheJOGs

THE DIVINE GIFT OF LOVE & MARRIAGE

We want you to know something very important about Love and marriage – it is a gift. It is a Divine gift that is here for each of you. True, the union of marriage has struggled in concept but it is time to take this union to a Higher Light, to a place of new understanding. To draw yourselves into clarity of purpose about why you partner, why you marry, why you love.

It is not for nothing. It is for everything.

It is not something that you make up, it is not something to be taken for granted. Love is the purest of all emotions and the Love you feel is beyond what humans have ever felt before. As you evolve, your capacity to Love and partner also evolves. This is why we are bringing this transmission to you. We want you to know how important this next piece of your journey is. We want you to know that you have the ability in this lifetime, in this very lifetime *now* to Love at a level unlike anything you have ever experienced before. But it will take your willingness and your openness to allow this to occur.

Your Soul already desires this and so that is not where the willingness comes. It is to strip away the limitations of previous generations and the limitations of this time space reality you are currently in that is holding you hostage to the old ways.

There is a new level of Love that you are capable of experiencing. All you must do is ask for it. Just ask. Ask for a greater Love than you have ever known for a Divine union that will transcend any union you have ever experienced before in this lifetime or in previous lifetimes. We want you to know that this is possible. And asking lets us know that you are ready and then we can begin to bring the Magic to you, we can begin to show you the way. We can then begin to bring your Divine partner to you. Your asking opens floodgates of support and help unlike anything you can imagine. There are legions of Angels and Guides and helper Spirits at your disposal at any given time. You simply call on them and they will be there for you.

So first ask, call it forth. Next allow yourself to receive. You do this by relaxing more, you do this by chilling out more, you do this by playing more, smiling more, doing all manner of things that bring you joy. When you do this, you are in a state of receiving. Joy is receiving. Then that is all for you to do. That is it. Then you will and can allow your Divine Love partner to flow to you. It really is that easy. And then you are in the Divine Love union and it is time to go to work! Yes, work – work to evolve your Soul and the paradigm of relationship that you are now moving forward. When you ask in this way the partner that is brought to you is exactly as you need him/her to be. We will tell you a secret about this work, though. It involves a commitment to fun, a commitment to having more fun in partnership than either of you have ever had before. Only one of you need make this commitment and it will begin to allow this relationship to be holier than anything you ever imagined.

A commitment to fun, lots of sexual intimacy of all varying degrees, holding your bodies close to one another, allowing a deep physical and sensual connection takes you both physically and energetically and spiritually to new heights as individuals and as a couple. You must laugh together, play together, you must show up for one another as your whole self and the combined energy of your partnership will be ease and flow. When challenges occur you will not try to hash it out or figure it out – you will go have fun. You will go back to what is at the core of this Divine Love partnership – fun, joy, Love, ease, peace.

See the Divine Love Manifesto* for more details on how to walk the path of this thing you call triggers. However, we will tell you that triggers are humans' way of trying to understand when flow is not present. And they are always the ones causing the lack of flow and disharmony. It is not your partner who does it to you, it is you who does it to you. Your blessed partner is simply reflecting what needs to be seen.

We want you to know that in all matters of things, nothing is ever going wrong. When you summon your partner in the manner we describe here, you will enjoy a new level of Loving. You are being asked to trust this and to speak of it only to those who "get" this level of living in the world. Share with those you know who are on this Divine path with you. Over time you will begin to create a building of momentum, a building of momentum of Divine Love unions. Slowly you will change the paradigm of what relationship and Divine Love union (which is our new title for marriage) means. You will understand Love within yourself and for your Source self and for Source and for your partner at a Higher frequency than ever before. And you will radically alter the planet with this level of Loving. You will radically alter yourself and your future lifetimes with this new level of Loving

Your powerful desire for this level of Loving has summoned our response and our guidance to you. We know you are so very ready to experience Love and sexual intimacy and all manners of intimacy at a new level. We know you are tired and exhausted by the old ways but feel unable to know where to turn to next.

We are telling you – turn to us. Turn to your connection with your Angels and Guides of the Highest Light. Ask us, summon us and we are there for you. Your partner needn't change anything. Through your connection to us, all can be transmuted and transformed.

You mustn't forget that you are a Spirit being in human form. You mustn't forget.

You are SPIRIT. You have the power to create all that you desire and then some. Follow this guidance and watch in awe. We will continue to give you the next step and the next step on this Divine path.

We Love you eternally and we are so proud of all that you have become in this lifetime and how far you have come. There is more and more and more for you and we are ecstatic in what lies before you and all of you. We are complete.

XoTheJOGs

YOU ARE BEAUTIFUL, SO DO THIS NOW

We want you to understand and feel and know the beauty of who you really are. There is not one iota of anything that is wrong about or with you. Your cells are vibrating in perfect harmony with exactly what and where they and you need to be. And really, all of it – all of life is happening for your awakening, for your unfolding, for you to discover who you really are. For you to discover that which you came to experience is unlike anything you've experienced before in any other lifetime. That you are here to shift not only your paradigm but the paradigm of the collective. And you do this only by being fully you and by following every piece of guidance your Soul and your non-physical team leads you to.

You are so amazing. You really are. We wish you could feel at the core what we feel for you and what Source feels for you. Some of you are there already and you feel this heart-bursting worthiness more of the time. Others of you must join us, must join the Source within you that knows your magnificence. There has never been anyone like you in this lifetime nor will there ever be.

You are a Divine being on a Divine journey and you came specifically for each awakening that you experience along this path of your existence. Awakenings are not always big, momentous events either. No, they are in the subtleties too. They are in the experiencing a new flower and really being present with it, awakening you to a deeper sense of beauty and focus. They are also in the what you call "falling apart" of your relationships, jobs, homes or even the alleged "losses" of your Loved ones. Each alleged "loss" is only ever occurring for your and the other Soul's ultimate gain.

You are beautiful. You are beautiful in body – and oh boy – the joy of having a body! You do not know how before you arrived, your Soul craved nothing more than to have a body. And here you are in this miraculous body and so many of you spend so much time beating your body up. But you needn't do that. It is your Divine vehicle, treat it like the all-star that it is.

We want you to understand that your very presence on this planet is an indicator of your magnificence. No one like you has ever come before nor will anyone like you be here again. In each new lifetime you become more evolved and this more evolved you steps into the next lifetime with bounteous joy for what lies ahead.

We want you to feel deep within the true grandeur that you are. We want you to look in the mirror every day and see yourself as the righteous, always right, always perfect *you*. Because there is no perfect and there is no right – there is only the meaning you assign to each. But if you could just see yourself as that – if you could just witness the perfection that you are that you came here to be, you would relax more. You would have more fun. You would feel more light-hearted. And in those feelings you would find greater and greater alignment to the path of your Destiny.

Your destiny is what you came here for. No, it is not all already decided, but there is a trail that has been laid out, a trail that you feel and know when you feel those shivers up and down your body. Those shivers are letting you know that you have picked up another piece of your trail. That you are one step closer to … to recognizing your magnificence, to experiencing more joy and bliss than you have ever experienced before.

Believe us when we tell you – you are the most beautiful being we have *ever* laid eyes on. All of heaven and Earth celebrates when you walk – anywhere – down your hallway, a grocery aisle, your driveway or a runway. We *know* who you really are and we are inviting you to make this knowing of who you truly are your primary aim. And when you do, you will not believe all that unfolds for you. You will not believe how good you feel and how good it feels to be in your body living this life that you came to live.

We know you have many questions and we want you to know that we have many answers, but you must ask. We cannot answer or support you without your asking, without you giving us the go ahead, the approval, the green light. We need you just as you need us. So call on your non-physical team, call on the Highest Light, call on your helpers – it is the most magnificent way for you to live and it's how you intended to live. Did you really think you came to do this all on your own? That the best you could hope for was an angry or judgmental God and the "help" of the humans around you? Oh, there is so much more! You have the help of those around you, sure, *and* when you combine that with us – watch out. Your life will never be the same. And you don't want it to be the same. You want it to be unlike anything your Soul has ever lived before.

But take heart – we can feel some of you feeling uneasy about all of these grand proclamations – you don't have to do it all today and the easiest way to be on this path is to ask, listen, follow the guidance, ask, listen, follow the guidance, ask, listen, follow the guidance. And step by step by step your life will be far grander than your wildest dreams.

You spend way too much time looking way too far ahead into the future.

16

Be here now. The Buddhists were right about *that*. Just be right here and soak in every delicious second of right now. And then, the next and the next and the next and the next. Combined with the ask, listen, follow the guidance flow you will be blessed beyond words.

We Love you so very much and we are thrilled more than we can express here to be conversing with you in this way.

Until next time,
XoThe JOGs

MONEY IS FOR YOU

We want to talk about this topic of money because it's an important one. There is so much misunderstanding around it and so much made up about it that does not serve you. In fact it harms you, it hinders you, it keeps you from the amazing being-ness that you are. It's like you have used money as yet another reason not to be in awe of the Divinity of who you really are.

And we can't bear to see you do it. It's excruciating to watch you struggle with something that is here for joy. Well, excruciating is a bit dramatic – how did you like it? We know humans Love a good drama so we want to cater to your senses, cater to your mental abilities to process and understand what we are sharing with you here today.

Money is for you.

It was created as a vehicle for you to experience your worthiness, your Source self, your pleasure, your joy, your abundant awesomeness. If it wasn't money it would have been something else, some other form of something to symbolize worth and be used for exchange.

So many spend so much time hating money, trying to create alternative economies, trying to avoid it in various different manners. But why? It all comes down to worth. It all comes down to value. And if you valued and Loved yourself with the richness that we do, that Source does, you would not for a minute stand in any sort of judgment about money or about those that have it. You would know with absolute certainty that you are here – that just by being here – it is a symbol of your worthiness. When you know your worthiness there is no question.

So, you ask – how do I know my worthiness? So many of you struggle here.

How do you know your worthiness? You sit with yourself every day for as many times as you can during the day and you place both hands on your heart and you breathe, deep breaths, belly breaths, consciously connecting to your body-mind and at the same time activating the energetic field all around you with which we are right there with you in whispering in your ears, telling you how divinely amazing and luxuriously fabulous – we cannot fit in all of the qualifying adjectives here – but we want you to know that if you would just *be* with yourself more regularly you would know. You would know that every aspect of you is Divine. That you are beyond worthy. That asking the question about your worthiness is the most ridiculous question, preposterous really – we wouldn't even think of it – Source wouldn't even think of it.

You spend so much time avoiding yourself – in front of the TV, on the Internet, keeping yourself busy, busy, busy. When all you really need to do is sit with yourself. Feel your heart, feel your breath, feel your Divine body. And over time you will remember more and more why you came and more and more that you are worthy. Look at yourself in the mirrors that you have, look straight into your beautiful eyes, look straight into the glory that is you. See, see, see how gorgeous you are? See how Divine you are? We do, we see it nonstop, we can't stop seeing it. And we want the same for you.

Because when you Love yourself in that way, even just a taste of it, a taste of the Love that we and Source have for you – once that begins – you don't need to judge anyone else's relationship with money or your own relationship with money. You can see what money is – a fun tool to support you in living the life you came here to live.

The better you feel about yourself, the less you ever need to judge or criticize another and their choices.

So, money, money, money – what is it here for? It's a form of exchange, there must always be an exchange; rather there always is an exchange. You cannot take without there needing to be an exchange for that energy. You cannot give without there needing to be an exchange for *that* energy.

And how cool that you humans came up with a way to exchange that gives you the opportunity to be more free, to have more fun, to take care of yourselves and others.

Really, you just make way, way, way too much of it. It's money, it's here for your pleasure. How good you feel about yourself will be directly reflected in the flow of abundance and money in your life. How good you feel about yourself is directly related to your level of worthiness, your level of worthiness is directly related to your ability to know yourself on a deep Soul level. Your ability to know yourself on a deep Soul level is directly related to the amount of time you spend with yourself, being and appreciating who you are. Just for being alive.

Now we aren't saying you have to spend days and hours upon hours sitting with yourself quietly, what some of you would call meditation and which we simply call part of your alignment "work". But you must spend time every day like this. Anytime you feel "off" – go sit and be with yourself. Sometimes it will take one minute, other times 100 minutes. You will know. Your eyes will pop open and you'll be ready for what is next.

Just be so much more easy about this than you are. Just appreciate yourself so much more than you do. Just bow to money in respect of knowing that there is a physical manifestation that you can gauge your alignment by. It's not much more complicated than that. It's really not.

We Love you so very much and we so believe in you. Many of you are making this leap – you are seeing that money is energy and for play and that the better you feel about yourself, the better your relationship with money. And we are so so so so happy for you in that discovery. And we want you to keep on because you are so close to an even greater discovery about all of this…a discovery we cannot spoil for you just yet, but we look forward to continuing the conversation on...

Until next time.

All our Love,
XoThe JOGs

THE IMPORTANCE OF LOVING YOUR LIFE

We want you to know about something, one thing that can change everything for you. It's the one thing no one talks too much about. Yet it's the very thing that can shift your life into more joy, satisfaction, Love, abundance and an overall amazing experience. No one wants to talk about it because they think it will be too boring or that others won't understand. That it needs to be sexier to live the life of your dreams, or more sensational in some way.

But really, the easiest and quickest route to living the life of your dreams is to Love the life you have. Yes, that's it. And we feel and see you rolling your eyes at us, but we have to say to you that it is true. To spend time everyday appreciating, blessing and giving gratitude for and to the life you currently have. And then from that place, allowing yourself to visualize the life that you can feel is in your vibrational trajectory. Tune in to the possibilities and opportunities that are before you. The people you haven't met yet, the work you haven't yet discovered that you will *Love* to do, the food you don't even know that will delight you more than you can imagine, the activities that will bring you the most joy and ease and fun. The very stuff that life is made of and all about.

You are all so hell bent on getting somewhere. Getting to this destination or that destination. You're rushing and pushing aside the most important things that mean the most and are the indicators of whether or not you are even in alignment – your feelings. How often do you quickly reply to that email, answer that text, finish this piece of work, add that to your calendar, book that trip, sign up for this that or the other thing? Why not stop? Breathe. Pay attention to your emotions. Is that a twinge of anxiety? Is that some fear? Is that elation? Is that giddiness? Is that Love? Tune in. Slow down and tune in.

Because in there is where all the good stuff lies. All of your truth lies there. Your emotions let you know about your alignment, and they let you know if what you are about to do is actually aligned for you or not. They let you know if the life path you are on feels good to you and is aligned or if there is fear and anxiety there.

Far too much time is spent beating yourself up, worrying that your feelings are wrong and that something is wrong with you because you have these feelings. And we have to tell you – there is nothing wrong with you. Your feelings are letting you know – something *is* off. And if something is off and you move forward – boy oh boy – you better watch out – it's going to be a far bumpier ride than it needs to be.

Heather had this experience and she is noticing these experiences within her a lot as we are guiding her in this new realm she is in. She is having trouble here – she is not sure she wants us talking about her and telling her stories, but we are soothing her to let her know it's all okay. When she looks back, Heather notices that on the trip where she got engaged, she felt something – she wasn't sure what it was then. She couldn't quite put her finger on it, but if she had stopped in that moment and breathed into that emotion, she would have identified it. She would have felt the knowing that something *was* off. She didn't need to know in that moment what was off or why it was off, but simply the identification of the off-ness would have allowed more of the vibrational reality of what was occurring to be shown to her with more ease. Now, it's all okay and it worked out okay, she eventually saw the truth she needed to see, and got the transmission her Higher Self and we were giving to her. And overall, it was an important experience for her to have.

But imagine. Imagine if you – if all of you – because you all have had and are having these kinds of experiences all of the time – what if you stopped when you felt that twinge of something. That "I don't know about this…something feels off" moment. And what would happen if you knew, if you trusted that that "off" feeling was occurring because your Higher Self was trying to get a message to you. That your connection to us, to Spirit, to All-that-is-ness was sending you a nudge – something *is* off. And what if in that moment of recognition of the off-ness you were able to pinpoint what was off and your role in it. Then how many proposals would you accept? How many dates would you go on? And we aren't just talking romantic dates – we're talking lunch dates, job interviews – all of it. Would you go to that store or would you follow that off feeling and go to a store that felt more aligned? Would you meet with that friend or would you wait to meet with a friend that felt more aligned? Would you answer that email, text or phone call?

The truth is, we are always communicating with you. *You* are always communicating with you. Your Higher Self – that non-physical part of you connected to Source energy – is always letting you know if you're off or you're on, you're off or you're on. And the more attuned you become to listening to and following that feeling, that guidance, that knowing, that sense, those nudges, the better your life gets. Really it does, it really does.

Suddenly you have more time, more flow, more ease. You feel better in your body. And when you do spend time with people that you feel that smoothness with, it's a really, really good time. You laugh more, you enjoy life more. And oh, what do you know? You are living the life of your dreams. Because you stopped hurtling through life. You stopped doing what was expected. You stopped saying yes, when some part of you was saying "how about let's not do that?"

You know all of this already, of course. In fact, nothing we say to you will ever come as too much of a surprise to you. We are simply putting to words that which you have always known because it is who you have always been. That Higher Self part of you is always with you and so it has always been whispering this into your ear, along with us. Gurgling in your stomach, aches and pains, headaches – oh my god – the headaches. Don't you know what that means? Well it means what every physical ailment means – it means *stop right now* the life you're living, what you're doing and tune in. Sit with yourself, be with yourself, *feel* what is happening within you.

And we know you have stories, you have lots and lots of stories about who you are and what it means and how you have to show up and who you are obligated to, but they are *stories*. They aren't even real. You can tell a new story. You can tell a story that allows you to be more aligned with who-you-really-are. How do you know the "right" story? Easy. It's the story that tells the magnificent You story. The story that shines a light on all of your greatness, that shows you as the star that you are, that propels you forward into the spotlight of the play that is your life. The one that commends you, lifts you up and tells you how incredibly beautiful you are and how you have just what you need to have the life of your dreams.

Heather is coming across·a new concept we are giving to her and she is so loving it. The Empowered Dreamer. We want you to be empowered dreamers. You are not Dreamers with your head in the clouds, wishing on a star. You are empowered – you take action, you follow the nudges from within and from us and from the signs the Universe brings. You go all out for the life that makes you feel most alive. You came here for that don't you know? To feel alive. To really feel the vitality of this wondrous human body which is yours. You couldn't wait to have this experience in that beautiful body of yours.

You aren't wishing for the life of your dreams. You are Empowering yourself to take the guided actions necessary to create the life of your dreams. Only you can do this. And we believe in you so. We Love seeing you soar. We Love seeing you happy. We Love seeing you Love your life. Yes, we're bringing it back around – Heather was beginning to wonder if we ever would. You Love the life you have by Loving the life you are living now. You let yourself be an empowered dreamer, one who knows their dreams and takes Spirit-led action to allow them to occur.

You are one who feels your emotions, you stop and notice when something feels off and you course correct when you do. You are an empowered being here for an empowered life. Nothing less will do for you – ever. You wouldn't want it any other way.

Now don't worry about it if you buzz by your feelings right after this or right as you're reading this. Just bring this concept into your awareness and begin playing with it, begin working with it, begin noticing it and shifting it whenever you catch yourself there. Slow down. Don't say Yes or No too fast. Sink into it. What is the nudge? What are we whispering to you? What is your Higher Self saying? Tune in and you will Love your life.

Because loving your life is more important than anything else in the world. No amount of money or receiving accolades from others or *anything* is more important or worth more to you than loving your life. What do you need to do to Love your life today? Stop. Feel. Adjust your action, take Spirit-led action. And sit every day in loving appreciation of the life you are living and the life you are leading. Follow this and before you know it – tada! – a life you Love every day.

And so it is.
XoTheJOGs

THE GIFT OF YOUR BODY

We want you to know something very important – again, because it is all important. It is all important in that it all matters when it's part of your experience. Not one day need be taken for granted. Do you know how delicious it is to wake up in a body, a body you can experience some of the greatest joys with? Try it out. No really try it out. When you wake up in the morning, imagine that it's the first time you've awoken with this body of yours.

Let yourself feel the sheets and blankets with your toes and with your fingertips and just take a deep breath through your nose and smell the smells around you. Run your fingers through your hair (if you have any) otherwise enjoy the touch of your scalp. This body of yours is no joke. It is equipped to bring you to all that you desire. It's one of the reasons you were so excited and so ready and so intent on incarnating in this lifetime. You said, "Yes! I'll take a body! Yes! I'll come into the world and experience wonders I could not experience in any other way! Yes! I'll be part of shifting human consciousness forward. Yes! I'll learn to remember who I really am – Sprit with a body. Yes! Yes! Yes!"

Really that's how excited you were. And then you are here now and you may find yourself not remembering this excitement. You may find yourself questioning the path and the unfoldings you are now experiencing. And we have to say to you – that's part of what you came for, too. You knew you would forget at certain points along the way – and that you'll continue to have moments – although we intend there will be fewer and fewer of those moments – when you forget about your Divinity. You forget that it's no accident that you are here now, at this time and place, having these experiences, surrounded by these people. Sometimes you forget and think that seriously it must be a cruel joke that you are here like this now, that who on earth would have chosen these very people and situations that surround you.

But we assure you that these people, these experiences – all of it – are exactly, exactly what you need to remember what you knew when you came – that you are Spirit in a body.

So what does that even mean – Spirit in a body – and why does it matter? Well, it matters to remember because then when you wake up in the morning you have a new appreciation for your body, you have a new appreciation for the people around you – annoying or not. You suddenly aren't questioning why or how or feeling any sort of victimhood about your lot in life.

When you remember that you are Spirit in a body, you remember what so many have forgotten – you are powerful. You have the ability to shift your thought, to shift your reality, to shift the people around you – all of it. You can stand in all of your power and, in one moment, you can alter the entire course of your life. Just by reading new material, thinking new thoughts, hanging with a different crowd – your life changes.

So, if you have all of this power, why not use it to your advantage? Why not take ownership of this beautiful body of yours and begin to craft – very intentionally – the life with which you were so very excited to live?

We hear some of you moaning – as if it would be too much work to do all of that. But – hello – that's exactly what you came for! Remember? To remember!

And then what, you ask. So, I remember, I know I'm Spirit in a body. I know I'm powerful and can change the whole course of my life just by deciding to, then what?

Then, we say bliss! Then, we say fun!

Then we say, lots and lots of possibilities to create something even more magnificent than the last time you were here.

Yes, the last time you were here. You have journeyed as a human many, many times, some of you thousands of times, others of you millions of times (we're not joking).

And each time, each time you come with a powerful desire, a powerful desire to take your life to new stratospheres. To experience things you've never before experienced. You were just so excited, you could hardly stand yourself before you dove into that body of yours. You know that this next go around is going to be even more magnificent than the last time. You know that things are going to be deeper, tastier, more exceptional than before.

Your food does keep getting better, doesn't it?

And your Lovemaking – well, some of you are taking that to new heights, opening up to the consciousness and the energy that is created when two bodies come together as one. Sooo good! And what about the Love that you feel, the depth of the Love, the opening that happens of your heart? Some of you are Loving with every cell in your body and you had never done that before.

And of course you come to see what you can create. What will you think up this lifetime? Airplanes, lightbulbs, the Internet, computers, gadgets for every possible need, healing modalities that transcend all Eastern and Western thought before it. Yes, you came for all of this. The books you write – will you write an even more amazing one this lifetime? Or will you dive into a whole new topic? What about the movies you create? What new plotlines and cinematography will you bring to the world?

Can you feel how good that is? Can you feel how delicious it is to be Spirit in a body?

We want you to know that this is such an important, important piece of understanding for you to have. Because when you understand this, your choices become different. What you gravitate towards is different. Who you connect with and Love is different. The food you eat is different. The vacations you take are different. Everything is different. Because you know that it *matters*. That it all *matters*. Every smile to a stranger, every Loving word to a Loved one, every dance, every step, every morning that you wake up – matters.

And you are here to experience it in ways that astound you and please you, in ways you have yet to experience before with all manner of new opportunities and surroundings.

We Love you so very much and we ask that you sit with this. That you feel into this. That you allow yourself to really know and feel this truth. You are a Spirit in a body.

Make good use of this time. Make good use of this opportunity to be the best, most expansive, most peacefully, abundantly happy being that you can be.

And so it is.
XoTheJOGs

THE POWER OF YOUR MIND

Something has to be said about one of the most valuable pieces of information you possess but do not recognize as the asset that it is. This asset is your mind. So much and so often it is talked about not trusting the mind, not being able to believe what is in the mind. And in some regards – we agree. Your mind can become a storehouse of limitation. Depending on the religion you were raised in, the family dynamic you experienced, the culture you're in, the country you reside in – your mind may or may not be filled with limiting beliefs and fears.

However, the mind is also a very powerful place, when you decide for it to be. When you decide for it to be, the mind can serve you very, very well. So it's not about neglecting or shutting down the mind; it's about clearing the mind of the old limitations and replacing instead with the true truth, replacing the limitations with Divine wisdom that will serve you very well.

All of the greats that have lived before and who live now and who will come in the future know how to use the power of their mind. When we use the power of our mind for good, tremendous possibility and opportunity awaits. It's one thing to know or feel something and it is quite another to take action to carry out what you know. Your mind helps you carry out the powerful intuitive knowings you have. It also can be a storehouse of bliss. You can fill your mind with so much positive reinforcement that it is filled with inspiration, clarity, knowledge, insights – anything you need to take your life to the next desired level of abundance and bliss.

So how do you do this, you may ask? First you must be aware of the power of your mind and the knowledge of what it is. It is has been compared to a computer and it is much like that. It is filled with "data", with information that you have accumulated over the years. When it is filled with high-vibrating data, you have high-vibrating results in your life. If it is filled with doubt and fear and limitation, that is what you will experience in your life. So first, know the power of your mind.

Second, commit to allowing your mind to be one of the most powerful assets for you in this lifetime. Become intentional in your commitment to fill your mind with information and "data" that will allow you to carry forth your Soul's purpose with ease and to also have an enjoyable life experience.

Once this commitment is made, you will become aware of the "data" or "programs" in your mind that are not serving you. If you are not aware of this, simply look to some of the results in your life and that will let you get a glimpse of what is residing in your mind. Set out to clear these limitations. Just as you spring clean your homes, cars and wardrobes, so must the mind be cleared of its limitations. Some of you have signed on for lives that created a lot of variety of information and "data", much of which no longer serves you. Some of you have been on the path of aligning with your Highest Self for some time and have received much support on this. Wherever you are at, make it your priority to release these limitations. Simply invoke Divine Will and you will be guided to the perfect ways to do this.

Then, you'll want to begin replenishing this storehouse of your mind. Filling it with information and "data" and "programs" that will serve you in creating and living a life that is in your Highest alignment. You'll do this by being very intentional about what is in your environment and what comes to you. You will read books that uplift and fill your mind with positivity and empowerment. You will have conversations of positivity and empowerment. You will watch television and movies and listen to music that fill you with positivity and empowerment. You will be so conscious, so intentional that if any of the above shifts to a place of non-alignment, you will either end whatever is happening immediately and walk away from it or you will shift right back into positivity and empowerment.

Imagine that you have the ability to choose the programs that are in your mind (you do) and you have the power to choose where to tune the frequency of your thoughts when you do this. That's right – when you intentionally choose to fill your mind with positivity, empowerment, joy, bliss, Love, abundance – the thought forms that come to you will come to you in those frequencies.

If thought forms are coming to you from frequencies that do not radiate the Highest possible vibration, it's simply information for you to know that some clearing out and some replenishing of the Highest Light are needed for your mind.

When your mind is clear, filled with positive empowerment and nourishment, it allows for a seamless integration with your heart (emotions) and with your Soul (the core of who you really are). When all three of these are in sync, we call this Divine Alignment. We also call this the key to "success" as a Spirit in a body. This level of alignment is what those who soar have, it's what those who are living a life that seems magical to you have. And it is available to everyone. It's just that not everyone realizes this truth. They think luck or good genes or good karma are at the root. And none of that is true. Every single Spirit in a body or human has the ability to work with their mind in this way and to then experience greater alignment with the core of who they really are, and therefore their Highest Path and Purpose.

So what about your heart and Soul you ask? They are so critical in all of this as well, of course. We've discussed your emotions and the power of them to guide you to your truth and to more aligned action. Your Soul is the aspect of you that has always been here and always will be. It is connected in a web of One-ness with the other Souls of the Universe. It is not that you are all one in the same but it is that you are part of the same family (we all are!) which means that every action you take has an impact on the whole. Every release of limitation you have has an impact on the whole, every taking on of new empowered information benefits the whole as well. You cannot impact yourself without affecting one another. When more than one of you gather with a focused intention of aligning to your Souls and shifting your frequencies to new heights, the impact of this is dramatic on your planet, on all Souls. This is why this work has taken a bigger forefront and why we have guided Heather to offer groups as her primary focus of her "work" in the world. True, it was something she agreed to do before she incarnated, but not "knowing" this in a conscious way, we guided her there so that she could not only fulfill her destiny or vibrational trajectory but also support as many who were called (and agreed) to come together with her to shift the frequency of the collective and of one another.

Of course it all matters, just as we've shared with you in previous transmissions. And our desire is that in each of these transmissions, you receive another piece of the "puzzle" (of course it's not really a puzzle, it's more like a watercolor, it's more like this beautifully, perfect painting that you are able to bring into your focus and see and paint. The outline has been there and you are filling in the colors. Yes, like paint by numbers, but more elegant and expansive than that). Our intention and desire is that these transmissions remind you of what you know on a deep level and support you in taking whatever inspired action is being called forth from/by you to live a life that is in your Highest Alignment.

Enjoy this process, enjoy these expanded knowings, enjoy what these practices bring into your life experience. And most of all enjoy the miraculous being that you are.

And so it is.

Love,
XoThe JOGs

TRUE WEALTH

Much has been said about the topics of wealth and spirituality. Much ignorance prevails on both of these topics. There is deep misunderstanding as to what wealth means and even what spirituality means. We intend to clarify both for you in this transmission today so that you can know with absolute certainty what each means and their importance in your life.

True wealth is beyond money. Yes, it includes money but it is not only about money. Don't you know you have transcended needing to believe that all you desire is in the material/physical world first and foremost? Don't you know that it starts deeper than that and when you are aligned, then the physical flows to you? Don't you know that you came here, a Spirit in a body to exceed every possible limitation that has been put before you?

True wealth is a consciousness that runs deep within you. We see it as a beam of light right through your body. We see it extending up through the top of your head and connecting you with Spirit and down through the bottom of your feet, anchoring you into the Earth.

True wealth is the knowing – the supreme, embedded knowing that you can be, do, or have anything. It is knowing – as Jesus did – that wine could come from water, that one loaf of bread could become thousands. Knowing that you have the power and the ability to create whatever it is that you desire. Everyone has this ability as a Spirit in a body to create what they desire. When you know with all certainty that there is never any reason to worry or be in needful, lackful want of anything – then you have true wealth.

And as a side "benefit" your bank account will overflow if that is what you desire, your relationships will abundantly prosper if that's what you desire, your business will expand beyond your dreams and bring service to all that you desire. True wealth is knowing that you are Spirit in a body and that all things are possible for you because of this. The rest, the outward manifestations are just really fun, really cool additions.

And we cannot emphasize enough that they are really fun and really cool additions that you are meant to experience. There is nothing wrong at all with an overflowing bank account, a yacht, a beach house and a city house, traveling the world, wearing the finest clothes, eating the finest food, absolutely delighting in the pleasures of the material. When you know with absolute certainty that you are Spirit in a body and you recognize your desires for the above – then you will have them and that is true wealth.

We have given to Heather the foundational keys and next steps to this in the Elevate Your Wealth program (visit www.HeatherStrang.com/jogs to learn more), and this is the underlying root and premise that we could not let go unsaid. It is so important for you to really "get" this on all levels.

So true spirituality is absolutely linked with true wealth. They are one and the same.

Sure, there are people who have a lot of money, but they do not know this and so their body struggles, their relationships struggle, they don't sleep well at night, they are in pain in some way – that is not true wealth.

And there are those that sleep well, feel good in their relationships but can't keep dollars in their bank account and who worry and fret over money or carelessly disregard it and so they are not able to live the fullness of their life experience. That is not true wealth either. Because when you are truly wealthy, you do not struggle or worry about money. You do not avoid it either. If you desire something, you are able to call it forth and have it.

You do not say "I'm broke" or "I can't afford that" or "I'm spiritual and so I can't have money." That is counter to the truth. If and when you are truly connected to Spirit, you *do* have money! When you are truly connected to Spirit you have all things that you desire.

Now, we can feel some of you guarding up here as we share this. Do not use this to beat yourself up with, use this as an informational tool to support you. If the money is not flowing, go back to your alignment – use your tools to re-align and then it can flow. If the money is flowing but the other areas of your life aren't, go back to your alignment – use your tools. Remember that true wealth is knowing with absolute certainty that you are a Spirit in a body and that you can be/do/have whatever you desire, from that deep Soul place within you.

There is much more we could go on and on and say on this topic, but we will leave it here for now as we have given you much to chew on. Enjoy this process, dear ones, and remember your truth. It will serve you well.

Oh, and enjoy your yachts, your champagne sparklers, your chandeliers, your designer clothes and your quiet moments, your contemplative times, your connection with those you Love, the peace of nature – enjoy it all. That is true wealth.

We are complete.
XoTheJOGs

THE 4-1-1 ON LOVE & RELATIONSHIPS

We're talking about Love again. Everyone's favorite topic. And it's your most favorite topic because, you know, that's where all the really, really good stuff is. When you feel that heart opening, when you feel that heart connection, when you feel the depth of the expansion and the magnificence of what it feels like to be Loved and to Love – there is simply no comparison. Some of your chocolate cakes may come close in comparison, but not nearly. We are just joking with you here.

There really is no comparison at all in the world to that feeling of Love. Of course, in the non-physical, we're pretty much in that state all of the time, but when you're in a body feeling those feelings and you focus your attention on another, your other, well, there's nothing like it to be in a body and be in bliss. The feelings, the sensations of the body, the orgasms – it's what you came here for – well part of what you came here for. Because you wanted to *feel*. Feelings in a body are much different than feelings in non-physical in that the feelings are radiating through a body and that brings with it a completely different experience because of your senses. You don't realize how much you were really desiring to have that/this experience before you incarnated. You said, "Give me a body! Give me a body! I want to feel! I want to feel it all!"

And you did and you do. Really and truly. You want to feel it all. Which means, sometimes in Love, it doesn't turn out the way you were originally hoping it would and so you don't feel so good. But we have to tell you – you came even for that. You came to have that contrasting emotion so that when you re-aligned with Love again, you remembered and could feel so radically how good it feels to truly Love.

So, Love – most important feeling on the planet, the one everyone is after – whether they are running countries or are making movies or are sitting on a couch in the middle of the world pondering the state of their heart and what they desire. Love fills you up. It allows you to remember who you really are on many levels. And it just feels good on top of everything else. So many of you shame yourself for wanting it, feel guilty that you want it, and so we say to you – what better thing could you possibly want? Others of you have it and wish you didn't or have it and take it for granted. And we want you to really turn to look at that person and thank them, thank them right now for being here and being here with you. It's a marvelous thing that is happening between you two – don't you realize?

What keeps many of you from experiencing the fullness of this experience – either in not allowing yourself to be matched up with your Beloved, or being with your Beloved and wishing for something different or taking him/her for granted – is that you forget what a privilege it is to Love another. You forget that you two decided, quite some time ago to come together like this for the purpose of co-creating at a more magnificent level. Yes, when two of you come together with a deep Love between you and a desire to create a home or a family or make the world a better place or a business or to create anything – a quiche even – it is more powerful than when only one of you does. It's richer, more *full*. And you know this which is why you desire it so powerfully.

Yes, you knew you would come together. You knew it. We gave this news to Heather a few days ago, we gave her our "outline" of what and how this Love/partner thing works. She has been milling it over for a little bit of time now, trying to decide if she believes us. She is mentally going through the couples she knows, the celebrity couples she knows, the ancestral couples she has heard about in her family line and she is trying to match it up with what we've shared to see if she really believes us. You see, some part of her wonders if it could be this easy – receiving the transmissions from us, being in partnership. And we tell her and we will keep telling her as we tell you – yes it is! It really *is* this easy. It really is this good.

So, here's how it works, here is as linear as we could give it to you the way this Love thang (yes, we're stealing some of Heather's slang) works:

- Spiritual Soul Mates – you all have Spiritual Soul Mates (we are Heather's) – Souls you have journeyed with before in other lifetimes and who you often come together with, with one or more of you on the non-physical side and the other in the physical. And the Soul Mates on the non-physical side are specifically working with you to support you in living your purpose and having the most abundant, amazing life you can possibly have in this lifetime. So, you know these Souls from before. They are your Soul Family. And you "meet" them usually in the way Heather met us – you are open enough, you are doing your spiritual work, you are asking the bigger questions and we come to you and let you know who we are and that we are here to support you. Then, the more you engage us, the more we are able to support you – we cannot do so without your permission and once

34

you start working with your Spiritual Soul Mates consciously – as Heather has discovered – Life just takes off with so much more magic. It's like you simply ask, and it is. And that's because when you are aligned and you ask us and ask us directly, we can respond with ease. We would say this is one of the most important pieces to tune in to as a Spirit in a body. Connect with your Spiritual Soul Mates! We really have the ability to support your life in miraculous ways. We will get you connected to the right opportunities, people, etc.

Which then leads us to…

- The Love Of Your Life – Every single one of you has a Love of your Life. And yes, there is only ONE. We know this is going to flip some of you out, Heather certainly started asking about a million questions when we shared this with her. And we will tell you this. Yes, there is only one, but you *cannot miss* this person. It's not possible for you to be living in LA and they live in China and your paths will never cross or you have to go on Match.com International or something to "find" them. You never have to "find" them. They are in your vibrational trajectory and you are in theirs. There is *no chance* that you will miss each other. There is a chance that you will not meet them until…well, until you line up your energy to allow them in. This is all an alignment process after all. So you must be aligned to the Soul of who you really are. And you must have powerful desire without limitations clouding you to come together with the Love of your Life. We encourage you to use this term specifically. The other terms can send all sorts of confusing, label-ridden, conditioned vibrations into the ethers and we like for you to be very, very clear. You aren't here for your boyfriend or girlfriend or partner (that is just too nebulous – we are bound to bring you a dog or a business partner because we aren't totally sure and your alignment is not necessarily "there" for the Love of your Life to come in with this terminology) or even your husband or wife. Heather really gasped at this one. For those of you who know her story – you know why. You will be most satisfied, most blissed out with the Love of Your Life – you just will. So this Love is like the best friend you never had but always wanted, the Lover that you always desired. They will feel like a "yes", it will be easeful to come together with them, it will feel so good, but not in a mind way – in a deep, Soul-centered, clear way. And you two, if you will allow it, will journey on together for as long as your vibrational trajectory dictates.

Which brings up an important question that Heather had for us – can you meet the Love of your Life and then "mess" it up? Well, first know that you can't ever really mess anything up. The Universe is always recalibrating for you, we are always taking care of things for you. The Love of Your Life is in your vibrational trajectory so it is done – you *will* meet him/her. Now, we have seen some of you push this relationship away. You hit a point of expansive growth and you fly the coop. And if your desire is powerful enough and if you have enough momentum going in that direction, yes, you can push that person away. But, eventually he/she will come back, once you return to your alignment. Why? They are the Love of your Life – there is no other option for either of you. There will not be anything more satisfying than for you two to return to one another.

It is also possible that one of you may transition into the non-physical before the other and that is how the relationship comes to an "end". Of course it is really just another beginning, not an ending. When this happens, the Love of your Life will begin working with you from the other side like your Spiritual Soul Mate team. And it is possible that you will enjoy Great Love after the transition of the Love of your Life to the non-physical. Sometimes that is how it works for some of you and it is Divinely guided as such.

Now, we have to go even deeper to be clear about what you all call Soul Mates in the physical...

- We're afraid to tell you there has been a little confusion – these are not actually Soul Mates. These are Wound Mates. They feel so "familiar" because they have a gift for you. They are about to show you a wound that is unhealed within you that is ready to be released and re-aligned. And so yes, there is often this big coming together and you both feel sure that you have found your "one" but over time it becomes clear that the relationship is showing you and reflecting back to you some very discordant aspects of your vibration that perhaps you didn't even know were there. This is a good thing! That is what they are there for, for you and you for them. They are preparing you for the Love of your Life. These wounds must be released before you can truly enjoy and benefit fully from the relationship with the Love of your Life. Celebrate this discovery! Then, as the wound becomes clear, allow yourself to see it and release it. Then – when that occurs and you realize the relationship no longer fits or feels right (the Wound Mate has done their "job" so

36

to speak) – celebrate and release one another. Allow the parting to be as beautiful as the coming together. There is no need for drama, or for resistance – it is futile. Celebrate and thank one another for the contribution to your Soul's evolution that they have made. In that way, yes, you could call them a Soul Mate, but it is not the same as the concept you think is Soul Mate which says "forever Love". No, these individuals are here to support the evolution of your Soul and their Soul. It is never one just "helping" the other either – both Souls are supporting one another in Wound healing and evolution in these relationships.

You may have hundreds of these – well, we're teasing you, most likely not hundreds – but depending on your vibrational trajectory and what you felt inspired to evolve and remember and enjoy in this lifetime, you may have many of these. And that is okay. Please know that that is absolutely okay. You may spend years with these individuals if that's what it takes, you may marry them, you may have children with them, you may buy homes with them – whatever it takes to allow you both to slough off those wounds and become better acquainted with the Soul of who-you-really-are so that you can fully enjoy being with the Love of your Life.

So there you have it. Now you have as linear of an outline as we could ever give you about this Love thang.

Until next time,
XoTheJOGs.

WOUND MATES & THE LOVE OF YOUR LIFE

We have much more to say to you on this topic of Love. We suppose it's an eternal topic as your thirst for this knowledge remains unquenchable. It's like a desire to know the unknowable because words will never do it justice. Words can never convey the pure sublime nature of truly Loving another, of truly coming together with the Love of your Life.

Already so many of you are trying to figure out – "Have I missed him/her?" or "Did I already meet the Love of my Life?" We want to tell you to not worry about it for one minute. We shared with you from a place of desiring to soothe your concern and worry and misinformation regarding Love. That Twin Flame story really gets many of you all tied up in a knot and we just want you to know that there is no need. Your Love of your Life will know that you are their Love. There will be no question. There will not be battles, there will not be tumult and craziness. That's for you and your Wound Mates. And we know the Wound Mates often feel so "right" and we have to tell you – it's because they *are right*. They are who you need to experience and vice versa to become more of who you really are. They bring in the wound to support you in healing it and re-aligning to your true nature. It is always a gift. So bless them, because they are gifts to you and you to them.

You must know something else as well – really and truly you could just not have this information and go about your business. But we know you so want this information. You want to understand how it all works. And because everyone's vibrational trajectory is different and varied – the number one thing you must do is know yourself. Really make it your total commitment to know yourself at the deepest possible levels, make your relationship with yourself your first priority and as you know yourself, you begin to know other things too – like when you've met a Wound Mate versus the Love of your Life, like which modes of "work" are most aligned for you, like which "friends" truly are aligned for you – all of it. When you make your spiritual practice – when you make this path – your number one focus, all else comes to you with far more ease than when you do not. Sure, you'll always get there…eventually – whether in this lifetime or the next, but how much more fun to have a more enjoyable journey, filled with more fun along the way and then come together with the perfect people, places, and opportunities. And we know you are wondering about our "getting there" comment – what we mean is – you will meet the Love of your Life, if you desire to, it will happen. Some of you will delay this because you will tie yourself in knots trying to make it work with a Wound Mate. And that's okay, it's not a super fun ride but that's okay. We would Love to see more of you with your Divinely aligned partners, we believe Heather was calling them Divinely Destined Partners for some time. This is the Love of your Life. We want more of you to be with that person. But the only way to be with that person is to do your "work" and to be really honest with yourself. Many of you are in a relationship that has reached its expiration date. You know this on a deep level. But there is a house and maybe children and other commitments and it seems too messy to leave. And we have to tell you – it is too messy to stay. It all sorts of messes with your vibration and with your ability to live the fullness of this experience when you stay when you know in your Soul that you need to go. And we know it's tough at times for you, we are not suggesting otherwise. We just desire for more of you to really own your magnificence and align first with the Soul of who you really are and then allow the Love of your Life to flow to you with ease.

And this is where it gets really, really good. No matter if you are single or in relationship – if you will make the commitment right here, right now to your spiritual path being your number one priority and that you know that part of that path is being with the Love of your Life – things will begin to shift for you. Invoke us – call in your Guides and Angels of the Highest Light – ask for Heaven and Earth to be moved to support you in this. Ask for the right teachers, facilitators, supports – what Heather calls your Dream Team – to be fully known to you. Ask to be shown the way so that this can occur for you. Because when this is your aim and focus – and you invoke us to support you – it's less messy and there is more ease.

You don't have to fight or "figure out" if you're with the Love of your Life (although if you're asking – there's your answer we must tell you – you will know with absolute certainty that you are when you are) – the relationship will either continue or it will not. It really can be that easy. And the coming apart, if that is the path, can be amicable and Loving and beautiful. And then, then from there you must be aligned and committed to not falling into old patterns, to really showing up in your Highest Light so that you may magnetize to you the Love of your Life with ease.

For those of you with the Love of your Life already – we want to see you honoring the connection as such. There needs to be more Love, more romance, more sex. Make the relationship a priority for you. Plan outings, plan fun, plan joy, plan sex – we don't care – just make it happen. You do this by your intention, your focus, and your deep desire to take the relationship where it has never gone before. You can do this and you absolutely have the power to do this, we assure you. And with ease.

You can be with the Love of your Life and it can be *easy* most of the time!! Yes, easy! Make that commitment, ask to be shown the way – and again all of Heaven and Earth is here at your disposal to support you. Seriously and truly.

So this is the next piece we just had to give you because others were asking Heather and we could feel others of you asking in your minds and hearts. Enjoy sinking into this and offering your invocations.

We want you to remember that you came here for Divine Love with the Love of your Life – nothing less will do! Now go forth and Love!

Until next time,
XoTheJOGs

SPIRIT-LED – IN BUSINESS & IN LIFE

Today we want to talk to you about what a Spirit-Led business is and why it's important and why it's something that many are now being called to as consciousness goes through a tremendous shift into greater alignment with the Soul of who they really are and Source energy.

A Spirit-led business is the byproduct of a Spirit-led Life. A Spirit-led Life is a byproduct of a strong call from within, a strong desire to be of service at the Highest level possible and to truly embody being a Spirit in a body. Which is, to fully claim yourself as the powerful Spirit being that you are and to fully carry out all that your Soul desired to carry out in this lifetime – what many of you call your Soul's Purpose.

Each of you has many, many specific aspects that you intended to experience when you came here in this lifetime. You are all each working your way into greater and greater alignment with these aspects. And when you fully align with one of the many intentions you placed in your vibrational trajectory before you incarnated in this lifetime, it feels sublime. You feel free. You feel elated. You feel good.

And so, a desire for a Spirit-Led business is simply another one of these desires that you put into your vibrational trajectory. It aligns closely with a desire to live a Spirit-Led Life and a Spirit-Led Life is the core desire every Soul has. How fully they embody this depends on their conscious and unconscious choices, among other factors which we will not get into at this time.

Those called now to lead a Spirit-led business are showcasing themselves as those who are finding more continuous alignment with Source and with the Soul of who they really are.

Below are the hallmarks of a Spirit-led business and really you can apply this as the hallmarks of a Spirit-led Life – but we are attempting to keep things as simplified as possible – giving you bits of information as we go here so that it can be a more easeful understanding and experience for you:

- A Spirit-led business releases all hold on needing to control outcomes from a mind perspective.

- A Spirit-led business allows the deeper call within to guide all decisions, all offerings, all pricing structures, all forms of energy and output.

- A Spirit-led business can be any type of business. It does not matter what the offering is. Anyone called can set the intention and run a Spirit-led business. And when they do – all manners not in alignment with Spirit (what you call Higher Consciousness, and Source/Higher Power energy) will fall away and in replacement – glorious new, abundant offerings will come to the surface. It's an ecstatically amazing process that we invite you all into!

- A Spirit-led business is fully intentional. It is filled with ritual. It is founded on a cornerstone of Spirit. Daily spiritual practices are key. All aspects of the business are treated energetically and spiritually – working with the core level of what buoys a business. This is the way you intended to treat everything in life! We are so thrilled so many of you are desiring to treat your businesses in this manner and from there letting it expand further. For many of you, this is the perfect place to start for a Spirit-led Life – take it piece by piece. This is how it has unfolded for Heather and it has served her very, very well. Now, she is on to extending Spirit-Led into every nook and cranny in her life and WOW is all she has been able to say to us and to many of you over and over again.

- A Spirit-led business does not defer to statistics, "experts" or "industry" – a Spirit-led business follows inner guidance wholly and fully. The only level of "experts" needed in a Spirit-led business are the one to two, maximum three guides or members of your Dream Team – as Heather calls it – that you are led to, to keep you as the owner of this business clear and aligned with the Soul of who you really are or what we would call your Source Self. All of you pick up and have accumulated limitations in beliefs and fears that over time no longer serve you. Releasing these and aligning to your core self is essential in a thriving Spirit-Led business. If you make your spiritual "development" – which is really and truly the only development any one of you ever need focus on – your priority and you let your inner guidance from a clear place guide you, your business will thrive. In fact, every area of your life will thrive. There is no other way for it to be.

A Spirit-led business feels good in your body. It feels like peace. It feels like calm. It feels like a big "yes". It does not scramble outside for clarity, it goes within for clarity. When it finds seeming roadblocks it uses practices and tools and supports to shift into the next Highest frequency. Because you know what those seeming roadblocks really are – don't you? They are a call to step into your magnificence further. As we described in earlier transmissions regarding your emotions, every manner of everything including your emotions are signs on your pathway, redirecting, guiding you, showing you a new something to uncover about yourself to release and re-align.

A Spirit-led business is the only kind of business we would ever run if we were in your shoes. We are beyond happy that so many of you are feeling the call for this. We know it will serve you and the desires you have for your life – for abundance and wealth, for greater health, for better relationships – for all of it tremendously well. In this tremendousness you will uncover aspects of yourself you never imagined and you will fly Higher than you have ever flown as a Spirit in a body. You will discover more of your true power and this power will bring you so much freedom and joy and good energy that you will not be able to keep yourself from sharing all of the goodness with all those you encounter.

Trust us, it is really that good.

In eternal Love,
XoTheJOGs

WHAT FEAR REALLY MEANS

We've got to address this business of fear. For so many of you face it, some daily, and some it surrounds your everyday life – on the TV, Internet, newspapers, magazines – everywhere. Why you do that to yourselves we'll never fully know, but what we want you to understand from today is that you do have a say in this fear business. You do have the ability to let the fear get its message to you and then release it. It is not an emotion that has to stay in your body and eat away at your tissue like it does for so many of you.

Fear is an emotion like any other. There is nothing to be afraid of, yet what keeps most fear active is the fear of the fear and what that fear means or says about you and your life.

Emotions are not anything to be afraid of – ever. They are simply guidance. They are another way that your Higher Self, Source Self – whatever you desire to call it – lets you know that there is some information coming up that desires your attention.

There are a number of meanings for fears when they pop up but the biggest core meaning is simply that there is a message for you. The message can be to get away from whatever is causing the fear, it can be that you've picked the fear up from someone or somewhere else, it can be that an old limitation is popping up now because you are ready to, as Abraham calls it, "Step 4" it – what we would call being the calm in the storm. As an example: you are in your life, a fear comes up and you have a choice – will you let that fear take hold or will you look right at it, with all of the calmness you have in your core and then choose to respond to it in a totally different way?

And guess what happens when you do that – when you are the calm in the storm – the fear vanishes from your cells and vanishes from your tissues.

Fear is really just like any other emotion – it has a message for you and once that message is received – not reacted to, but received – then it can release once and for all.

So many of you will push your fears down – "Well, I don't want to look at that," you say. And we aren't saying spend an inordinate amount of time dwelling in it, but do carve out a quiet space and some time and just see what that emotion wants you to know. It's getting your attention for a reason. And then, how about following whatever that emotion is asking you for? Sometimes the fear is excitement and your Higher Self desires for you to claim that excitement rather than stuffing it. Sometimes the fear is saying "leave! get out!" and upon further connecting to your Higher Self, you realize that is the most aligned action.

Only you and your Spirit Team know what each emotion means for you, but we so want you to really take time to play with your emotions. Let them guide you, they are simply giving you information; and if you will stop and tune in to whatever the emotion is and ask – from that calm in the storm place – "What do you need me to know?" you will get so much more richness out of your life. Your life will become fuller because you are no longer zipping by and pushing through, and rushing to/from. You are stopping and allowing what needs to come up to come up. You are not buying into an overreaction – you are not believing that the emotion is "real" from a perspective of – "Oh! Something is wrong!" No, you are taking it as communication from the deeper part of you.

And when you can work with your emotions in this way – oh wow – so much more opens up for you. First, you just feel better in your body. Second, you are more on purpose. You don't make decisions that aren't fully aligned for you anymore. You really take the time to feel and move through it and then create and choose from that more aligned place. Working with your emotions is one of the most powerful tools you can use to stay aligned with who you really are.

And as to our earlier comment about surrounding yourself in news or what we would call fear consciousness – please stop. Make a commitment to only take in information that lifts you up. Stop watching it on the TV, in the movies, in the newspapers (if any of you are reading them other than online anymore), on the Internet – fear and heaviness is in many of these forms of what you would call entertainment. But we have to tell you – if it doesn't lift you up into the truth of who you really are – is that really entertainment? And do you really need the information of every little thing that is happening out there? Couldn't you be a more powerful creator in your own life and therefore spread powerful positive ripples to all you encounter when you are in a state of upliftment more of the time than not?

We know, you cannot avoid it all entirely, but we would like to ask that you avoid it as much as possible. So many of you are feeling fear that isn't even yours. It's fear you've absorbed from those "entertainment" and "news" forms. It's fear you've absorbed from your religions, from other organizations you attend "meetings" at, from your parents, from people you've allowed to be close to you. And we are encouraging you to clear the clutter. Cut out the fear-based anything wherever it shows up. And then when you feel it in your body, it will be much easier to assess what is yours and what is another's and it will allow you to release any fear in your body with greater ease.

Fear is really about communication. Just like any other emotion. And we want you to treat all of your emotions as Divine guidance that is meant to lead you forward into the bliss that you came here for.

We Love you.
XoTheJOGs

GO HIGHER INTO THE TRUE YOU

Today we want to talk to you about terms that we are enlightening Heather on. Terms that Heather has used much of the time (and no we won't be dissecting her overuse of the word awesome – we tend to like that she is so exuberant with her 80s lingo) and that in your culture are used much of the time.

The first word has been used for quite some time in Western culture specifically to describe something as better. The word is big. All uses of this word – big, bigger, biggest – have been used to describe something growing, often exponentially. And we like growth, and we know you like growth – well, most of you do, and certainly those of you reading this like and desire growth as a part of your life experience.

But we want to present to you another way of looking at this term as well as the term Higher, which Heather uses quite often. We want to further clarify what these words truly mean when you are living a Spirit-led life, when you are connected to the Source within you, when you know what many know but are too afraid to admit – that this life thing is first and foremost a spiritual journey.

So, Big. When we are talking about going Bigger or going Higher, it would seem to imply some diminishment of something or someone else. It would also seem to imply going somewhere outside of where or who you are. This is the point we really want to highlight here.

When we are talking about going Bigger or going Higher, we are talking about *within*. Heather didn't understand this at first, she thought Bigger *was* BIGGER – the context with which she had been raised to know it as. She applied it, understandably so, to manifestations outside of her. The manifestations needed to get bigger to show alignment. Now, we'll tell you when you are on this path – yes, many of the manifestations will or can get bigger if you desire them to, but we want to go even beyond that.

Imagine if what Big and Bigger and Biggest really identified were ranges of closeness in and to the Soul of who you really are. What if the Bigness was the Bigness in your capacity to Love, in your capacity to know the truth of not only who you are but of who everyone is? What if going Bigger was synonymous with going deeper? What if when you went Big, you went Big inside yourself first? And you know how this works, don't you? So is within, is without. So when your focus first is feeling the Big-ness within and really marinating in that, a natural byproduct will be Bigness in the external manifestations as well.

For many of you and honestly for all of you walking this path, it will result in a Bigger bank account, that will just naturally occur. It may not be millions or billions of dollars (unless you so desire that) but it will be much bigger than when you were not letting Spirit guide your life, when you were not tending to the garden of your Soul as your primary relationship. So that will just happen. And for those of you who desire it – bigger houses, bigger cars even (for many, including Heather, luxury cars would be the same as bigger here), bigger impact, bigger acts of service, bigger audiences, bigger lists. Yes, all of these things can be part of the Big-ness. But they are not the primary Big that we desire you to focus on. And not all external manifestations will be the same for everyone. You've got to let yourself be okay with this because not everyone's path is to have the same things. We are smacking your hand a little here –stop comparing yourself to others. Their Big is not meant to be your Big and vice versa. Tend to your own Soul, that is the only thing you need ever "worry" about – if there was anything to ever worry about (there's not).

If you put your focus on going Big within, to feel the Big-ness of your heart, your beautiful, radiant heart and the Big-ness of your Soul, your massive, connected to all that is-ness Soul – oh my, oh my, oh my – really it will just be wondrous what happens from there. What happens for many is their focus is on creating or manifesting the big-ness outside of them – the car, the house, the audience, the list, the stuff – whatever it is. And while – because the Laws of the Universe are what they are and they are unchanging – they may experience the manifestation of these things, but there will be something missing. They will experience this as a feeling of a hole within. A hole that no outward manifestation can – nor will ever – fill.

And that's simply because they forgot that the most important Big-ness to tend to is within. It is truly the only Big-ness that matters. Because when you feel that, when you know that, when you are fully connected to that Big-ness that is You – and oh, it is so Big and so beautiful and so expansive and so luminous and so – it takes our and everyone else around you's breath away – nothing else matters. And when nothing else matters – all things that you desire in terms of outward manifestations can flow in unimpeded.

It's just how it all works.

The same with Higher. Higher would seemingly imply that some are lower and this is not at all where we want you to focus. When we say – or

Heather says – Higher, what we are talking about is Higher in your connection to Source. But that would even seem to imply that you have to leave some aspect of yourself down there or leave others "down there" and really, Source is not even up anywhere. It's a term to use when again you are discussing going deeper into Source, deeper into Spirit, deeper into the all-that-is-ness. So we could just say deeper, but sometimes we like to say Higher. Sometimes you like to say Higher and we want to be clear that this is not black and white. This is not, "I desire to go Higher," which must mean, "I am lower." No, not at all. It means you desire that ever expansive connection with the all-that-is-ness that you can feel is all around you and running through you. You want to expand *into* that One-ness because you know there is a feeling of home unlike any feeling of home you have ever known before.

You can go Higher into Loving, which is really the same thing as saying Higher into Source or All-that-is-ness. Higher allows you to transcend the limitations that were keeping you locked out of the knowing of your Divinity. Higher is leaving behind old stories and fears and beliefs that did not allow you to feel the fullness of who-you-really-are.

So when you desire to go Higher, you are desiring to go Higher into the heights of what is possible for you as a Spirit in a body. You want to stay in that beautiful body and reach and expand and experience the depths of Source.

And we say Bigger and Higher – in the contexts that we have given you here – are the most wonderful of desires to have. They will take you places you could not have imagined prior. They will show you the truth of who you really are, of Source, of the Magic of this life, of the miracles that are here for you in every moment and so much more. May you go Bigger and go Higher, within and with Source.

All our Love,
XoTheJOGs

YOU ARE SO LOVED

We Love you. We Love you more than words can say. We Love every single one of you and we want you to Love yourselves as much as you are Loved. For when you know Love, truly know the Love that is within you and all around you, you can do nothing but be overjoyed for all that you have lived and will continue to live. You are so supported in every way. In ways you cannot imagine, in ways big and small. You are so well Loved and adored for the whole of who you really are, and nothing can or ever will change that. Only the Highest Love and Light is yours at all times and you are so supported in experiencing this.

Please know that there will be times when you forget this and that is okay, that is what we are here for and what the Universe will move heaven and earth to support you with. You are so Loved and adored and we want you to know that you need not forget this as often as you do. You truly can be Loved and adored for all of eternity for the magnificent brilliance that you are

But there is one important thing you must do. Remember. Remember who you really are. Remember that you are a Spirit in a body and that means you have all manner of abilities to live the life of your dreams. You have the ability to will what you desire right into fruition – not from a place of efforting or trying, but from a place of peace and joy and Love and relaxation.

You get to have your best life ever right here, right now. Just choose it. And then take the next step and the next step to choose it again and again. We want you to know how Loved you are because maybe then you would be able to Love yourself as wholly and truly and deeply as we do. We want that for you so totally and completely. We believe in you so totally and completely. And we know that it may seem like things are going wrong in your life at times or not going the way you want it to or you can't understand why things are happening the way they are or how it will all turn out. And we want you to know that you do not have to know any of that at any time. It really is as simple as taking the next step and the next. Taking it moment by moment.

Your daily life doesn't seem to allow for this though because there are all of these schedules and plans and things you "must" do. We would like to see you schedule less and just be and let the next impulse lead you forward more.

Perhaps you can start small if your life is heavily scheduled. Perhaps you can start with taking one day a week and have zero plans and – from the moment you wake up until the moment you go to sleep – you allow your guidance to lead you. You just follow the natural impulse to do this next thing and that next thing and take this next step and that next step. You keep letting yourself be led. And as you are guided you get to enjoy a day unlike any other. You get to have experiences you may not have had otherwise. You get to relax, rest and come together with those you may not have if you had followed a plan based on what you usually do or what seemed like the "right" thing to do. How marvelous this is for you! How magnificent it is for you to allow a day to unfold with such ease and grace and wonder and surprise!

We know you are going to be so surprised by what you experience and so surprised by what happens for you with this practice. Maybe after that you add two days a week of unscheduled bliss. Or two days and an evening. And it's not about doing nothing, unless that is totally your impulse. It's about connecting to and allowing the Soul of who you really are and your connection with your non-physical team to lead you forward. To allow you to just feel into what's to come forth from you next. Maybe it's dancing or cooking or laughing at silly YouTube videos or maybe it's calling an old friend or going for a walk in nature – whatever it is – it will be perfect for you. And you may be surprised really by how perfect it is. How effortless your life can be. And that's what we want for more of you. More ease and effortlessness. Less hustle and bustle and making things happen. More allowing, more letting your deep impulses or intuition lead you forward. Letting your days unfold in the most magical way, in ways you could not have dreamed up on your own but that which were meant to unfold with the utmost of ease.

We know that this can feel a little frightening to some of you – those of you especially who are so very scheduled. And so while early on it may be a little uncomfortable, over time we promise you will come to regard your days and evenings of unscheduled, unplanned time as the most blissful. And soon you won't want to have anything but. Can you imagine? Spontaneous gatherings as the norm, honoring the impulse within you at each moment so that you never know what may happen next but always trust and honor that it will be the most perfect for you?!

How Divine!

Try it out, give it some time and space, air it out, try it on – we promise you will find this to be one of your most favorite practices.

XoTheJOGs

EVOLVING IT FORWARD

We are so excited about what lies ahead for us all in this incredible co-creative, expansive, Soul-elevating journey that is Spirit in a body "working" with Spirit to go Higher than any lifetime before.

You know that's what you're doing, don't you?

Taking this lifetime into new stratospheres that you've never ever ever ever journeyed to previously. Some say, "Oh, we had it so good back in the day," – meaning your culture was thriving more in earlier times and we have to tell you – that is not the case. Never in any lifetime before has consciousness thrived in the way that it does now. Never ever before.

Every lifetime, not only the Soul of who you are evolves forward, but the collective consciousness also moves forward. You do see some things evolving more slowly, don't you? Like marriage for instance, it took a bit of time to get marriage to even be about Love, but you got there and then it was the wrong kind of Love. Not the fleeting, wound-mate Love, but marriage is meant – in its initial intentions that most people bring to it – for you and the Love of your Life. You don't need to worry about getting it wrong or it ending when it's the Love of your Life. But so few of you will hold out for that person. Or you dive in, sure you have found that person but you haven't taken the time to really and fully develop your relationship with yourself and with your Spirit Team and with the whole of who you really are. When you take the time to sink into that relationship and that bliss, the Love of your Life is one, more identifiable by you & you by them; and two, it will always work out so very much more beautifully and effortlessly for you.

There are other aspects that the collective consciousness is eking forward in its evolution – but it is still moving forward nonetheless. And what's the hurry anyway? You are all doing a beautiful job and we want you to know that any amount of attention and awareness and light that you shine on any area of your life greatly benefits not only you but all of you as a whole. That's this One-ness piece that can seem so tricky to talk about – but you really are connected in that everything you do affects not only you but the whole of you and the whole of the ability for the collective to evolve forward in the Highest Light.

We share all of this to inspire you into recognizing the power of your actions and your abilities to really shift consciousness – even as seemingly "one" person. Let this inspire you to more greatly align with your core truth. And when you do – oh wow, wow, wow – so much more joy for you in your life and for the collective and for the lifetimes to come.

So we are talking with you today about how each lifetime propels you forward, how it's never been better or more aligned than it is right now. And even if you feel like you're struggling – oh boy – you should have seen what was happening the last go around. You are always moving it forward. Now as we shared in the collective consciousness example, how much you are evolving your Soul forward is solely and wholly dependent on *you*.

Some folks, they don't so much feel called to go within or elevate their consciousness. They still evolve things forward but it is a drop in the bucket compared to what those of you who are fully aware, conscious and living your life working with the alignment of your Soul and your Spirit team are doing. Now of course, this was all how it was meant to be. Meant to in that it was as you designed it to be. You came into this lifetime with ravenously huge desire to take your Soul, consciousness and Spirit to places we all had never been before. And that's why you come in so hungry, really starving for Spiritual Truth. You know that the more you align with Spirit, the more You your life can be.

There's a reason why your research cites spiritual beliefs as a key to longevity as a Spirit in a body. Any type of connection to Spirit – religious or otherwise – enhances this life experience because it's more fully the truth of what you are experiencing. Even religions that you all may deem inappropriate, if they are teaching and focusing on a Higher Power as a primary life focus, that alone is supporting others in living a life that is more aligned.

Now, where it gets all sorts of whacked out is when Spirits in a body start trying to control the definition of what Spirit is & how Spirit operates in one's life. None of you have the right to do that to anyone. You can make your requests sure, but it's not up to you to tell another individual how to be or live or who they can Love or have sex with or what they can do or not do in the world. That's just too much and too fully opposite of the Divinity of who you really are.

If everyone was connected fully to the Soul within and to their Spirit Team there wouldn't need to be all sorts of rules and regulations and laws – from governments or religions. But because there are those who are not yet fully aligned (but who are gradually working their way there at various paces), they create non-aligned structures which then keep people from being aligned and then they create more non-aligned rules and laws and then more people are not aligned and so on and on the cycle goes.

We are not encouraging anarchy as Heather is starting to bristle up as she is grasping some of what we are stating here. We are encouraging Alignment with the Soul of who you really are. We are encouraging you to desire total alignment in every way possible – that desire alone brings you closer to your alignment – and to enjoy every moment you are aligned and to make your actions come from that place. Just don't do a thing until you're aligned. So what, maybe in the interim you spend more time in meditation – this is not a terrible thing at all. Make alignment your Soul intention and your Soul's evolution will not only be more abundant and exuberant, but all of your relationships will flow with more ease, your wealth will soar and you'll enjoy your life more fully. You won't have to read up on rule books because your alignment will lead you to Love and peace and harmony with all.

It really can be that easy and that good.

We promise you.

Enjoy this Divine unfolding. Remember who you are. Remember that your Alignment with the Soul of who you really are is everything. And then enjoy it some more.

And so it is.
XoTheJOGs

YOU CHOSE YOUR BODY, NOW HERE'S WHAT…

In your continued life unfolding you are able to have many experiences. You have experiences in Love and in relationships, in your work in the world, in your day to day unfolding. And we, we are always wanting to encourage you to bless all of these experiences. Bless all of the people, all of the transactions, all of the unfoldings. Because it is what you came here for. It is a gift in and of itself to be in a body and to be able to have the in the body experience.

Even experiences you would label as boring or experiences where you wish you had another by your side to share them are valuable for and to you. The very act of getting up out of your bed or going to sleep at night or waking down the hallway or brushing your teeth or preparing yourself food, all of those what you would call mundane actions are truly a miracle in every way. And driving those machines you call cars or trucks, can you believe it? You sit inside of it and it takes you places. Or what about airplanes shooting off into the sky and getting you to where you desire to go? And your computer systems. There is so much negative talk about screens and computers and Internet but truly dear ones – can you even believe that you can be connected to any single piece of information you desire in almost no time at all? It is truly astounding.

And so every moment of this life that you are in a body you have much reason to give thanks. And we can feel and see some of you sort of rolling your eyes or sighing loudly knowing with your mind that yes, we are correct, but also not willing to be that present with each moment of your life to feel the richness of the moment of brushing your teeth or putting on your clothes. We understand and yet, if you want to live the richest life available to you, then this is what you must do. You must allow yourself to be fully in each moment that you are in, not desiring to be somewhere else, not desiring to have someone else with you, not trying to get out of whatever moment you are in to get to another one, but to be truly, fully and completely present with what is before you right here, right now.

Being able to do this will add years to your life in a way that we cannot fully explain to you in the here and now. Taking conscious focused attention and placing it where it most deserves to be, in this here and now moment lengthens the experience of aliveness that you are in. It allows you to tune in and feel the incredibleness of your body. Those hands, that face, those toes, that grass outside beckoning you. Walking, talking, breathing, laughing – all of it is miraculous. And all of it was a reason why you came. You cannot do those things when you are not in a body. When you do not have a body you do not have the experience of deliciousness that you have available to you in every second of being in a body.

Of course being Spirit has its own perks, but if you are in a body now it's because you so wanted to be. And some of you really fret over these beautiful bodies of yours. You are paying attention to every little thing that seems to be wrong and then doing your damnedest to figure it out – by going to doctor after doctor or healer after healer or just using your own powers of analysis to try to figure it out. And we desire more peace for those of you so concerned about your body.

Your body knows what it's doing, our dear ones. It is a beautiful, miraculous vehicle. It is like your Earth. Your Earth is not run by you. She is affected by you, yes, and she will communicate with you when you are out of line or need to adjust course as she has. Your body is the same. It's good, dear ones. It is solid, it knows what to do. It is set up and created to heal itself. If it does not heal itself it is trying to get your attention. It is trying to let you know a message and it is nudging you to adjust, align and take action.

But so many of you with chronic conditions get into a habit pattern of constantly seeking to heal your body, constantly trying to fix your body and that does not bring you the joy that is needed. And so, that is why we opened this transmission with our encouragement to stay focused on the miracles that your body performs every day. The miracles of having a body. Whatever that is, rejoice in it, even if it is quite limited for you at this time, rejoice in it. And do not worry about the intricacies of your body – what this fluid or that cell is doing.

Stay present to the moment before you. Do your – what you would call – "due diligence" to care for your body – bringing on any healers of any kind that you feel a deep Soul resonance with. Follow your intuitive nudgings on all of that. But do not worry about your body. Can you hear what we are saying here? We have told you that when you worry about others you bring both of your frequencies to a lower level and we are telling you the same is true of your body and your planet for that matter.

Remember the wisdom that created your gorgeous body. Remember the wisdom that created your gorgeous Earth. And be present to that. Be present to all of the wonders of both of those. And when you feel a strong inclination to go this way or that way, follow it. But until then, marinate in the now moment no matter how "mundane" you "think" it is or how your mind may try to take you out of the beauty of it. You are in control of your focus and you can redirect your focus to whatever feels best to you. Use your power to redirect your focus to the knowing that this moment is precious. This body of yours is remarkable in every way, no matter how it is showing up. Remember that your body is created to heal itself and that if you will keep your focus on the present and what lifts you up and the Light that is within and all around you, your body will thrive at new levels.

You needn't be kept down by diagnosis or limitations around your body. Nothing is irreversible, there are no incurable illnesses, there is only your perception of these illnesses as such, there is only what Heather would say "your buy in" to these illnesses as such. We do not know – well, we do know and we won't go too far into it – but why in the world Spirits in a body go to such great lengths to study and label and then forevermore put on another Spirit in a body this belief that you have this disease forevermore.

You do not have this disease or that disease or any disease forevermore! Only if you choose to believe this do you. If you would work with your Higher Self and with your Spirit Team and follow their wisdom wholly and fully you could and would "cure" any form of dis-ease in your body-mind. Any of it. We do not care what the supposed experts say. True experts truly connected to the Source within and around them would never, not ever tell another being – human or animal or otherwise – "You have this thing which has no cure, you must live with it," and then throw toxic chemicals at them as the means to sustain their aliveness while dealing with this alleged disease.

We wish you would all stop participating in this charade once and for all. We have told you, quantum physics tells you – this life experience is a hologram that is malleable and perception based. You get to choose what beliefs you anchor into. And just as sure as someone can hand you a diagnosis, you can hand yourself the Source truth, which is that with alignment and with Source, anything is possible. Anything and everything is possible at any time.

So do not worry so, do not fret. Your body knows what to do, you must only give it the climate in which to do it and you do that by following your deeper nudges and by following the guidance from your Spirit Team. They will align you with the proper healers and doctors, they will align you to whatever you need to do to allow your body to thrive in the way that you meant for it to thrive when you came here. We want this all put into perspective for you, because there is far too much fear and far too much worry and far too much heaviness around these bodies – these wondrous bodies – that are yours, that are meant for you that you specifically chose.

You know that right? We have told you this before as well. You chose the body you have. You said before you incarnated that you wanted the body you have. You knew the vibrations that were in your trajectory would have an impact on your body, you knew the limitations you picked up along your way would affect your body and you even knew how that might go. But you still wanted that body that you are in now because you knew it was the perfect body, the perfect guide, the perfect teacher for you. That you could not live the fullness of this life experience without this magnificent, wondrous, glorious body.

So dear ones, follow what we share here. Take it to heart. Shift your perspective on this most important topic – you are ready for this and your body is, can you feel it? It is breathing a deep sigh of relief in your acknowledging and fully receiving our transmission.

And so it is.
XoTheJOGs

PURE LOVE & LOVING

There is much to be said on this topic of Love. We know it is a strong asking within so many of you, so many of you eager to understand and know more about this thing that you cannot *not* desire in your experience as a Spirit in a body. We have said, as have many others, that Love is the core of why you're here – because it feels so good to Love and because Higher Consciousness in whatever form you resonate with is totally and completely Love. How did Jesus heal so many? How do other great healers heal so many? It is through their focus and connection to Source energy – which is Love, pure and total Love. And it is through this connection to pure and total Love that any great, radical transformation can occur. When you Love in the purest form – without agenda or desire for anything to be anything other than it is – all manners of your world can align with the core of what they are meant to for you.

And yet so many of you have such very specific ideas about what Love is and how it looks and who you can Love and how they look. And we say – that is not pure Loving. That is loving with agenda and we want you to be able to take a minute right here right now to feel into your heart, deep, deep within your heart to that place within you that is purely Loving. That is pure Love, where no other agenda than to Love resides. Just sit with it right now. Feel it deep within you.

This is buried deeper for some of you than others, depending on how much encasing you have placed around your heart, how much protection you've created – protection from what we cannot fully understand because with pure Love, there is no need to protect. With wound-Love yes, you feel that strong desire to protect. But we want you to know that the more you can be pure in feeling the Love within you and then for yourself, then you will radiate that outward and then nothing other than pure Love can ever come to you.

So if agenda-ed Love comes to you, it's only an indication that there are some beliefs or aspects within yourself where you are also loving in this way.

No big deal. Just information, information you can use to shift and adjust into greater alignment with the whole of who you really are.

Letting yourself feel this Love deep within you is something we would recommend as a daily practice. Everyday sitting, lying down – however you are drawn – and stating your intention – stating it out loud even: "I wish to feel the deep pure Love within me," and then just see what happens. Notice the sensations in your body, notice how you feel, notice what comes up for you. Maybe it's tears or chills, or any range of sensations. Be present to whatever comes up. Some of you will say "but I felt nothing" and we say to you "that's impossible – you are always feeling something" – it's simply a matter of how connected you are to your feelings and what they feel like.

So, daily sit with this desire to feel the Love within you and then as you get more comfortable with this, ask to feel the Love that you have for you. You have for you, you may say? Yes, the Love that the Source within you (Higher Self, Soul Self, or whatever you prefer to call it) has for *you* as this current incarnation of a Spirit in a body. And again, notice the sensations, notice what you feel, let whatever emotions want to roll in, roll in.

The more you do that, the more you allow yourself to feel the Love within and for yourself, you create this light of energy all around you that is radiating Love. And when you are radiating Love, do you know what comes to you? More Love. More Love that matches that deep Love within.

And we know – you were never taught to do this – but you are now and consciousness is at a place to receive this information in the Highest Light it has ever been able to receive it. So, since you are receiving it now, do it now. And teach this to your children. Teach this to your nieces and nephews and neighborhood kids – all of them. Of course it would be wonderful if everyone's parents taught them this, but not everyone's parents know this on a conscious level. So teach it to any and every child you can. Because the Love within and the Love for yourself are imperative for you to feel and to know what the Love from another could ever feel or look like.

So these ideas you have about what Love is and how it feels – they come from what? Past experience of being "Loved". And for many of you, your past experiences of feeling Loved have not been as seamless and pleasant as you would like. Because many of you were raised by people who didn't have this practice either, who didn't know what pure Love felt like. And so, you grow up thinking, "Well, that didn't feel good a lot of the time – but they say they Love me, so that must be Love." And then you go into the world radiating that version of Love and therefore attracting that version of Love and you wonder as you become more and more aware and more and more aligned why it feels terrible more of the time. And it feels terrible more of the time because it is not truly Loving. It is not pure Love, it is not the true Love within you. So the Source within you is letting you know, "Nope – sorry – there is more pure Love you could be feeling and it's not happening here."

And it's not the other person's fault or anyone's fault – it's just what is when no one has taught you about how to Love and feel the pure Love within you and allow yourself to feel the pure Love that you have for you.

So try it out Loves, let yourself practice this practice. Forget about going on dates and trying to snag your guy or girl or or change your current guy or girl – do this for 22 days straight and watch as Love strolls right in without a care in the world.

And so it is.
XoTheJOGs

DECISION-MAKING 101

Whenever you are wanting to know how to make a clear decision or how to get clear to make a decision you must first remember this truth: there is no wrong decision. Heather is gasping at this right now because this transmission is emanating from a strong desire within her to make the "right" decision in an area of her life. And we Love telling you and really what we're doing is reminding you because at your core you know this – there is no wrong decision. There really isn't. True you can choose a path that has a bumpier ride, but even so, it's not a big deal. You can always get your bearings, you can always recalibrate, it will always work out for you.

So many of you are paralyzing yourself in trying to make decisions about all manner of things that are "right" and so in your effort to find the "right" path you block the flow of the Magic that can lead you forward in just the direction you need. You're often – and we are watching you while this happens – you are often rushing to make a decision, as if you pull the plug quickly enough somehow you'll escape any "wrong-ness". And truly there is not a wrong decision for any of you on this planet.

There are decisions that evolve you, there are decisions that bring in drama, there are decisions that bring in joy, but if you have a pure desire and wanting for clarity of purpose, you will always arrive at the general intended destination – which will then evolve into another call for a new destination, but we'll come back to that at another time. Some decisions may be bumpier than others, but often that is exactly what your Soul wanted so that you could evolve forward in big ways. So, so many of you are saying – "Well, if I have a less bumpy ride than that means I did it right." And we are saying, "Come on – you think it's that black and white?" Well, we are more gentle than that, but really – it is not at all like that. It's not right or wrong, black or white. It is following the vibrational trajectory that is here for you that you chose before you incarnated. Well, it wasn't just you who chose it, it was you and your Spirit Team, but we digress.

You are wanting to find alignment with the choices/decisions that most accurately reflect the vibrational offering that your Soul decided it wanted in this lifetime. And you can tell where you're at in relation to that trajectory by how good it feels. And yet! And yet, you can be in the midst of something that does not feel super good…and yet you can also feel something really big, juicy and exciting en route to you even from your position of not good feeling. Ever had that happen? Heather had that happen with the breaking off of her engagement. There were moments of her feeling awful and then at the edge of these moments was this distinct, clear knowing that she was evolving something massive forward for her Soul and her family line in this choice. There was a part of her, that Higher Self part of her that was shining through even still in those moments where she seriously doubted herself and what was happening that was shown to her to let her know that a Higher Calling was in fact calling her. That she had not done anything wrong in being in that relationship and she was certainly not doing anything wrong in leaving that relationship. In fact, both were the "right" choices for her!

Yes, that's right – two seemingly opposing choices and decisions can absolutely be the right decisions for you. Now we know you are wondering and questioning us here – like didn't you all just say there's no way to make a wrong choice, so how could there be a right choice? Yes, let us clarify our transmission further for you here.

A right decision feels good to you in your body when you make it. A wrong decision feels not good to you in your body when you make it.

Aha! You say – but you said Heather was feeling awful about her break-up decision so how could that have been the "right" choice?

You must go deeper than the surface feeling. So, what was the thought Heather was thinking that made her feel awful? The thought was, "I'm such an idiot." That thought felt terrible, and it felt terrible because it was as far from the truth as she could get (or just about). The thought of not being in that relationship felt GLORIOUS to her, it was the best feeling in the world to her, it was the other thoughts about being a failure that were making her feel terrible.

So yes, you must go deeper here, that is why we are saying it is not a black or white ever. It's not go here is right, go here is wrong. It's boiling it down to what are the thoughts at the root of these good or not good feelings and when you can distill it down to "taking this action feels good" and "taking this action doesn't" – then you know which way to go. And sometimes the only clarity you can get is for the next baby step forward and that is okay. You do not need the clarity for the end all be all, in fact, that would defeat the whole purpose of this glorious life experience you are having.

Here is the thing about being a Spirit in a body – you have the mind – the mind can tune in to a variety of conditioned frequencies from your culture, religion, childhood, etc. So you are in this process as you are evolving the Spirit in a body forward ever more, of distilling down to the Soul within you and your Higher Self – that part of you that remains in non-physical and that is what you let guide you. This is why release of this conditioning is so valuable and why Heather's Soul Alignment work has been so successful and profound for so many and also for others who are offering from a High vibrational place clearing and release of conditioning – it makes getting to that clarity so much more effortless. And of course you came for effortless.

Okay, so let's say – as we feel Heather asking us. Let's say you just cannot feel the alignment of what you call right-ness in your decision. You go do what you need to do until you can shift back into a Higher vibrational place. Not knowing splits your energy all over the place. So when you know what we shared with you and you are feeling into it, distilling it down and you still feel unclear – go for a walk, go dance, go watch a funny kitten video – just force yourself into a new environment that will preferably get your body moving or get you into a totally different space – like comedy. Then come back to whatever it is you are trying to get clear on and you will have better clarity.

We gave Heather a decision making exercise for her Live the Magic retreat this year and what we are sharing here takes that to a deeper level. You see, this evolutionary process and what we've shared in earlier transmissions is that going bigger is now about going deeper. Deeper into the truth of who you really are, deeper into the truth of who all are, deeper into your connection with all that is and with yourself (one in the same really).

This gives you more to chew on. Play with it, try it out as we encourage you to do with all that we give you. Let your own experience and guidance lead you forward from here with this.

And for heaven's sake – trust yourself more. You are so much wiser than you know. And really you cannot get it wrong. We will and are always recalibrating for you. Don't beat yourself up, just keep choosing what feels the most aligned, feels the best – the most fun, the most glorious and know that it will always work out in your favor. Every time, no exceptions.

And so it is.
XoTheJOGs

CHOOSE THE HIGHEST ALIGNMENT

In this life you have special choices to make. You get to choose a number of things – the delicious, Divine food to put into your body, the delicious, Divine drink too. You get to choose how to adorn your body and how you wish to present yourself to the world. You get to choose your thoughts – a lot of them anyway. What do we mean by that? We mean that you get to choose which thoughts you get to engage. Once there is enough energy behind a group of thoughts they begin to auto-populate if you will and take you in various directions.

We know sometimes folks feel like they can't get a handle on their thoughts. To those we say – go sit, be still and be quiet. Focus on your breathing, listen to soft music, place one hand on your heart and one hand on your belly. Do this every day for 11 to 22 minutes and watch what happens over time.

Time, your version of time, is a beautiful thing for you as a Spirit in a body. Because daily focus and consistent action build over time, they build to create their own energetic field or vortex or matrix and that energy can carry you to whole new worlds if you let it. But the content of these thoughts is up to you and your connection with your Spirit Team. If you find yourself in streams of thoughts that do not feel good to you, and you are unable to choose something that does feel good to you – you can always call on your Spirit Team for support. And by all means – please do! We are here to help and we want you to call on us! In fact – did you know that if you do not call on your Spirit Team they cannot help you? We are Heather's Spirit Team and we were thrilled when she first began to utilize us. At first she had trouble interpreting our transmissions as clearly as we desired but just like any exercise, over time, day by day in her asking and her desire to be Spirit-led – we could come through clearer and clearer. Now she can hear us most of the time. She will go to do something – like repetitively check FB and we will say to her – "Don't do it," – we did that just before she went to bring this transmission through. She saw she had some FB activity and went to instinctively check in and we brought in the message "don't".

Heather has learned over time through some of her own trial and error to listen to these whispers and knowings. She sees and "hears" them but there are a number of ways your Spirit Team may communicate with you. What it takes is practice. It takes day by day asking and being open to receiving. It also helps to be clear in your conditioning and static from media, culture, religion. So we recommend having some type of daily practices that allow you to be as clear and open as possible. Early on in Heather's journey she was not open, she was not receptive. When she came to us in Brazil seven years ago she was wound so tight. Her mind buzzed, she was running on autopilot by conditions and programs that she had amassed through her intense religious upbringing and her family life and her culture. All of you are like that. But all of you are also like Heather in that – with desire and consistent day by day asking and openness – your life can be one that is Spirit-led or in the Magic as Heather calls it.

When you live from this place, your life becomes more effortless. It is not that everything goes exactly the way your mind wants it to – oh no – but it does all happen exactly as your Higher Self intended when you incarnated so that you can pick up the pieces you need to become the Highest, most joyful, most vibrant, most fun Spirit in a body you have ever been in any lifetime. So your choices are real and your choices do matter. As we've told you, you don't want to get yourself all wound up by worrying about choosing wrong. You do want to make your focus on your alignment. Alignment. Alignment. Alignment.

When Heather began her journey she was so focused on healing. She felt broken. Her childhood was a mess, her parents were a mess, the men she was attracted to were a mess – she wanted to be healed. But we guided her, gently at first and then more directly to shift out of that malarkey. That's what it is – it's just not true. The only thing that matters is that you are aligned to the Soul of who you are which automatically will align you to your non-physical supports or what we are calling your Spirit Team. You have your Dream Team with your physical entities and you have your Spirit Team with your non-physical entities. We really like that. It makes us smile.

Well, if we had cheeks we could smile, we are making Heather smile to let her feel this fully from us.

So, you can choose what you wear, the thoughts you engage, the people you engage. And if you listen or tune in or feel or allow yourself to know, you'll notice that your Spirit Team is there with you guiding and nudging and directing. There are some stores that Heather can't go into any more. We simply won't let her. When you focus fully on being Spirit-led there will be places and people that you may have had in your life for a long time or stores you went to for eons or travel or hotels or restaurants or homes and then one day you just can't go back. You literally cannot do it.

Heather has a tendency to want to look back and ask why – what changed? When was the moment this shifted for me? Why did it shift? We remind her that it doesn't matter. What matters is acknowledging and knowing that it has shifted and that is enough to honor that.

We know many of you on this path have had this experience; you used to be able to do something, to "choose" it over and over again and then one day you wake up and you can't anymore. That's us. That's your Spirit Team, that's your Soul guiding you, letting you know when you've out-evolved something that used to be commonplace for you. And you will never stop doing this. In this lifetime, in the lifetimes to come, it will always be like this for you. You are ever-evolving beings on an eternal, everlasting journey.

Even in the Spirit realm there is choice, this ability to choose from a certain vantage point and then as we too evolve, we can no longer choose from that perspective any longer. The choices are usually far different than yours – we are operating in a whole other vibration of course – but it's similar. You never get to stop choosing. You are never not empowered.

So nothing happens *to* you – not thoughts or people or situations. Yes, things may happen that you feel like aren't what you desire, but you can choose how you respond to that situation. And depending on your choice, you rule the vibration of that experience.

Notice the tendency to go into blame, victimhood or self-disrespect. And then as you notice it make a choice to not go there. Make a choice to tell a new story.

We are working with Heather on this. She will notice a not good feeling thought come in and she will want to dissect it, "Now where did this come from? Who put this here? What does it say about me and my path if this is coming in?" And we have to stop her and say, "Enough – just choose a better feeling thought." Pick a fun thought. And then, fun she could do, fun she knew. So she found a thought that was fun and she got back into her fun visualization and we immediately sent her physical manifestations that showed her that she was lining up the energy in a more powerful and supportive way for her.

And your Spirit Team does the same for you. Choose the Fun thought. Choose the thought that brings a smile to your face. Choose the clothes and the food and the people and the opportunities that do the same. If you lived by this one principle alone your whole existence would change – you would be forever shifted into a frequency that is in far greater alignment with who you are.

And we feel some of you right now saying, "Oh no, I'm not there a lot of the time." Stop that! Don't use what we share as a reason to be hard on yourself. You're not going to only feel one emotion all of the time, you are going to have a variety of emotions at various times – enjoy them. And when you notice the thoughts inside of you and you don't like them, choose a fun one. That is all. That is all. It really can be that simple.

Remember your Divinity and everlasting-ness. There is no hurry in all of this and yet there is urgency. You can feel it, can't you? You can sense it, don't you? You are shifting at a rate that is faster than human consciousness has ever shifted. You are evolving the current vibration forward in a way that they have not been evolved forward before. You can sense your bigness amidst all of this, can't you? You know that you are Divine when you allow yourself to feel this frequency, don't you?

There has never been a time like this – ever before.

And what you are doing in this lifetime matters so supremely much because it is literally changing the face – literally and figuratively – of what it means to be human, aka a Spirit in a body. And that is not something to frown upon, it is something to feel mighty proud of. You are doing this. You are part of the greatest time on your planet that has ever been known. Your Soul chose to be here at this time because it came for the radical big-awesome-ness – as Heather would say – of this time.

So choose. Choose fun. Choose peace. Choose joy. Choose expansion.

We Love you eternally,
XoTheJOGs

YOU CAN HAVE WHAT YOU WANT

There is something especially important for us to share with you today. It's so important and today is the day because the energy in your cosmos is making it ripe for this to come through. Your asking has been strong and we have heard you loud and clear and we have felt you, too. You have powerful desire because you are powerful creators and your powerful desire aligns you ever further towards your desire. But sometimes this powerful desire serves as a block for you, it actually seems to push away that which you desire.

Why is this you might ask? Well, we're going to tell you. We are going to clearly share this with you in a way we have never shared it with anyone at any time before. It acts as a block because wrapped up in that desire is this – your belief that you cannot have that thing which you desire.

It's contradictory we know – you want something at a deep level which you must know means you are *meant* to have it and experience it. Yet, somewhere along the lines of this lifetime – and trust us, in other lifetimes, too – you have picked up this belief that says, "I can't have what I want," "I'm not worthy of having what I want," "There's something wrong with me which is not allowing me to have what I want." And none of this is true, of course, and in your logical mind even now reading those words you know that this is not true. You know that there is no way for that to be true, because deep, deep inside there is a part of you – bigger and brighter for some more than others – that says, "I am Divine. I am here for a Divine Purpose. I am a Divine Creator. I come from Source. I am Source because we are all connected in this universally magnificent way." But you choose to ignore this a lot of the time.

So these creepy crawly fears, those whispers that say, "You can't have this," "You don't deserve this," – oh my – what a bunch of hogwash that is. And we Love using these words that are coming through – we had malarkey in a previous transmission and now hogwash and Heather is asking us very gently in her thoughts, "Where are you guys from anyway – the 50s?" And we say – oh, much, much further back than that my dear.

In any regard – there is this part of you that knows and yet a part of you that denies. What is that? Why is that there? Here's what we can tell you – it is part of this game of Life. It is part of what you came for. There has been this evolution of humankind, of Spirits in a body. And there has been much desire along the path of the physical that has built and built and built. And each one of you are carrying pieces of this amassed – over eons – desire because you all come from the same Source. And because you all come from the same Source, you are connected with many of these same/similar beliefs and fears. Why? Because you all agreed to evolve them forward. You all agreed that you would come here and you would expand and align whatever piece(s) that you are carrying. Some of you are carrying it for an ancestral line, others it's just something you (aka your Higher Self) agreed prior to incarnating in this life that you would help us all out with. This is why it is so powerful and so important when you show up for your life fully. When you commit to living an extraordinary life or what Heather calls the life of your dreams. Because you contain within you many pieces of the puzzle in this game of life. We are calling it a game because we want you to realize that it's meant to be fun. For a long while many people were calling life a School where you're here to learn "lessons" and we just say "ick" – who wants anything to do with that? Doesn't that sound limited?

Well, we can tell you it's far, far, far from the truth. You aren't truly learning anything – it's more of a remembering and a co-creating. And it's meant to be fun; in fact, fun was built into it all on purpose. But we watch you get so serious and so worried and so concerned. And we are saying to you – you have your pieces that you're here for. You're going to have fun along the way – at least that's what our desire is for you and what your Higher Self desires as well, and you are going to evolve it forward. Some of you will evolve all of the pieces forward that you came for. Others just a few – it all depends on your desire and willingness and awareness.

And if you're reading this and you've been following Heather's "work", you are definitely evolving all of your pieces forward. It's not hard, you see. It wasn't set up to be hard or to be a trick you can't figure out. It was set up to be fun – for you to discover this and delight in it and be like, "Wow, this is the coolest ever – I get to eat, drink, have sex, experience all of the momentous beauty of life *and* I get to support the whole consciousness of being a Spirit in a body to become more of its Source self? And that by my noticing what the shadow is in myself (which is really just various aspects of the shadow within the whole of humankind) and giving it to Source and also turning away my focus on the shadow in the world or in others, by doing this alignment, by making Soul alignment my primary intention – I bring more light to the world, to Spirits in a body for the generations to come – wow – what a cool deal!"

And it really is the coolest deal we want you to know.

70

You are surrounded by beauty everywhere you turn. Your incredible minds have brought forth so much advancement in technology and medicine and travel and all the wonder of what is possible when you focus and apply the wisdom of the ages and of the here and now to your desires. It's truly magnificent. It's truly and utterly awe-inspiring.

And then the way you Love and the way you can Love and the people you get to Love. Oh my, do you know, do you know how this feeling is unlike any other feeling anywhere? That when you are Spirit in a body feeling a feeling of Love it is one of the most transcendent feelings you can have? Of course you know this and that's why Love is so important. It's why you have phrases like, "Love makes the world go round." You know, it's the best. And when you have moments where you feel and allow yourself to feel the Love that Source and/your Spirit Team, and that the Higher Self part of you has for you – oh, it is utterly … we are speechless – Heather is searching for the word that could encapsulate the vibration we are sending her on this. She had that experience just now before this transmission came through. She was sitting here meditating and we were just hugging her and wrapping her up in Love and she could feel it so strongly and tears came to her eyes like they are right now and her heart expanded and she feels waves and waves of chills everywhere and knows she is Loved more than life itself. She is Loved more than anything on the planet in that moment.

Of course, you all are. And you all have your Spirit Team and your Higher Self and Source beaming that Love to you at all times. It's just whether or not you'll allow yourself to feel it. And feeling it is one of Heather's most favorite things in the world. She tells us how much she Loves us – she tells us she would Love to hug us to pieces and, we quote, "kiss our faces off" if we had faces. It's so much Love you just want to do something with it because it's expanding and pulsing through every cell in your body.

And when you're a Spirit in a body you get to show another how you feel. You *do* get to physically hug them and kiss them and wrap them up in your Love and warmth. And we would like more of you to do this more of the time with one another. Hug more, kiss more, touch more with the people you Love. Let yourself express this Love, let yourself show this Love in the delicious ways that only you as Spirit in a body can. Enjoy this experience; enjoy all that is here for you in this experience.

There is so much here, so much here for you right now in this moment. And we Love you so very much and we see you and feel you and hear you. And your Spirit Team – they are with you (that's the "we" we are talking about) and they are wanting to wrap you up with kisses and hugs and warmth. And that translates into chills and tears and this deep knowing that you are Loved beyond compare. Because you are.

And so it is.

XoTheJOGs

YOU ARE NOT ALONE

We are with you now. And in truth we are with you in every moment. Your Spirit Team is always by your side. We are always at the ready for you. So what's the difference between someone who knows this and someone who does not? Well, if you know it, then you're making requests, asking, working with us, asking for guidance, asking to be shown and you're enjoying a host of magical occurrences and decoding fun messages and knowing that nothing is only what it seems at face value – there is always a beautiful message wrapped up in it. And if you're not, you are missing out on a huge chunk of the brilliance that is this life.

If you're not, you are like many people who walk around thinking they are alone and that the world is against them or that they don't have anyone, and that could not be further from the truth. You actually are surrounded. You're surrounded by Loving energy and support that desires to be part of your experience in this lifetime. In fact – that was the plan all along. Do you really think your Soul would agree to incarnate with the hope of winging it? Do you really think anyone would think it a great idea to let you go at it alone? You're babies, and when you are a baby you've got a whole host of people, in the most ideal of situations, but you have someone, you need someone to support you, to guide you, to show you the way. In this regard, it never changes, only that as you get older, and your parents or close supports also grow further on their journey you have an invisible, non-physical team surrounding you and supporting you at all times, and at the ready to guide you through the next chapter, the next moment, the next "bump" in the road or the next question that comes your way.

But so many, and it saddens us to see this (Heather is asking if we actually feel sadness and we say perhaps not in the same way one does when in the body, but we still have emotional responses and while we know it will always work out for you, we always want the best unfolding for you and when we see it not going that way it is not the best of feelings for us), so many have forgotten this truth. And so they go searching in things where support does not live and they have a much harder time of it than is necessary. But, don't you know that somehow some way we often find a way to get to them, as well? Don't you notice all of those stories of people who "hit bottom" and then at bottom they have a transcendent experience and then they Love life in a whole new way? It happens to a lot of you Spirits in a body, doesn't it? And while that isn't us or anyone doing it to that person, it is that person doing it to themselves so they can remember. And then when they remember, it is such a huge vibrational shift that they are like from another time and place, they are transformed. They are transformed back into the core of who they really are.

Depending on where you're at, the bump up or over or whatever you want to call it – the bump back into alignment feels so breathtakingly exuberant it's just the best thing that has ever happened to them. And some, some Souls just decide it's easier to make their transition into non-physical rather than go through all of that. Of course we are simplifying it here because there is a whole team (that individual's non-physical Spirit team) that make the decisions around when to transition and when to stay in the physical. One person's choice to make their transition isn't only about them, it's about the individuals in their lives who also will be transformed and will go into a deeper alignment with who they are.

So, it's like this and it's like this with everything and we've said it before and alluded to it in other transmissions and we'll go into it now further still.

You aren't only here for you.

It isn't that your path, that your vibrational path or trajectory is just for you – it *is* for you – and in its is-ness for you it is also serving the collective. It is also serving the people around you and the generations to come and if you are aware and desiring to live at a Higher frequency, your path can have a ripple effect that extends much further than you can imagine. Because we are all in this together, we are all connected, we are all so very much impacting one another with everything we do.

So when one decides to make their transition or "hit bottom" and bounce back – it is for that individual *and* it's for all of the ripples that extend out. All of the lives it impacts. And we hear some of you saying, "Well that's not fair. I didn't need to be affected by my parents' or partners' (or sometimes both if that's the vibrational pattern you're here to evolve forward) alcoholism or drug addiction of whatever their "bottom" was." And we say – yes, you did. Yes you did and yes you do. Because the ripple from them was setting you up for the ripples that you will send out into the Universe. And if you're aware and if you're asking and if you're willing you will rise to a new level of you from that experience. You will transcend that pain, you will transcend what happened and all of the implications that it could mean for you that would not be of the Highest Light.

You set yourself up. You are setting yourself up for success, though, and many forget that and they believe that, "This 'bad' thing is happening to me." And we shout at you – and really we are shouting sometimes but you can't hear us if you're not willing to ask for us – so we are shouting, "Only good is happening *for* you!" This situation or this person transitioning or this addiction or whatever it is – is supporting you in becoming more *you*. It's supporting you in remembering the *you* that you are, the *you* that you came here to be.

Heather wrote about this in an email to her community and she talked about this concept of becoming more fully *you*. This *you* that you are is the you at the core of you. And when you can be *that* core you *and* be in a body – oh well now – you are doing exactly what you all came here to do. And when one of you does it – that ripple is far reaching. It supports generations in being able to rise to the same frequency. It shifts whole consciousness aspects and pieces and thought-forms.

You being you is what you came for – it's the simplest way we can ever say it. And it is a journey, it's a journey where every person, every situation, every occurrence in your life is all showing up with the tall order of allowing you to become more you.

So how do you make the choice to become more you?

First you start by committing to it and committing to being you no matter who it upsets, disappoints or pisses off. Because remember – you being you is going to support them in being them. So you do no one any favors when you do anything for their benefit. You must do anything because it feels like a full "yes" to you. It has to be a full-body, in every cell yes – if it's not, don't bother. Hold out for the full-body yes. And when you demonstrate that – no matter what another may think/say/do in response – you are holding now a frequency that opens the space for them to live from this vantage point. Now they can live from their full-body yes, or be inspired at some level – no matter how big or small to do the same.

Let's start there. Only do the full-body yes. You feel the right-ness of it within you. And some of you are so used to living from the mind or the subject/topic has so many threads of others' thoughts attached to it that you will need to stop yourself wherever you are and close your eyes and get quiet and feel into your body. Ask, "Is this a full-body yes?"

We have been doing that with Heather. Literally, unless it's a full-body yes, she's not doing it. And it frustrates her at times because well, she has "obligations", she has people waiting on her, she has people expecting things from her and she has spent the majority of her life seeking not to disappoint any people in her life. And yet, here she is, on the Spirit-led path, and she knows this is her commitment above all else and so there are perfectly nice people asking her to do things and perfectly nice opportunities coming her way and yet, unless it's a full-body yes, she can't do it.

She tried recently to overstep this, because she had signed up for something several months back before we had her in this position where this was the only way. And so she bargained with us and hemmed and hawed about how she couldn't go back now – she had spent a pretty big chunk of money on this thing and so she would just "make the best of it". And as she lay in bed the night before, she knew – this was not good, she wouldn't be able to do it because her Soul was not in full alignment with it. And we watched her, she tried, she went back to efforting and it just felt so awful to her. Sure enough, her body let her know she was out of alignment, she started having some interesting body sensations and she knew immediately what it was. So she walked away, she did the hard thing that she needed to do all along and from that experience she got this at a whole new level. No more. Never again. Can't do it. Full body yes or she won't and can't do it.

And you see, sometimes you're not going to catch it in time. Like in this case with Heather, she just caught it too late. The message was there, if she had really let herself hone in more deeply she may have caught it. But it's okay because it's always being recalibrated for you. It's always being repositioned. So, you catch it late – you find yourself in the middle of an experience and you realize, "Oh, this is not a full-body yes," – no big deal – get up and walk out. Be polite, be nice or not – it's up to you – but go. And then in a time when you are feeling more relaxed or in meditation you can go back to that experience and see – oh yeah, that's where it was, that's where I chose to hurry past the lack of full-body yes and dive in anyway. And then, sure enough, another opportunity will come your way and then you can try it out again.

That's all this life thing really is – you're remembering as you go, you've got up-lifters around you with words like this to remind you, you've got books and podcasts and radio shows and the Internet all filled with – well, filled with lots of things but if you are in alignment with your Soul you'll find those that are here to remind you of this truth.

So now you have a new practice. Do you like it? Full-body yes or it's a no. Play with this, enjoy this – we will enjoy watching you. Watch how it shifts your world. Watch how you react to it shifting your world. And then really let yourself sink into the expansion and the new adventures and the spaciousness that results from this. Oh, you're really, really going to Love it.

Until next time,
XoTheJOGs

HOW TO GET OUT OF YOUR OWN WAY

One of the aspects of your journey as a Spirit in a body that we watch time and again is that you all have moments where you get in your own way. You know this don't you? You "know" or say you "know" the intended way to allow you to have and experience and be/do all that this magnificent life has in store for you and yet, and yet you find yourself focusing on aspects that do not serve you. You find yourself asserting your will when you know that doing so blocks the energetic flow. You find yourself bad-mouthing another or yourself and yet in your heart of hearts you know – you know with absolute certainty and we know that you do know – these behaviors only hinder *you*.

And while some of you are prone to berate yourself – discouraging yourself, talking about yourself in a less than positive way when you notice the above behaviors in your life experience or just in general – that too only holds you back. There are so many ways that you do this unnecessarily to yourself. Focusing on another and their success and using that as a reason to feel bad – to make them or yourself wrong – is yet another way. And all of this really serves you not one iota at all.

Again, you know this, but so many of you go to these behaviors again and again and they do not serve you.

And so we would like to ask of you something very, very important – we would like to ask you to stop doing that. And yes, it seems as though this would be easy to do and yet you say it is not. We would like to ask you to do something else instead. We are going to make this easy for you and allow it to quickly replace the defeating behaviors we have already outlined here.

We want you to focus on one thing and one thing only – what feels good. "Ahh…" you say, "I already know about this. And if I could, I would." And we say, "Ahh…but you do not know about this in the way that it is intended, about it in the way that will serve you above all else."

You have the powerful ability to shift energy through your focus. Many of you know this and if you're reading this you probably work with this concept in your life. But your thoughts are powerful energy forms, and when you can focus your thoughts on energy forms that feel good in your body, you literally can create new and more aligned and more magnificent external manifestations in your life.

So let's say you see something that instantly takes you back to an old habit thought form of yours – it gets you beating up on yourself or looking down on yourself or another. All that is, is a mass of energy that has preceded it – a reactive programmed response – someone else is having success that makes me feel like not a success or whatever it may be. Who cares where it came from or when it started let's just work with where you're at right now. That information while mildly helpful usually throws you more off track than putting you on track. So you notice this and here's what you can do in an instant to shift this – you can come up with a phrase that reminds you of what your true intention in this life is. For Heather this has been the word "fun" or "millionaire" – both words lighten things for her, they make her feel playful and light and easy.

Align with a word or phrase that makes you feel light and playful and easy. It doesn't matter what it is. Maybe it's a word that makes you laugh out loud – it doesn't matter. What is most important is the vibration this word puts you in. So you say this word once you notice yourself doing the above non-helpful response and then maybe you tap Cortices or you dance or move your body in some way – imagining you are "shaking out" the old thought-forms and habit pattern of response. You use your word, you move your body in some way and you consciously choose to follow the thought pattern of the word you have chosen which calls forth easy and light and playful energy from you.

This is truly and really one of the best and easiest ways to reprogram those old thought-form patterns. You may notice them rearing up and trying to get your attention more once you start doing this – it's only that vibrational frequency rising more to the surface before it completely expires. You literally can discard old thought-forms forever in this way. It needn't be tedious or difficult or trying to do this. All of you have these quirks, these aspects of thought that do not serve you, these triggers as some may call them. This is a piece that you are again evolving forward not only for your journey but for the collective. The more who are choosing not to engage less than supportive thought-forms, the more they will not be accessible to other Spirits in a body. It diminishes the power of these lower vibrating or frequency thought-forms which makes them less accessible to the whole. That's why the collective or group energy is so powerful. When many of you are focused in one particular way, it sends out a ripple of thought-form energy that others of similar vibration can be affected and influenced by if they choose to latch on to the thought.

If you notice thought-forms coming your way that do not feel in alignment with you, you can simply use this process to shift right around them and not take them on.

Heather is wondering how anything could come to you if it is not in direct alignment with your own frequency. There are many reasons for this. In Heather's case, she is an Uplifter of others, so others may bring to her their experiences asking for support. Heather can feel the mis-alignment of the energy and yet it is her role to support the other in remembering who they are – someone who is not a true energetic match for whatever experience they are bringing her. These experiences may be called to you because – as is the case with Heather – it is part of your Soul path to support a certain group of other Spirits in a body. All of you need support in one form or the other. We do not encourage nor do we believe that anyone should ever have to do any or all of this journey solo. It was never meant to be that way.

So yes, you may be a direct vibrational match to an experience because it's part of your Soul's path or journey, or because it's something you have experienced previously in this lifetime or in a lifetime before and it is wanting to be fully released – and you can do so with this exercise we have given you and in other ways that we will share in the future as well. You may be a vibrational match because it is a reflection of something within you, as well. There are so many possibilities before you and it helps for you to tune in to your own deep wisdom to know the perfect aligned response for you and to use a tool like the one we share here to support you in letting go of unhelpful thought-forms once and for all.

We want you to know that there are so many ways that you can shine more brightly in your experience. You can choose so very powerfully where you desire your intention to be, where you desire your focus to be. You can summon through your powerful focus all that you desire – if you have zero resistance to it coming to you. If you have some resistance it is okay and that's where these tools come in handy for you.

Know your power, remember your power and remember that every piece of anything and everything that comes your way simply gives you an opportunity to remember the truth of who you are – without exception.

In Love,
XoTheJOGs

ALLOW YOURSELF TO RECEIVE MONEY

Tonight we have a transmission for you regarding money. Money – this thing that so many clamor for, so many desire, so many feel desperate with or without. The process of money and acquiring money is so simple and yet it can evade so many and rule so many others. The trick with this Money piece is to first stop giving it so much power over you. It's so important to recognize that it is just a thing, another thing just like anything else. And because so many place it in a state of high value and because it is how you transfer energy for output and input, it has risen it's desirability by all or most.

We are not in criticism of money or the system of exchange. Exchange is a natural law of the Universe. You see it in everything. There is always some aspect being exchanged for another – rain leaves the clouds and the flowers blossom. The flowers blossom and the bees thrive – and on and on it goes in ways big and small. So exchange is an important component of anything in the Universe. Not in a transactional way, mind you, but rather in a way that allows each participating member to thrive. That is why the big component – or trick as we are calling it – is that all money must be connected to allowing another to thrive in an expanded way.

So that when you are giving or receiving money you are inherently connected to the knowing that this organization or person or company or system is going to thrive at a newly expanded level because of the abundance you are giving to it. And you, you in your receiving of said service or item or aspect will also thrive in a newly expanded way because of it.

We felt this transmission was most appropriate as so many of you in the United States are making your tax payments – something that culturally is looked down upon with much disdain. Much negativity is directed at these organizations or governments as you call them. Heather just finished her tax payment blessing ritual and she called us in exuberantly and with much insistence to support her in feeling fully aligned as she wrote checks – some of the biggest she's ever written – to these organizations. She wanted to be flying high as she wrote them; she wanted blessings and light to surround the payments so that she felt so aligned and so High and so good about what she was giving to these organizations as well as what she was also receiving. She began to connect with – out loud – all of the benefits that she receives as a member of her state and of her country. And as she talked out loud about all of the benefits, she could feel herself going Higher and Higher in her appreciation for these organizations. She felt her appreciation for her wealth grow Higher and Higher as she did this as well.

And we guided her to this ritual and have guided her to share this ritual with others (in Spirit-Led Money) because it is a primary & necessary component of money and wealth. There is always an exchange and the exchange must be in service to both. And if you cannot directly feel or know the service that is occurring or the exchange of benefit to you, you must stop yourself and get yourself into that feeling place of gratitude and connection with the benefit to you of what you are paying for. Just as you shall get into alignment with the benefit you are receiving.

For those of you in businesses, as you call forth your wealth you will receive it at a Higher rate and level if you take the time to connect to the service you are providing, the gift you are giving, and your absolute commitment to giving this gift to the world in the Highest Light and best of your abilities. Whenever you receive money from an employer or anywhere, not only give thanks and gratitude in the receiving of it but stand in recognition of the service you provided so that this wealth and abundance could come to you.

It is all exchange you see. Nature is not holding one another up in resentment or ingratitude because it didn't feel like it got a "fair deal". Nature is not holding back or withdrawing because it is convinced it could have gotten more for less. No, nature gives in service to the cycle of life.

So it is with your money exchange. It is an exchange that is part of the cycle of life. And how fun it is! Some of you argue adamantly in favor of trading services and argue that money should be eliminated. And we say – lighten up, don't you see how perfect this really is?! Don't you see the freedom that is allotted to you beyond trading? Trading services always and for everything enslaves you – with the addition of money you are free.

Let us explain more.

If bartering or trading were the only form of economy, that would mean you would have to align with each, separate individual to provide for you everything that you could give in direct proportion and alignment with. It would be near impossible for you to give at the same rate as others could give to keep things equal and "fair". With the advent of money – or cash-money as Heather likes to call it – you receive money and give money which allows the provider to be free to spend it however he/she would like and with ease. You are not bound to give your lifeblood in that moment or in a moment in the future. You are immediately free to receive said service, pay with cash-money and the transaction is complete! It simplifies things tremendously and frees up all involved to have more of the experiences they crave and desire, and to be free to spend their money in any way that feels most aligned for them.

You see, the advent of money created freedom, it created spaciousness, it expanded what was possible for you. And so, despite there being many who gnash their teeth and complain about the use of money in your cultures, we say you would be so much better served by embracing the evolution and using powerful alchemical focuses of gratitude, blessing and more gratitude to attract all that you desire (& more!) to you.

You would feel so much freer if you would just embrace the beauty of money and the possibilities it brings into your life. If you would take the time to line up your energy and your gratitude with anything and everything you spend money on – you would experience a deeper joy with those items and aspects and you would thrive in a new way in your life.

Deeper joy and peace, greater and more expanded experiences in life – aren't those the things you all desire? And is it no surprise that money leads to all of this when you take the time and energy to line up with it? When you make it a priority to appreciate and be in gratitude to that which comes to you – it allows you to have a Higher quality of your life experience. And don't you all desire that?

The money then becomes a part of this Divine journey that you are on. It is not the means, it is not the end, it is not everything. It is a fun and distinct part of the journey. It needn't be a focus of stress or worry or even the enslavement that occurs when that is all that one focuses on. Money is meant to be part of your expansive journey. It responds like all of nature and all Spirits in a body to gratitude, to enthusiasm, to positive talk. Money, just like nature & all things, is energy and so it responds in kind to your focus and attention on it – positive or heavy (negative).

In fact, as we take this a bit further for you, everything responds to your focus and attention on it. So what you think about your government organizations as you write those checks, what you think about the services you receive from the companies you do business with, your beliefs about the people you are receiving products/services from – all of that energy goes out and comes *back to you*. So what are you putting out there? Bless your transactions, bless the organizations, bless the governments (no matter what country or area you live in), bless the people you are giving the money to because all of that blessing goes to them *and* comes back to you. This is a Universe of exchange, energy flows out and flows back in. If the energy and focus you are giving anything – money, organizations, people, etc. – is negative or heavy or dark or sarcastic or cynical, that energy will come right back to you. If it is light and positive and happy and supportive and in gratitude, that energy will come right back to you.

The fantastic thing about all of this is – you get to choose. You are choosing. In every moment you are choosing what energy you are putting out there, which helps you know the energy that is coming back to you. You can argue with this, you can disagree, you can scoff that it's not fair, but it does not matter what you say – it is law. It is how this blessed Universe works that you are in and we will encourage you to follow and work with the laws of the Universe because only then can you experience the life you so desire and that you so deserve.

All that you put out will come back to you a million-fold. We suggest, encourage and ask that you make it as High-vibrating, beautiful, as in gratitude as possible. And when you do that, your life will be one beyond your wildest dreams.

Happy check writing and blessings and bliss,
XoTheJOGs

DIVINE TIMING SUPPORTS YOU

Beloved one, we're here with you today for a great purpose and for a great reason. There is much we wish to tell you, so many things we desire for you to know. And yet, we must carefully lay out the pieces – giving you piece by piece wisdom that you have access to with your connection to your Higher Self and your Spirit Team, but with which it can be so much easier to hear and digest when it comes from another.

You see, all are like that. You can know something in the core of your being but your mind may doubt it or people you consider important people in your life may doubt it and so it causes you to doubt it. And then, you ask or we hope you are asking, and then your Spirit Team and Higher Self – who work together on your behalf – will send you a sign – some kind of nudge or tug or pull to let you know, "You got it – you know this thing that is being said to you right now is true."

And that's what these transmissions are for you. They are reminders of the deep wisdom that is available to all. That is why so many are able to do this kind of "work" in various ways – because their perspective will allow a specific group of people to hear their transmission clearly. That is Heather's role here, too. There is a group of people that Heather can reach in a way that no one else can – a way that will shift them into a Higher frequency of alignment with the Soul of who they really are and so that is why she is doing this "work". And there are others who are the same. They are contracted to reach a certain group of people that only can hear the transmission from them in the way that they bring it through.

That is why there is no competition ever, our Loves. There is no need to worry about will this one get it or that one get it or if I don't hurry and do this or that someone else will take it. No, no, no, no, no. It's not like that at all.

And we can feel the desire to know more about this term contracted that we use. You see, before you came into this body that you are currently in, there was an outline, if you will, of specific experiences and specific people that would be important for you in order for you to experience what you desire to experience in this lifetime that you agreed upon. And often, part of this outline would include key "contracts" or agreements, if you will, of experiences/people that you are here to support or come together with in some way. And so that is what we mean. It is not like you can get this wrong either. You can't miss a contract just like you can't miss the Love of your Life.

It is set up so that you will in fact come together with these people, it can't *not* happen. Now, the timing of it and the exact manner in which it happens is up to you and your ability to follow the signs and honor them and trust your gut, as you call it, or your intuition. You cannot get this wrong of course, as we've assured you many times. Spirit will always recalibrate for you; it will always shuffle things around if you "miss" the message – or aren't able to align your energy is the more accurate way to frame it – to take the next step on your path.

For instance, Heather was told by an intuitive before she even became a BodyTalk practitioner that she did not need BodyTalk – she could do it if she wanted to, but that she already had what she needed to serve large groups of people and support their shifting into a Higher Frequency. Heather could not believe this. The woman told her she was going to lead large groups and would be part of supporting the collective in raising to a Higher Frequency of Consciousness. Heather thought she had just wasted her money! But really, that was us trying to let her know this was part of her path. Only she did not have any conscious desire (her Higher Self sure did!) to lead groups and she certainly didn't believe she had anything to offer a group of people without at least knowing BodyTalk. So, she pushed ahead and all worked out really, really well for her (we wanted her to know she was on the right track and getting closer to where her Higher Self deeply desired to be). But we are telling you right now – one way or the other she was going to end up here like this, translating these transmissions, bringing them to all of you. She was going to be guided to bring massive alignment to massive amounts of people whether it was BodyTalk or not.

This still stuns her as she feels she did not have any of this capacity without BodyTalk, and we assure her and you she did – only she had not and did not know how to line up the energy so that she could. This was always inside of her; this was always part of her path.

And so it is with you. There are certain technologies or modalities you can choose to study and learn and expand into – if it lights you up, by all means, do it. But know that the modalities and their power are their power based on your trajectory and what you are here on this path to do. Some are studying things that are of no use to them. They are only doing it because others have told them that it will have the best return on investment and that it will allow them to be this or that level of successful. And we say – that isn't so. The only way you will know the right path for you is that it will feel like the most natural thing in the world once you lock into it. Now that Heather is here, she is wondering how she was never not here. But prior to that, she thought it was ridiculous to believe she would or could guide anyone anywhere or translate transmissions from Spirit or have anything to do with non-physical energy.

And that just shows you how misaligned she was with her true truth. And that's okay, because she found her alignment and you always do. We are nudging you, we are guiding you, and so every moment of your life is not some random occurrence and certainly the big things that happen to you are not random occurrences; they are *all* happening – believe us when we say this – they are all happening to support you in becoming more of who you really are.

Heather's conscious mind and personality needed the framework of BodyTalk to have the confidence to see what was possible for her and the impact she could have. Fine, we acquiesced to that. We were there with her watching her go through the coursework and cheering her on. But always she was going to be here.

And always you were going to be here, right where you are now, reading this transmission. You – it was sanctioned as such long ago – are one of the ones that is ready for this transmission. You are one of the ones that said – I want to have big experiences in this lifetime, I want to go where no one has gone prior to this lifetime, I want to be right there on the edge uncovering the deepest and most exciting facets of this existence and not only that, but I want to be *creating* new experiences and objects and subjects and topics and joys and laughter – things that have never been known before.

And that's why you are here.

Welcome.

We are so happy you are here, and we are overjoyed at your desire to know more and live more and expand more and Love more and really do all that is available to you as a Spirit in a body. Because there is so much. And sometimes these things happen in your quiet moments in solitude or in quiet moments with those you Love or in big wins in your life experience – this knowing, this alignment, this bliss is available to you in any and every moment.

So what will you do with this?

How will you allow yourself to expand from these knowings that we are bringing to you? Will you take the action that your Soul is asking for? Will you slide deeper into the core of who you really are and enjoy the absolute glory of it? Will you make new choices and will you summon the power that is around you to have a life that is one you may have or never have been able to dream of?

It is our intention that you will.

It is our intention that you will remember this call within and you will allow these transmissions to inspire you to the greatness that is you. That you will remember that there is plenty available for everyone – really, there is – there is no shortage of anything on your planet even though it may be told to you that there is. You are powerful creators and so the minute you decide and align the energy for your full alignment and the full abundance for you, your family, your community, your state, your country, your planet – it is so.

Follow these words and prosper, we promise you this. There is no shortage. There is only abundance.

And so it is.
XoTheJOGs

YOU ARE BEING FINE-TUNED

We entreat you, kindly to lean in and listen closely to what we are about to share with you. It is something that will shift every area of your life if you will follow it and take this guidance, this Divine guidance to heart. We know that many of you are desiring, really yearning for a feeling, a feeling that exceeds all other feelings. It is the feeling of Love. Of true Love, of true alignment with the Love that you are. The whole of who you really are, of your essential self, of your Source self. There are many names of this Divinity within because it is so difficult to use words that accurately convey the Highest Light that is within you and that of which you are made of. So we try here in this way and sometimes the words really land and you feel it. We will keep doing our best here because we so want you to feel in every cell of your body that which we are desiring for you to fully feel.

This feeling of Love, this feeling that is *you* – the true you – is the feeling that you are searching for. It's the feeling you are searching for in almost everything you do. Slow it down, take a breath, and allow yourself to feel this truth. What is the feeling you are going after when you eat that food, when you go to that beach, when you take that walk, when you go to that restaurant, when you call up that friend? What it is that you at the core of you are wanting to feel?

You are wanting to feel you. You are wanting to feel the truth of who you really are.

And the action sometimes can get you there. And sometimes the action doesn't get you there and you feel disappointed. And sometimes it does and you notice it doesn't last as long as you would like, so you perhaps take another action again in hopes of feeling or aligning with that Love within.

And we say – you can just cut to the chase here, and fast-forward to get to the Love within you.

But how do you do it you may ask? And again, you are wanting an action to get you there.

And we understand because how else can it happen? It is a fine-tuning that is happening here, an uplifting of your frequency into greater alignment with the core of Spirit that you know at a very deep level and that is accessible by all of you. So we will give you a new expanded understanding now on how to feel the Love within you.

You first must ask to know and feel the Love within you from your Spirit Team aka your Guides and Angels of the Highest Light, and you ask to carry this Love with you wherever you go and in whatever you are guided to do.

And then you meditate, every single day you meditate. And perhaps your focus is to feel the Love that is within but we would like it better if there was not agenda of achievement for this. You meditate because you know deep within that it is most in alignment for you.

And then from this place you take any actions that feel good to you.

When you now know with this new knowing that the whole emotion you are after, what you really want to feel is the Love of yourself, the Love Source has for you, the Love all of Spirit has for you – then you've now shifted your frequency. Yes, this seemingly slightest of tweaks in your understanding, this actual expansion in your understanding is what can make all of the difference.

What you'll find – as Heather is finding as we are guiding her day by day, sometimes moment by moment with this – is that you do not need to "do" as much as you did before. In fact, you may find as Heather does that there is not much that you even want to do other than simmer in the enjoyment and the pure pleasure of feeling the Love within and all around you.

And that in itself shifts you and your life into a frequency that aligns more fully with your vibrational trajectory and allows more of what you desire to flow to you.

Then when you do take any action, you are feeling so in that place of Love that you just get to enjoy whatever it is – whether it's going to the gas station, or sitting on your deck staring at the trees blowing in the wind, or it's going to the grocery store. And you will find, as Heather has, that so much just comes to you when you live from this place, so that somehow the details of life sort themselves out in new and surprising ways, making merely a fraction of the action you use to take needed to bring in "bigger", more aligned manifestations than when you took a whole bunch of action with little results.

We want you to prepare every day like this. To set this new focused intention, to tune in to the frequency of Love that is at your core.

Often you will make another person – romantic or friend – as your way to feel Love and let yourself feel Love and we understand that because it can seem easier, but then it is just like the chocolate cake or the other actions you might be taking to feel Love – it won't and can't last.

It is far better to feel it already within you and let that emanate from you in your life.

Even better to know is that this Love is not somewhere outside of you –

even in the ethers of what you may call "heaven". It is all within you. Earlier on in our transmissions to you we asked you to feel this Love for yourself. And now we are guiding you in a fine-tuning of what that is really about.

Because we see you, we so many of you doing, doing, doing, doing, doing. And you know the principles of Law of Attraction, you know how this stuff works. And yet, still you are overly focused on this achievement/doing wheel – a hamster wheel, really – that is not allowing you to really and truly feel the bliss that is you.

The other day, Heather was in meditation and we, in concert with her, supported her in going deeper than maybe she has ever gone before – her meditations are becoming more and more like that now that she is at this place in her unfolding – and she was in such a state of pure bliss in this meditation she could not even fathom moving out of it ever again, and when she noticed it she was just so astounded, but then – almost immediately in her noticing this Love Bliss – she began to pull herself out as she noticed her mind wondering how long it would last to feel this good and contemplating how she had meditated before without feeling this good.

We share this with you because we want you to know that this is a process. This is a process of remembering the core of who you really are and what you're here to do/be/have in this life from a place of not having to do but from a place of alignment. Ah, we hear you worried about not taking action and what that would mean for you. You can't help but take action, we are just asking you to tune your frequency to a Higher level so that the action you do take can be more aligned. Which makes it all so effortless.

It makes it as such in that you'll think you are going to go "do" something, and then you sit with this knowing of Love in meditation, and then you come out of it and you no longer need to go do whatever it was you thought you needed to do because you realize that the whole reason you were even going to do that thing was because you hoped you could feel like this. And now since you feel like this, you can marinate here in this bliss and Love and then see what wants to be called forth from you from this fully and wholly aligned place. And maybe as that happens the phone rings, a letter arrives, a knock is heard on the door, your phone chimes and the next beautiful unfolding is delivered to you.

That's how we would like more of you to live.

Not meditating your life away, but aligning your life into further and more expanded bliss.

We know that there is no better way that you could or can live than this.

And so it is.
XoTheJOGs

BRING EASE TO YOUR RELATIONSHIPS & RELATING

One day soon we intend that you will know and feel with every cell in your body how Divinely Loved and honored and cared for that you are. It is our deepest desire – or one of our deepest desires – for you to know while in the body how Loved you truly are. How perfect you truly are, how miraculous you truly are. We want you to know in every cell of your being-ness just how much reverence and Love that all of us have for you. And by all of us we mean Source and your Spirit Team and all in the Highest Light in the non-physical realms. And if you let yourselves really sink into it and feel it, you too would feel this Love, this bounteous, deep Love for all of the beings around you.

At times you get irritated or annoyed or agitated with one another – or you think you are, anyway – and really underneath those emotions is a deep Love for each other. A deep Love for the other simply because they exist. We would like you to tune more into this emotion than any other emotion. When you find yourself annoyed with another, or responding in ways that perhaps you don't even realize why you are responding in such a way (we would call that your unconscious or subconscious at work), we would like you to stop for a minute and place both hands on your heart and ask to be aligned with the deep Love and reverence that your non-physical self has for this being. And sure enough, if you call on us – call on your Guides and Angels of the Highest Light – you will be able to feel this. And then whatever happened can be "dealt" with in a way that is far more easeful for everyone. Solutions instantly appear, and sometimes the need to do anything releases as well.

We are not saying that you should never speak up when you feel tension or discord in your relating with others; it is important to speak up if you feel the full alignment – the full body yes from Spirit to do so. And it is important to share your feelings or make your requests – yes, of course. And we need you to know that the step before all of this – before you reach out and share – is to feel into and connect to that deep Love for the other, and then reach out from that connected place. And when you do that, the other can hear you and receive you in a new, more aligned way and can honor and align with a solution that honors you both. You are bound to bump around with each other in your environments because you have all agreed to help one another in this way. You help bring the unconscious to the conscious, you help to go deeper in to your connection with one another with these instances. What we are suggesting and saying is that before going to any of *that,* anchoring in to the tenderness and Love that you truly feel for the other will serve you all far better. This can be more difficult – we hear some of you feeling/saying – when it comes to family relationships where what you call triggers may be rampant, or in intimate, romantic relationship if there is a history or seemingly so a history of patterned triggers.

We understand. We know that it can seem challenging to you and yet we want to invite you, to implore from you, your also Divine ability to connect to the Divine Love that you have for them first, before approaching the situation.

At the heart of it all, there is a deep Love. Even those who are hurting or killing each other in this country or in other countries. If they could stop for a minute and feel into the heart of who they are, they would find there, maybe just a small spark of Love at first, but upon further alignment with it they would feel a well of Love for the other that they are "supposed" to hate or feel they must hurt to feel safe in who they are.

It is at the core of each and every one of you. This deep Love, this Love that knows no bounds. It is the Love that binds us all together.

So yes, you may get on one another's nerves. You may feel annoyed or angry or rageful even. But those feelings are just indicators of misalignment. And perhaps that individual *is* misaligned for you. Perhaps they do not need to be part of your intimate circle or experience. Or perhaps the emotion is letting you know that you are misaligned in the work you are doing or what you are offering or in the forum that this occurrence is even occurring. Whatever the message of the emotion is, trust that it is simply giving you information about your alignment and that you can easily shift that into a place of more alignment. Tuning in and allowing yourself to feel the Love of your brother, sister, friend, Lover, mother, father, daughter, son, coworker, Loved one, stranger you "do not know" will serve you, and all manners of solutions will be made available to you.

We hear some of you saying it's just not that easy, and again we hear you and we encourage you to begin to work with this. It is of course a practice that builds on itself, for as you open up to your deep heart Love for all beings, it begins to expand and expand so that you can feel it at greater and greater depths. You were born this way, you were wired this way, you were made this way, you all incarnated onto this planet with a deep ability to Love each other. You all came in knowing that you are Love and that you Love all beings. You *all* have that within you. Over time, conditions and experiences may guard up or clog up this ability to feel this deep Love inside of you, but it is still there. So as you crack it open more and more, more and more of it can be illuminated into your consciousness, and therefore bring solutions and flow and ease to all manner of friction or tension in your world.

We promise you, it is within you.

And we promise you that you can Love another very, very much and also choose to be far, far away from them. You can Love another so much and also know they are not the Highest Light for you. And that is okay. What is important is that you allow yourself to feel the Love and then from that place you can choose – in or out? Do I want this person in my sphere or swirl, as Heather likes to call it, or do I want them far away? And you *can* choose. But when you are choosing to push them away from an angry place, or a "triggered" place as you call it, more and more of them will come to you – either that person or more like them. When you can feel the Love that is within you and bless them from that place, and then feel the misalignment of having them in your world, then they go and stay gone and it is all easeful and good for you and for them. Then each of you can live out what you're here to experience separately, without ever needing to or having to or ever seeing or connecting with one another again.

Really, it works like this and is so easy. But if you do not take the time to do your personal alignment first, then it creates far more bumps, far more potholes even if we're using the road analogy. And you just don't need that. You have far more important things to do than hang out in pothole-ville.

Trust us on this one.

Go forth and enjoy, and know that you are Loved so deeply and so truly by all –whether or not they can express this to you.

Love,
XoTheJOGs

LIVE THE LIFE YOUR SOUL CAME HERE FOR

There is an important transmission that we have for you today. And you may notice we say repeatedly that these are important transmissions. They are. Every single one of them has the ability to allow you to remember the core of who you really are, to remember your Divinity, to remember why you came here at this time on this planet. You incarnated in this lifetime for a reason, for a purpose, for a Divine unfolding. It was something you set into motion long ago – a strong desire to come forth and manifest in the physical. A strong desire to see what was possible as a Spirit in a body. A strong desire to support all of the energy that is here on this planet as well as others in becoming more aligned with Source while in a body. It's not a test or a challenge or a school even as some have thought. It's a strong desire. It's a pull that you may not even be able to understand fully. But it is core within you. This desire to create. This desire to play with possibilities, the desire to experience deep emotions and to let them flood your body.

All of this lights you up, all of this is why you are here and why you came.

And you will notice, if you let yourself, that there are other individuals around you that you resonate with deeply. This again is part of this Divine journey you are on. These are Souls that you have traveled with for many, many lifetimes and who many of you will continue to travel with in future lifetimes.

We have said this before and we most likely will say it again and again and again and again. You did not come here just for your trajectory, in fact, not one of you did. It is always to support all in becoming and embodying more of their Source self.

Some of you are holding particular strong anchors for a number of Spirits in a body. Some of you agreed before you came that you would be so fully focused, so fully focused on supporting the collective that your life would be a testament to this, that your life would showcase what is possible as a Spirit in a body. That you would, with the support of Source, shine a light brighter than had been previously shown before and you would inspire those around you to remember their true path and their true Divinity. And in doing so, all go Higher; in doing so, all know more fully what it means to work with energy and to be in a body and to "work" with Spirit. And this is a path that lights up so many, including the Soul it is in. And many of you are carriers of this and you know who you are, you know it fully and you can feel it within you. You've had it within you from an early age, this knowing, this pull, this undeniable thirst for the why, for the healing, for the alignment, for the support of so many as you, too, rise to a new level of understanding of what it means to be a Spirit being and to have a body.

It is our wish, our desire, our deep hope for you that you will heed these words. That you will take these words to heart and will allow them to imprint upon you the call that is deep within you. You have many distractions; you have people telling you what you should be doing in the media, on TV, on the Internet – oh wow, there are so many distractions there – your family and friends, magazines and movies.

There are distractions a plenty, but those who are listening to the call of their Soul finds a way amidst the distractions to stay connected with their Soul and with their Spirit Team. We aren't suggesting you abandon all media (although, we would like you to abandon anything that is not in the Highest Light, that is not uplifting), we are asking that you make your number one focus living fully the trajectory, the path, the YOU that you are here to live fully. Each of you know deep within – some more deeply than others – what this is.

Check in with yourself regularly – are you living the life your Soul came here to live? Do you feel expanded and open and filled with joy most of the time? Do you feel guided? Do you experience magic daily? These are the questions to ask. Ask to know what your Soul truly desires and then begin to follow those steps. Doing so will open doors and open possibilities that you could not have imagined previously.

Until next time,
XoTheJOGs

CONNECT TO WHAT TRULY MATTERS IN YOUR LIFE

When you're in the world that you're in you are often trying so hard to manage so many different aspects of your existence that you forget about what truly matters. You get caught up in things going wrong or potentially going wrong or what this one said or what the other one said and we want you to know that we can understand how it catches your attention and yet we want you to know this very truth – it does not matter.

Here is actually what does matter:

- How do you feel in your body right now in this here and now moment?
- What would make you feel more joyful than you feel right now?
- What thoughts do you need to focus on right now to align with this joy?

That is what matters.

Without a connection to the truth and core of who you really are, there is no way to really know the answer to any of those questions. There are so many people and they want to tell you what to do and which way to go and what program to take and what tips and tricks will make you perfect and fabulous, and then others who are closer to you who want you to make this choice or that choice because they believe it will serve you (and them).

And so, so many of you are running yourselves right into the ground doing, doing, doing, doing for everyone but yourself. And we want to encourage you, to ask of you, to entreat you to really take this time and take time every day to connect with what your true desires truly are.

And we know and we hear you as you say, "But there are new tires to get and kids to pick up and this deadline, and they demand that I do that which I do not desire to do." And we say – that is your work. Right there. Your work is to create a life that does not demand of you aspects that are not in full alignment and full harmony with your Soul and the path for which you are here for. Your job – if there truly was one – is to identify and know and create all that lights you up and takes you Higher.

But some of you, some of you just let yourself get so taken out by the things you perceive are going wrong or not taking you Higher. And we get it, and yet it is not meant to take you out. It is meant to incite you to powerful, creative, joyous action.

"Oh, I'm sick," you say.

"Yes," says the doctor.

"Oh, okay now this is really something else. Think of all of the trouble my body has gone to to get this message to me. Think of what it must be trying to tell me. Think of the joyous-ness that must be on the other side of *this*."

That is the response we are desiring from you.

And when your Lover leaves, "Oh wow, would you look at that. Look at what must be in store for me if this Lover had to leave like *that*. Oh wow, it must be something really amazing because I know that it and all is always working out in my Highest Good. So this – this apparent, alleged drama – is only an indicator that I am one step closer to the all that I so desire from the very core and heart and Soul of me."

And we say, "Yes! Now you've got it, now you get it. Now you understand. You understand that tuning in to *you* is the most important piece of this life journey."

And sometimes there will be pieces of You that you are not so readily and easily tuned in to. Aspects that seem to be hidden from you. Others would call this your "shadow" self, and all we would call it are the parts that still await your acknowledgment and attention and Light. That is all it is. And sometimes the ways these aspects get your attention is a sickness or a Lover leaving or a job leaving or a new person showing up.

But whatever way it happens, you can be assured that if you are more attuned to the core of you the more you would know this truth we are giving to you now. And so, no matter how annoying or aggravating or saddening, you would know that those emotions were not necessary. You would stand in the middle of this said wrong thing happening – this is the calm in the storm that we have talked about previously – and you would know with absolute certainty, "Well, this must be happening so that my life can get even better. Something really fantastic is certainly in store for me now."

It can be as "simple" as your electronics not working properly or a driver cutting you off in traffic. All of it, every single bit of it is just one step or a few short steps or maybe some long steps – it all depends on your trajectory – but either way, it's on its way to your bliss. Every single time. But you miss this because you take yourself down so many tough roads with the stories that you tell. Stories that say you are less than or unworthy or somehow you have screwed things up. And you listen to experts tell you about diagnosis of what is wrong with you and what it means if you have what you have and if you act as you act and it's just twisting you into a knot. And we say – it's within you. Your Soul and your connection to your non-physical – what we are calling your Spirit Team – is what will anchor you into your truth, into your joy, into your bliss far more than anything else.

So for the Love of us, for the Love of Source, please ask yourselves the three questions we started with today. Remember that it's all on the other side of wonderful. Even the wonderful things are just showing you that more wonderful is in store. Don't worry, we'll pick up the "other shoe dropping" topic soon (Heather is wanting us to go there now) but we will leave it here – in the perfect spot that it needed to be in. Soak this up and we will be with you again very soon.

XoTheJOGs

YOU MUST ALLOW WHAT YOU DESIRE IN

Hear this – almost always when you are trying to make anything happen, it simply cannot happen. Do you hear that? Do you understand what this means? What we are calling forth from you here is a way of holding and carrying energy that will allow you to experience that which you desire, and we want you to get this very, very clearly. When you want something so badly, when you are trying to make something happen, when you need this something to happen – it cannot, and will not come to you. The very act of needing and wanting repels that thing that you want.

We are asking of you – we are asking of you kindly but firmly – to stop doing that to yourselves. Instead what we are suggesting to you is this – have the presence of who you really are with you so firmly held that the minute you find yourself pantingly, wantingly, demandingly wanting something, you stop what you're doing and you acknowledge, "This energy, this vibration will not allow me to experience that which I am wanting."

So we know you are asking – well how am I supposed to manifest anything if I can't have anything I really, really want?

And we are saying – no, you did not hear us correctly then. You can absolutely have everything you want, but when you are trying or efforting to make something happen, it cannot come to you.

We are also clarifying here – and this is something we shared with Heather a few moons ago – you are not manifesting anything. You do not manifest anything. You co-create everything. So even if you are not aware or not conscious, everything that has manifested in your experience was a co-creative process, because you have a team that is working with you whether you know it or not. And you can disavow that team and ignore it and push it aside, but your team will do whatever it can to support you whenever it can. And when you consciously begin working with your team, when you are actively co-creating together that is when the magic happens. That is when things flow to you. That is when life just keeps getting more and more and more and more of what you truly desire and will continue to do so for as long as you will allow it to.

So let's say you want something. And we know you do and you cannot help but want it; after all, you incarnated here in this lifetime because you had things you wanted to experience. You had a plan of sorts, a vibrational trajectory that was and is carrying you forward. So you didn't come here to stay inside all day and watch TV. No, you came here to live fully your purpose and experience the magnificence of every moment. And yes, we know there are occasionally those moments on TV; we are not saying TV is wrong but we are saying that if that's all you're doing – you are missing so so so much of what is here for you.

So, to continue, let's say this thing that you want does not seem to be coming to you. All of you have something like this because you were not meant to experience everything you desire by now. Because you cannot. Because everything you desire continues to shift and change and expand and unfold in new and surprising ways. We did not want you to get bored after all. We are kidding here, for anyone who is bored is simply unconscious to the Light within them and is simply avoiding the power of what is all around them and within them.

So if it is not coming and you are trying to decide how to make it come, you are already off track.

Here is what you do instead:

You say to your Spirit Team, very clearly – Heather does this with us all of the time and it works so very beautifully – "You know that I want this thing. You know I desire it from a deep and powerful place (and if you do not desire it from a deep and powerful place it's most likely not actually yours to have, so let it go as soon as you identify this truth). And I am now surrendering this thing to you, my Guides and Angels of the Highest Light. If it is Divine Will and if it serves my Highest Good to have this thing, then please bring it to me with ease and grace. If it is simply not the Divinely inspired perfect time for me to experience said thing, please send me a sign by tomorrow night at ___ (name your time here) to let me know you hear me, you understand and to let me know that it is en route to me. If it is not in my Highest Good to have this thing, please release my desire for it with ease and grace. And so it is. Amen."

And there you have it. You will then receive communication if this thing is part of your path and if you are open to receiving from us – which, if you are making this prayer, then you certainly are – that will let you know that this thing is en route you.

For example, Heather Loves the radio. She Loves it so much. We gave this to her early on; in fact, it has been with her since she was a teen. She wanted to go to Mt. Hood Community College's radio broadcasting school program, but her religion would not allow her. She married a radio morning show host. She has been on the radio in so many different formats and ways and she absolutely Loves it. And so, we have been giving this to her throughout her life in varying manners and again we are bringing it back around – she has been doing all sorts of interviews and just loving, loving, loving it. And she says to us as we have been nudging her, "Maybe I should have my own show?" This is actually not something she has ever considered before until now. And we of course know that this is in her destiny that this will happen for her. And so…it starts showing up in her dreams, opportunities flow to her, and recently an opportunity came in that felt like it might be it. And she really felt alignment in many ways but not completely. And she asked our permission to investigate it more and we gave her the yes, which gave her a lot of excitement because we hadn't given that before when she had asked. So now she is thinking, "This is it – this is possibly the opportunity to allow me to expand in this way that I have been desiring since I was a teen but didn't even really know or understand that I was desiring." And she investigates and talks with some people and does her research only to find – no, it was not the opportunity for her.

And she was a little irritated with us. "Don't send me on wild goose chases," she said to us. And we said to her – that opportunity coming in was the most closely matched to any opportunity that has come your way. And we gave you the all clear to move forward with it because we wanted you to feel the joy of that and the delight of it, and we also wanted you to see what made it not right for you so that when it is the Divine timing for this, you will know it so clearly there will be not one shred of doubt in your body-mind-Spirit.

So sometimes dear ones you get the all clear and you are delighted and excited and you are like, "This is it!" And it *is* it, but not in the way you always think it is. You do this with relationships and jobs and all manners of opportunities.

Relax. Everything that is coming to you is coming to you for a reason – it is giving you information that will serve you very, very well. And some of the opportunities will last a lifetime and other opportunities will not and both are perfectly okay.

Now Heather could have efforted, she could have tried to make this opportunity that came in work for her because she wants and desires this experience. But that would have put her down a road that she eventually would have to bail on because it was not fully aligned with her Highest Good; and it would have been really bumpy and not the joyful experience that is really here for her. So just don't do that. Just wait it out for the full and complete alignment. It is so much better for you when you do. You feel so much better when you do. Your life is filled with joy after joy after joy when you do.

And so it is.
XoTheJOGs

CHOOSE TO LOVE

We are going to pick back up the topic of Love today. It is a topic that impacts every single one of you, and some of you don't even realize how deeply it touches and affects your world. Because when you willingly and openly choose to Love – even those who appear or may seem unlovable – then you are transformed by a power that is greater than yourself. Almost all of you have had the experience of deeply loving another, some of you may guard up or self-protect but in every instance every one of you knows what it feels like to Love another in a deep and profound way to some extent or the other. And Love is something that all become better in the having of it.

It is something that many of you are actively seeking – whether you are in a relationship or currently looking to be in one. And we have discussed with you previously how Love is at the heart of everything and that means that you must Love yourself first and foremost and then radiate that Love to all you encounter – again whether you are in a relationship or not. And also we have shared with you that every single one of you has one Love of your Life. And that has lifted some of you up, and triggered a whole storm of worry and convoluted thoughts for others about your ability to "keep" this Love of your Life when you come together, or others still are worrying that perhaps you have messed it up and have already met and rejected the Love of your Life.

Oh, and we have much to say to you on this. First, there is no keeping of anyone or anything. There is your Divinely aligned path with the people, places, opportunities and the like that are exactly for you and there are those that are not. You are not here to keep anyone or anything – ever. They are aligned and you dance together in this life, or you do not.

And we want to remind you – as we will repeatedly, again and again – there is no messing anything up. Because the Universe is always recalibrating for you. So let's say you are disconnected from your true Self long enough to end the relationship with the Love of your Life, and let's say that your Beloved is also disconnected from who they really are – because it will take both of you being disconnected from the Source within for the relationship to ever end. One person may be disconnected and try to end the relationship in a state of total misalignment but there will always be the other who will hold the Light for the partnership so that it may stay intact. So, let's say you are both sufficiently disconnected from your Source Selves and the relationship must end.

That's okay. It's not great, but if you're disconnected from your Source self, you're not feeling so great as it is. So what then? You then embark on a journey to return back to who you really are. And, depending on how much resistance you have around this, it can take any length of time. Once you return back to who you really are, you will feel the call and the pull of the Love of your Life again. Now depending on how connected or not your partner is from his/her Source self, they will be able to hear and respond to the call or they will not and it will take more time. But we are telling you – it will always come around.

How will you know? Well, you are intuitive beings. Remember you are Spirit already – you have access to an incredible wealth of knowledge. If the Love of your Life is already in your life and you return to your Source self, you will just know and there will not be anything that can or will possibly deter you from aligning with them again. This happens all of the time. And so again, there is never any need to worry about messing it up. There is always the time factor because you can delay things significantly for yourself when you are disconnected from the truest version of you, but again, it's okay, you can always – and we mean always – re-align and hop back on to that place of utter easeful streaming alignment.

When you meet the Love of your Life, you know. It is a return to who you have known all along was yours. Many of you have had this experience or are in that relationship now. There is just no parting from it because the knowing is too strong. You will want things you never knew you wanted because this individual and the two of you coming together aligns you both so beautifully, so effortlessly that there is simply no denying what is occurring. It is beautiful and we Love to witness this.

What we really want to encourage you and ask of you is to connect to where you are right now. Are you feeling mostly aligned with the core of who you really are? If you have a partner, is your partner mostly aligned to the core of who he/she is? Do you know with a deepness within that your partner is the Love of your Life? If you are unsure we want to encourage you to make your full connection with who you really are your number one priority so that clarity can come. Because when you are fully connected with this aspect of you and you maintain it the majority of the time, that individual and you will go Higher together into Loving. And if you are not, one or both of you will know it is time to go separate ways.

For those of you whose Love of your Life made his/her transition into non-physical – what you are calling death or passing on – earlier than you would have liked, you too follow the same practice. Are you connected to the core of who you really are the majority of the time? If so, does that deeper part of you desire for a Great Love to share the rest of your physical experience with in this lifetime? Tune in and see. If the answer is yes, open yourself up to experiencing the beauty of two Spirits in a body coming together to experience the wonder of Loving.

Now there is another matter of importance here that we must address when it comes to Love and deeply Loving. It is regret. We see and feel so many of you with such severe and serious regret about how you treated this one, or what happened with that one or how you are with your current partner even. And we want you to know that that feeling of regret weighs you down, it weights you down, it makes you heavier and it does not allow you to connect to the true Love that is before you and within you. So we want you to tap, breathe and consciously release the regret because it does not serve you one iota. When you can clear that heaviness from your body-mind you have the exceptional opportunity to free yourself into deeper Loving – of yourself first and then of a partner – whether he/she is the Love of your Life or a Great Love.

This life that you came here for is worth living and living fully. Loving is a big piece of this experience that you purposefully came here for. You all know this inherently which is why there are millions of dating sites on the Internet and millions more eyes open at grocery stores and restaurants and bars and festivals, seeking and wondering – are you my one? And the seeking and trying is unnecessary because when you see the Love of your Life, you know. And there is no denying it. Depending on how connected you are to the core of who you are, that is – you will feel and know it immediately, and – as we said before – nothing could or will stop you from taking action.

If you are not deeply connected to the core of you, your Higher Self will be whispering in a shout to get your attention to alert you to this person you will Love and have Loved for lifetimes prior. That is why making your alignment with your Source self your utmost priority is what makes all of the difference in any area and facet of your life experience. Then you will, then you can be guided. Then Love will bless you instead of frustrate you.

Know that this Love is eternal. We shared this with Heather recently and she so just Loved this. The Love of your Life is your Eternal Love. That means you have come together lifetime after lifetime loving in new and surprising and sometimes unusual ways. Sometimes romantic, sometimes as friends or family but always a special, special bond. And in each lifetime you evolve that bond forward; you experience a new, deeper dimension of this great, profound Love. And since you are on an everlasting journey – which means your Soul will continue on for all of eternity – each time you meet up with the Love of your Life, it will grow or evolve in new ways that it had not before. That is why this one feels like no other one feels. That's why there is a softness, a relaxing, a knowing, a feeling of home, an ease, a flow. It is like everything that comes into your experience that is aligned – it feels right in your body. It is, this person is, a full body YES.

So no need to push or force – you will evolve as much forward with the Love of your Life as you are both able to in this lifetime, and then you'll meet up in the next and get to "work" on some other new depth of Loving that you came to uncover. And as you do, you evolve the Spirit in a body's – or what you call human's – capacity for Loving forward. Every couple who ascends Higher and deeper into Loving not only evolves this forward for their Soul's journey – as individuals and as a couple – but for the collective. This is how you have grown into Love, this is what it means to grow deeper into Loving.

It is magnificent. It is Divine. It is exactly what you called forth for yourself on this life journey you are on.

We are loving you ever so much.
XoTheJOGs

LIVE YOUR DIVINITY

There is no question that the most important focus for each of you is to remember your Divinity. And from this place of remembering your Divinity you can affect all manner of aspects of your life experience. No area of your life will not blossom and expand when you know and honor your Divinity. And this, you often say to us, is challenging because of the requests and demands of you as well as balancing your emotional stimuli and responses. And we understand. We too have been a Spirit in a body at one time. We too can hear your concerns and have also been there ourselves.

However, true spiritual mastery, true mastery of self is what you all came to experience and it is most certainly the journey you are all on whether you consciously acknowledge it or not. To be in your body, to have the "challenges" arise and to not beat yourself up over them but instead to actually stand in glorious delight and honor of them because they are leading you forward. They are opening new doors that you cannot even imagine just yet. They are providing you with an opportunity to know yourself on new levels and to know us, to know Spirit, to know Source on entirely new levels. This is both exciting and refreshing and exhilarating for you.

What would it be like if you could look at your so-called problems this way? What if you could look at everything that occurred in your life as Magic? As what is allowing you to become more you? We want you to play with this. We want you to look at your life through this lens. As it is the lens with which Source and all in the Spirit realms see what is occurring for you. We know that you have your emotional experience and we say also look at your emotions from this vantage point. Observe them, feel them flood through your body, watch and witness them – do so with the eyes of Source and in doing so you will remember so much more about your Divinity.

From this practice, you will know with even more certainty that you are Divine. That this life experience you are on is Divine. That you have no choice but to continue forward as a Divine being of Light. If you so choose.

You see, you can choose not to follow this path. You can resist it. You can drag your feet so to speak to avoid it. But it is always available to you. It is always an option for you to choose *you*, to choose your Divinity, to choose your Highest and most expanded path.

Take a look around right now. Who do you know who is fully living their Divinity? Who is living a life of Spirit, of being lit up by the power of being a Spirit in a body, of being so connected, so entwined with their Source self and their Spirit team? And look at those who are not. Do you feel the difference? Can you see the difference?

We would describe it as merely an absence of light or a heavy feeling when you encounter one who is not embracing their Divinity. In truth, they are believing the lie, the illusion, the silliness – we want to make it as light as possible here – that says there is something wrong with them or with life or with the world or with those around them. They are focused on "problems" to fix and people to fix and on things going wrong.

And we encourage you to choose a Higher path. To choose the path filled with Light. When making decisions choose the option that has the most Light attached to it. You are trying to decide, "Do I do this or do I do that?" And we say – choose that which feels Light. Which feels full of Life and vitality and just like you could float on a cloud along with that decision? These decisions will serve your Highest and best good. These decisions will make all of the difference in the world for you.

We so want to see more of you living in this manner because all things can be made available to you – that are on your vibrational trajectory – when you give yourself this gift. We Love you and we are forever holding the space for your Highest and most profound alignment.

In Love,
XoTheJOGs

YOU HAVE FREE WILL, USE IT

There are many things that you can know that will serve you well. And there are many things floating about and around you that do not serve you well. And you have a choice. You have a choice in each moment of where you put your focus. Your focus can expand your experience and your focus can diminish your experience – it really is up to you.

In fact this entire life experience is up to you. But not in the way that you think. It is up to you in the way that you get to choose what you let in. Your free will is – will I let this thing/person/opportunity in or won't I? Whether it be what you classify "good" or "bad", what you allow into your life is the hallmark of what your free will choice represents.

And that leads us to an important aspect of choice, a pinnacle that all will reach in their free will choice ability. And that is the role of your Spirit Team and how you can better utilize this important, powerful, always here for you aspect of your Spirit in a body – or human – experience.

You have a team around you. It's a team that has been with you since the day you entered this physical plane. A team that has been waiting patiently for your acknowledgement and for your permission to work with you more actively in your life experience.

When you are a little one in this life experience you can see us and play with us and you are aware of our presence. You know that you have an incredible support system around you because you can see it, you can feel it, you just know it. You have your mother and father – in many scenarios that is – and you have a whole slew of non-physical energies around you cheering you on as you take your first steps, begin to enjoy and experience food, as you begin to explore with more vigor this physical domain all around you.

Over time, your ability to perceive us becomes less and less. Since your physical eyes can only see that which refracts light off of it and that which you expect to see, your conditioning over time from your family or home environment teaches you that those are "imaginary" friends, and that who you see and talk to that is unseen is actually not real. And so your ability to connect with us becomes less and less.

This is how it was meant to be for many of you, so do not mourn this. You currently live in a very exciting time where now greater and greater numbers of you are waking up to this truth about your non-physical team. Many of you will be or are parents and can encourage your children from an early age in this area that no one supported you with – that you are meant to enjoy and evolve and enhance a strong relationship between you and your non-physical team that is all around you, that is here for you. In fact, you can and will be most served by consciously and intentionally "working" with this team to create a masterful life experience.

And so, for most of you as you grow and evolve in your Spirit in a body experience, time goes on and you go through a host of life experiences – some of which serve you, some of which do not. And if you place your focus and what you talk about and what you think about on the experiences that do not serve you – the heartbreak, the pain, etc. – you begin to attract more and more experiences like that. The same goes for if you choose to place your focus, attention and what you talk about on experiences that light you up and do serve you.

When you get to the point where you are reading or listening to a transmission like this, you have come full circle – you have anchored back into the truth that there is non-physical around you that is here to support you. You recognize that life becomes richer, sweeter and a lot more fun when you stop going at it alone and instead choose to align with the non-physical team that you have around you.

So now how this works is that you must ask for our participation in your life. When you are not asking we are there and we are throwing in nudges and shifting things this way and that to support you in recognizing us and recognizing your Divinity, but that's as much as we can do. We cannot become overtly involved because we do not have your permission to, and that is what free will choice is about.

Often, you'll have a major health crisis to wake you up and get you to open to working with non-physical energy. That is what happened for Heather. She wasn't going to get here without that. And now she can see what an absolute blessing that so-called health crisis was. It was her opening into who she really is. Many of you go through the major loss or what you call death of a Loved one and that is part of their gift to you – to wake you up. Others of you have a major Love relationship crumble or lose a job that was an identity to you – all of these are ways that you are being opened up to your true truth. All of these are ways that you get the opportunity to meet your Spirit Team and really rely on your non-physical support to live the life you were meant to live – the life of your dreams as Heather often calls it.

So what do you do now that you know all of this you may ask?

The first piece is consistent and regular connection with your Spirit Team through prayer and meditation. Every day we ask that you meditate – as little as 11-minutes – and Heather has many 11-minute meditations to share with you as needed.

11 minutes you sit, and your intention is to know yourself more fully and to be connected to your Guides and Angels of the Highest Light. That's all you need. Breathe. Relax. Be open.

After you meditate, state a prayer – give gratitude, thank Source for all of the good and abundance in your life. Bless those you Love and who are around you. Then ask that you know your Highest Good and that the way be made known to you with ease and grace.

It is quite simple, and the above practice opens the door for greater goodness in your life experience.

Recently someone Heather has been working with on this said to her after a powerful 11-minute meditation, "It's the best feeling I've ever felt in my life," to connect with non-physical in this way. Tears ran down her face.

This is what we wish for all of you – the best feeling in the entire world. And when you connect with us – when you make a focused intention daily to be led by the Highest Light of Spirit – there is no stopping what is possible for you.

In Heather's own life she has experienced this to a new degree as more and more of her control is released and she surrenders into living a truly Spirit-led life. Tears of joy. Deep gratitude. The best feelings of her entire life. More flow than she can realistically understand. More Magic at every turn.

You have a team of non-physical beings that is here for you. Here for you. All for you. You don't have to know everything about them – you often will get hung up on what your Spirit Team's names are and who they are and blah blah blah – it does not matter, we tell you. Over time, that information may or may not come to you, but that is not the place to start. And if it never comes to you, that's okay, too. Set your intention to connect to the Highest Light energy and allow it to flow to you, trusting that it will come in in exactly the way that serves you the Highest.

For those who are connecting with your Spirit Team on a regular basis we want to add this to your practice – we want you to ask your team to show you what you need to know that you have been unwilling to know up until now. You all have those areas that feel scary or frightening or like you would rather not know. But that is no way to live – hiding out from your true truth. Ask to be shown with ease and grace what you have been avoiding knowing so that the knowing comes to you effortlessly and with ease. And then commit to taking whatever action you are guided to when this knowing comes through.

And be prepared. Be ready. Open your arms wide to receive. Because your life has now taken a dramatic turn to more goodness than you can currently now imagine.

It is so.
XoTheJOGs

YOU PLANNED IT TO BE JUST LIKE THIS

There is much to be known that we want to share with you, and much of which you know already – in fact, as you read our transmissions you will often feel as though you are remembering what we are sharing with you from long ago. In truth, you are, because locked within each of you is this clarity, is this knowing and above all is this ability to connect with the Source within you, with your core self, with your non-physical self who is intimately connected to your Spirit Team and there you have an incredible wealth of knowledge that is available to you. So few realize this or feel they cannot access this wisdom and so we find ways to come in to share with you to bring to you messages and nudges and clarity that will support the ease and flow of your life experience. We know it may be challenging at times to fully hear or disseminate the information being brought to you but we assure you that your Spirit Team, that Source, that your Higher Self are all united in their deep desire for you to know the fullness of who you really are and the path with which you are here to experience in the most aligned ways.

And so ,there are those that bring these transmissions forth. Those who have agreed before they incarnated that this would be part of their path. There are those highly and completely and fully dedicated solely to this path who are here to support as many as they have agreed to support and who have agreed to be called forth by them to be seen and heard and expanded through the voice and the messages of Spirit.

Each individual who brings these transmissions through has a specific flavor we would call it, or a specific aptitude to bring forth transmissions that are more clear, concise and applicable to those they are here to serve. There is never any need to worry or fear about not receiving the "right" transmissions at the "right" time, or missing a part of your path that is critical to your overall happiness and purpose. Because it has been decided on and you were part of that decision that you would intersect with specific messengers and messages at specific times that would allow you to remember what needed to be remembered so that you could experience greater alignment and joy and bliss on your path.

You also agreed before incarnating that you would be drawn to a Spirit-led path – which Heather refers to it as – although we would like it if you all just called the Spirit-led path "the path", because really and truly it is the only path worth living. Oh, you can and many of you have tried and tried to do life on your own and tried doing things the way you think you should and the way you've been taught and conditioned to believe things should be, but it is not worth it, we tell you. Too much hardship. Too much pain. Too much strife. We say it is not worth it and we would request that instead you make it your sole aim to live the life that you fully intended to live, the life that the core of you came here for. There is so much for you to experience, there is no sense letting the collective mind non-sense pull you out of your true, unwavering alignment.

And yet so many do, so many are thinking that it is all up to them. And we have told you and will continue to tell you that you have an entire team of non-physical beings around you just waiting – like really and truly just hoping and praying you are going to request something of them – that an opportunity will arise for them to jump in and support you and watch as you flourish in a new unfolding on your path. Yes, that is really and truly how it works.

And even so, even with your team and even with those of you who are aware and are connected to your Higher Self and your path, there is still a need for upLiftment, for support, for reminders of that which you know within you to be true. And that is why we are bringing these transmissions through and why others also bring in transmissions from their Spirit Team. It is because you all need one another and you are all in this together in many regards. You all have days that feel not so good and when those days occur it is so very helpful to receive those reminders that remind you above all else what you are here for and who you are here for and how it all is really meant to go for you and how you really and truly can and should delight in the Magic of this existence.

There are times when you will be soaring, absolutely soaring in the Magic and in the Love and in the abundance that is *yours*. It is so truly and completely yours. And we Love watching this, we celebrate and soar with you when you are in that state. Can't you feel us with you? Can't you feel the crowds of us cheering and the delight that is emanating from us to you? We hope that you can and we ask that you tune in to this more. In your most joyful moments, stop and tune in – what do you feel and where do you feel it?

Tonight Heather was having the experience of sitting on her deck and she was so happy. Overjoyed really. And she was watching the boats floating around and listening to the birds singing and then the neighbor cats all wanted to be out with her and she was reflecting on how happy she feels and there is no reason. No reason at all. Nothing particularly out of this world happened today and yet her heart is beaming wide open. And she can feel this pulsing within her heart and then all around her heart. And that is us. That is us feeling her happiness too and rejoicing in her now moment in which she – a once self-proclaimed go-getter and doer – is simply happy, because she is and she is doing nothing to have the experience. It is simply occurring through and around and within her.

And those moments – whether they occur when what you would call big or magnificent things are happening, or when you are simply like Heather, sitting outside feeling happy for no reason – we are there celebrating with you.

We would Love for you to be in your body more, to really feel the pulsing, feel the energy swirling around you. Feeling the loving hugs and support there for you. So often you all on this path are feeling chills and yes, that is your Soul saying yes, and it's also all of us hugging you, too! We are hugging you and so happy for you as you have aligned with another core truth or action that is part of your Destiny. That is part of what you came here for – to delight in your *yes* in this lifetime. You know when one of you says something to the other of you and you are covered in chills – yes, we are saying yes, yes, yes, you've got it! Follow that knowing, follow that guidance, follow that offering – you are on the path of your Destiny.

We will continue to share with you all of the delightful ways we all get to play together. Our intention is that in reading these transmissions you will have a newfound appreciation for the power of this relationship between you and your Spirit Team, and that you will expand the ways you work with your Team and the ways you ask for your Team to be present and to be part of your life experience. We always sneak – not exactly the right word choice here because we really want you to find them, so they aren't that sneaky – new practices and techniques and knowings that will further support your evolution and further support you on being on the path that is most aligned, most fulfilling and most fun for you.

Our intention in bringing these transmissions through Heather is so another segment of the population that were perhaps untouched by our transmissions in earlier years or in previous incarnations are touched now. Are supported now. Go Higher now.

And so it is.

Love,
XoTheJOGs

YOU ARE IN THE PROCESS OF ALIGNING

The topic of infidelity is one that must be addressed, as it's something you see on your movie screens, in your homes on television and in your novels, as well as down the street in your neighborhoods and communities and many times even in your own home. What is it this predilection around infidelity? What of the excitement and thrill that seems to come from these clandestine affairs?

There is much to say on this topic and we are grateful for this opportunity to share with you what we know to be true.

Infidelity is not about what you think it is about. It is certainly not about the sex (although many of you will say this is so) and it's not even about the relationship that both parties have allowed to stagnate that opened them up to a person entering their union (although many more will argue that is in fact the case).

It is about one thing and one thing only and it is the one thing that everything is about – it is about lack of alignment to the Source within.

Lack of alignment to the Source within causes one to marry and make a vow they cannot possibly keep to someone who is not the Love of their Life. Because, dear ones, you do not experience infidelity with the Love of your Life.

Lack of alignment to the Source within causes one to stay in a relationship, in a partnership that is not nourishing and uplifting them to their Highest Heights as they also do for the other.

Lack of alignment to the Source within opens one to actions and activities that cause great perceived harm to many other parties – children, families, communities.

Lack of alignment to the Source within causes one to break commitments of all kinds through dishonesty of all kinds.

Truly all causes of what you would call suffering in your world are from a lack of alignment with the Source within.

So this is what we have been getting at all along. We want you to be so fully aligned with the Source within *before* you take those vows, before you make any and all commitments. So that when those commitments are made, you are so connected to who you really are you know without one miniscule of doubt that you are absolutely and completely making the best and Highest decision for your path. And then, poof! Just like magic – there is no more need for infidelity.

Infidelity – like most discordant behaviors, attitudes and actions – is simply a symptom of the greater "problem" – too many making choices about who to commit to and who to be with that are not based on being fully aligned with the core of who you really are. Alignment must occur first before all other things, and then the ride will not be the bumpy ride so many of you experience.

Now we know and we understand full alignment is not what everyone on the planet – yet anyway – is striving for. No, they are confused, striving for people and things and status of achievement which really are all rooted in the search for the incredible, expansion, ever-joyful feeling that only true alignment with Source brings.

We get it. And besides, we know you all are evolving this forward. And this transmission is supporting many of you in doing so.

So if you, like Heather and like many others, have chosen partners in the past form a misaligned place – no biggie. Shrug it off. Let it go, don't give it a moment of thought. And then right here, right now, make your alignment with your Source self your number one priority and really tune in to who you really are. When you meet that person, when you're in that relationship – are you aligned? Are you vibing at a frequency that is the true you?

See what comes in, see how your partner acts, see who is magnetized to you when you are there.

Now you are all continually aligning in this way, and it will continue forevermore to evolve as you become more of who you truly are – a Spirit being who inhabits a body. So please again, do not egregiously beat down on yourself for what you deem as errors or shortcomings. Be here in this now moment and move forward from here.

If your current partner is the true Love of your Life – as you become more aligned with the Source within you – he/she will align with you and your relationship will become more harmonious. If he/she is not, he or she will fall away and there will not be much for you to do to make or adjust that from happening.

Listen to us closely here – we are not haters of divorce and we are not haters of break-ups and we are not even haters of infidelity or of anything for that matter. It is all part of the evolutionary journey to becoming more of who you really are. We are just saying you do not need to go through all of those bumpy, unpleasant experiences to get to where you really desire to be. And we want you to know why you have had these experiences, and then from this now moment on, take action that will allow you to wholly and fully live your Highest and most profound life experience. The truth of this life journey for you is: how would you know what pure alignment felt like if you had not had the opportunity to dance – sometimes it feels like dancing far too often, we know – with mis-alignment? Really, you wouldn't fully know the exquisiteness of pure Source alignment without having had it.

So, you come together, you break apart, you align more fully, you come together with a new other, you break apart – the dance will continue on until you are the most aligned version of yourself and your true Love of your Life is the most aligned version of his/herself that is lined up with the Divine Timing that you two agreed to meet under.

We would not encourage any of you to engage in infidelity because all it does is create bigger messes, bigger bumps along the way. We would encourage you to line up your energy fully to Source and when you do, you'll know the direction to take, you'll know the way. You'll be clear. And the right people and places will fall effortlessly into place for you.

So now do this – make this one commitment, make this the most important commitment of your life:

"I fully commit on this day of _____ of the month of _____ of the year of_____ to only being in any form of romantic relationship when I am the most fully aligned to my Source self as I can be. I understand that this alignment will mean that there is always total and complete honesty, respect, trust and holding one another in the Highest Light. I understand that when I am fully aligned to the Source within me, I honor every living thing inside and outside of my partnership with complete honesty and respect. I fully commit to being in the Highest alignment first, and then coming together with another. And so it is."

And so it is.
XoTheJOGs

SEX & SPIRITUALITY IS A PRIORITY FOR YOU

Sex is often a topic that follows Love almost immediately and we are eager to share with you the Highest Light vantage point of how sex factors into your Love partnerships. For so much of the time sex has been distorted and used in various forms, but rarely as it is intended to be used. And this is difficult for many of you – it is difficult because it is so far out of alignment with what the Source within you knows is what sex is meant to be used for and what purpose it serves for you.

First, we will say what you know deeply to be true, the purpose of sex is pleasure. It is one of the most incredible ways that as a Spirit in a body you can feel pleasure. You feel pleasure with sex in a way that is beyond the realms of what is possible with food or other sensual delights. Where things go awry for most is that the pleasure becomes the sole focus of the act and this is when things are completely out of balance with your innate wholeness and what you know fully and solely to be true.

Yes, sex is a deeply pleasurable experience that is unlike any other experience you can have on the planet. And it was created not for the act of mere pleasure nor even for the sole act of reproduction – although many of your religious texts will tell you otherwise, but they are incorrect in that assessment. Sex was created to allow you to connect on the deepest possible level with another Spirit in a Body and through that connection to experience the One-ness that you can only feel coursing through your body through the act of sex.

Would it surprise you if we told you that when you are in Spirit form you feel the orgasmic pleasure of One-ness on a daily, almost moment by moment basis? That when you are fully connected to Source, when you are living as that Source, that you are experiencing that extreme One-ness that Spirits in a body only experience during that radical moment of orgasm and climax? Well, it is true. And when you are in a body you want to remember that feeling, you want to remember that One-ness, you want to be able to lose yourself in a moment of pure bliss. And those moments are not always available to you in your everyday life, because there are so many other aspects catching your attention and asking for your evolution and for your delight and enjoyment.

And so this is why sexuality and spirituality are so closely entwined for you. They are a pathway, a gateway to experience God, Source, All-that-is-ness. When you are without a body you have this recurrent experience always because you are it and it is splendid. It is just so the norm of how it is for us that we think nothing of it. And we know that is not the Spirit in a body experience.

Things get all sorts of convoluted, exaggerated and distorted when it comes to sex because so many have forgotten this. So many have forgotten that to experience their pure essence, they must simply be with the Love of their Life and allow their bodies to lead them there. Now of course you can experience orgasm and climax with any partner you choose, but you do know and you do feel the difference in the orgasms when you are connected to someone deeply and when you are not and you are using the sex act as a means of pleasure only bypassing the depth and Spirit that is available to you when you come together in a deep connection with another *and then* orgasm and climax. We needn't draw you a picture on this, we know you know what we are saying.

And this is why we would encourage all of you to make sure that before you are intimate sexually in any way with anyone that you are feeling fully connected to your Source self and that you know that the other is a deep Soul connection. It is the only and best way to align sexually. It's the only way to create new life – whether it's a child or a project or a business or another manifestation. The power of two who are Soul-ly connected – and most definitely when it is two Loves of one another's Lives together and they are creating sexually – there is the potential to create so much together. To experience God together, to experience the fullness of Source, to experience the feeling of who you really are together – that energy, that power is the power that creates all things.

It is the power that supersedes all. That is why if we were you, we would make sure that our sexual attention, energy and acts were with the Love of our Life. We would in the meantime experience the pleasure and orgasm and climax and connection to All-that-is through self-pleasuring when we felt the alignment for such. You can most definitely experience this One-ness when you stay present in your body and allow the sensations of pleasure to guide you to your One-ness to your All-that-is-ness that is so readily and easily accessible to you.

Now we will say there are many levels of judgment by many around sex – judgment of yourself and of others. And we do not see it that way. We want you to be fully aligned and then align with your Beloved. Fully aligned and then have sex. Fully aligned and then go into whatever conversation or connection you wish to have with your Beloved. When you are fully connected to who you really are, there is absolutely nothing to fear or judge or worry about. And what happened in the past is in the past.

Take a deep breath now, and release with ease those past regrets or mistakes or whatever comes up for you around sex. Let it go and step into the now. The now where you know more, you know a better way, you are clear and you are committed fully to your Highest Path and Purpose.

Those in partnership now, make your sex about more than simply the pleasure. Be with the pleasure, enjoy and sink in to and celebrate the pleasure and also remember that it is the way you can express your deepest Love to your Beloved and the way that you two – together – can experience the bliss that is only ever felt when you are not in a body. See the sacredness that is available to you here, feel the depth that is possible when you allow sex to be the vehicle that opens you up, that opens your Beloved up, that opens your partnership up to greater harmony and connection with Source. When both of you are aware of the power of sex and you take this knowing into your sexual time together, you will notice a deepening of your intimacy and expansion of what you are able to create together, you will notice that the harmony and the joy and the pleasure available to you both accelerates from this conscious awareness and placement of focus on the power of your sexual union.

Have fun with this and enjoy honoring the sacredness of sex. Because it is one of the most Divine ways to connect to All-that-is-ness that surrounds you while feeling extreme pleasure in the body-mind. It is often referred to as the place of no-mind. It is the place many wish to go in meditation but which is truly available in its fullest form through orgasm and climax.

It seems funny then, doesn't it, that religions for eons have worked so hard to repress and stuff and stymie sexual expression. Perhaps they did not want others to fully know their power? What would your world look like if individuals knew the sacredness and power of sexual intimacy and so they only shared this with the deep and true Loves of their Lives and in the interim allowed their own self-pleasuring connection to take them Higher on their journey until their Beloved arrived? Your world would be a much different place.

So we say, you have this information now, use it now, start this now. Watch what happens now to your existing Love, to your future, to all the shifts that will occur when you engage the power of sex in this way.

XoTheJOGs

YOU ARE SUPPORTED IN LOVING WHO YOU LOVE

We've got to address this "issue" about who you Love because it has been so prevalent for so long amongst so many of you and it is one of the wackiest, silliest, aspects that Spirits in a body often try to control in one another. And this need to control comes from a desire to want uniformity, for singularity for something that is just not possible. And this comes from a deep wound within, a deep wound in the human core that is being evolved forward step by step. This deep wound says, "I am inferior and in order to not feel my inferiority, I must try to control all outside circumstances that do not line up for me. These aspects that do not line up for me exaggerate my own feeling of inferiority and so I must do whatever is necessary, namely control, so that I can feel superior. Because superiority is the only place I feel safe."

Of course this is a lie, as all wounds are. Compassion is needed here for those who suffer from this affliction, acknowledging that they are carrying it because they are supporting themselves and those who can see clearly in healing this wound once and for all. Someday it will no longer exist, for now you must acknowledge it and step into your own Light to support the evolution of it forward.

Early on, this means of control and uniformity was aimed at trying to make everyone the same religion, then the same government and same race and now same sexual orientation. And we have to tell you – you Love who you Love and it does not matter their gender or their race or their political affiliation – none of it matters. Because you see, you agreed long before that you would be with the Love of your Life – the Love you have incarnated with again and again and so trying to control that person to look a certain way or be a certain gender or act a certain way is a sure-fire way to make yourself so uncomfortable, so unhappy and so miserable. You all have ideas of how the person you Love should look, be, and act, and you've got to give that up. You've got to surrender fully to the path of Spirit, to the path that you – before you incarnated into this specific body – were wholly and fully aligned with. In fact, you said, "Yes, that one! Yes, I Love it. I Love how quirky they are. I Love how different they are from the lifetime before and the lifetime before. I Love, Love, Love that Soul so much and I'm so excited to dance with them again in this lifetime!"

You were not putting rules and constrictions about gender and identity together then. You cared about none of it, because you understood what so many of you are needing to remember right now.

You are all the same. You are all Souls in a body, Spirit in a body. You are all Source in a body. And you have your trajectory, aka Destiny, that is lined up to support you in evolving forward so much beauty that you came here for along with wonderful experiences and joys to nourish you and uplift you into the remembrance of that which you are.

So really Love who you Love. Don't worry about who anyone else is loving or why they are loving them. Bless them, honor them and then get back to the one thing that is your utmost business, which is the relationship you have with your Source Self and with your Spirit Team and with this path, this Destiny that you are here for.

One day we know that those in the body will have the worldwide epiphany that they do not need to control anyone. That alignment is the only focus needed, and that – with that focus – no need to control is necessary. In the meantime, shine that Light now, hold that Light now, become that Light now. Be a shining example of someone who is not trying to control others' actions and who others Love and who others have relationships with and how others feel and act.

Do not try to control who you Love. Do not constrain yourself to believing that there's only one gender or orientation or race for you. Open yourself to the infinite possibilities that your Higher Self created for you in concert with your Spirit Team. Hold yourself in the Highest Light offering, and know that whoever the Love of your Life is, they are amazing and they are perfect for you. And for those in a partnership with your Love of your Life – remember this when you think they should pick up more or chew with their mouth closed or whatever it might be that you find yourself trying to control. When it is the true Love of your Life this will be easier to do, although sometimes not so much. If there are things about your current partner you wish to have changed we say go to work on shifting and changing within yourself. Change how you perceive them, what you think about them and what you desire from them. And focus in on what you can control – you. Focus on making your life the magnificent experience it is meant to be and let the rest, rest.

And if your partner then goes away, then we tell you – either they will be back or they were not yours to have anyway.

Honor your Divinity at all times, our Loves. For yourself, for your Loves, for your community, for your world.

We Love you.
XoTheJOGs

IT'S ALL MORE FUN THAN YOU THINK

In your time in this life experience you have the opportunity to soar to new heights, to ascend to new levels to, in truth, become the fully integrated Spirit that you are while in a body. This is an opportunity not every one of you realizes is in front of you, but that is available to every single one of you. Why would this be important, you might ask? Why wouldn't you just want to be in the body and let that be your sole reality, your sole focus, your sole way of being?

Well, there are some of you that do so. And these ones, while they may be enjoying the delights of the physical experience have yet to know the exquisiteness of being fully integrated as the whole person that they are. You see, when you are simply existing from a physical perspective, and not recognizing your true power and your true nature, you suffer more than is necessary. You are unable to understand why things happen the way that they happen, and you often – understandably so but not rightly so – blame non-physical or Source or the government or other people around you for these alleged wrongdoings. Being in the body we know is a Divine experience all in itself, but just like you cannot help but voyage to new areas in your world – like the explorers of your time – you cannot help but begin to wonder and tiptoe into what an expanded body experience looks like.

And an expanded in the body experience means merging with Spirit, it means consciously co-creating with Spirit, it means allowing yourself to taste the delicious food and smell the delicious smells and make the delicious Love, but while also engaged with your Source self. And from there, the sensations, the pleasures, and the expanded knowing and understanding of all that is permeates your being. And in that process you are inspired to go forth and create aspects that have yet to be created before. No longer from a single-minded perspective of, "This thing solves this problem." No, quite the opposite. Now you know that there are multi-dimensions at your disposal and available to you, and so now you can look at anything in your world and focus in on how you can bring more of that multi-dimensionality to your in the body experience. And when you do this, you are now creating a new frequency that has never been created before. And when you do that not only do you expand and other Spirits in a body expand, but Source, the creator of all that is, also expands right along with you because you yourself are what Heather is calling a slice of Source. You yourself are causing all things to expand from this aligned co-creative level.

So part of your in the body experience is happening because you Love being in a body, it's true. And the bigger part of you, the Higher Self part of you wanted to come for the purpose of experiencing the multi-dimensionality of being a Spirit in a body, with the conscious knowledge of that truth and with the conscious ability to transform and transcend what has not been transformed or transcended in previous lifetimes. And this is not a heavy thing. This is not a weighty thing; this is what the Soul of you, the core of you, longs for.

This is why you will find things you may not understand fully lighting you up. Because you came fully and solely to expand and co-create in the multi-dimensionary way that has never been done before. And while the inspiration for whatever you are creating may not be new to Spirits in a body the way that you bring it through, the way that you create is. Because never in all of your lifetimes have you been this one that you are now, and never in all of the world has anyone been you in your previous lifetimes – this one included – and has been such a powerful creator.

Except so many of you do not realize this. You often fall into limited thinking that says that you are flawed or broken or need help or need fixing. You believe that your body, when things are going "wrong" with it, that that means something is wrong with you. And no, we say that is not the truth. You are being called, you are processing and integrating through your body, you are experiencing another fundamental aspect of having a body. You cannot ascend to the Higher dimensions without your body going with you while in a body. So sometimes your body may seem to struggle with this or it may seem to need more time than you would like it to have. And we say – there is nothing to fear with this, our dear ones. Give your body what it needs. Take it easy and give yourself the Love and nurturing you need.

And laugh. We most would like to see you laugh more. We desire to see you letting it all be light-hearted even when you do not feel from your limited mind state that it is. We want you all to see and feel more clearly this notion and this true notion that you are a slice of Source and so whatever your body must process, whatever you must process, really needn't be heavy or weighty. It can be what it is while you keep your knowledge and focus on the fact that you are a Divine multi-dimensionary being and even whatever you are feeling that is not feeling good *is* living the fullness of this human experience. And nurturing yourself, caring for yourself, taking it easy when you need to is so part of your expansive life experience.

And true, you could try to shrug it all off , you could try to just live from the body experience – meaning that when something goes wrong with your body, you fly into action to "fix" it, that when something goes "wrong" in your life, you fly into action to "fix" it. Or, or you could laugh. You could acknowledge your in the body experience. You could bless it. And you could say, "Okay, show me the way. Show me where you'd have me going. Show me the multi-dimensionary way that I can create, that I can experience more fully what I always intended to experience. I know that I can. I know that I will."

You can say all of this to yourself to pick yourself up, to elevate yourself from whatever is swirling around you.

This is more fun, our dear ones. It really is. We know you don't always think so, we know you don't always believe us. But it is. Heather has had these conversations with us and she will mull it over for a bit and then say, "Well, what else was I going to do? Of course I was going to come here and have this odd and weird and Magical experience. Of course I was."

And we say yes. We applaud this. Of course you were going to come here and you were going to have all sorts experiences and they were all going to give you the jumping off point to be more, to be deeper, to be more expanded, to Love more fully, to feel more fully, to create more profoundly than you have ever done before. Not because there is this "look at this" tangible "there I did it" thing, but for the joy of it from the time it popped into your mind to create whatever it was, from the time that it delighted you with its arrival in to the world. For all of it, for the whole of it.

It is all fun, our dear ones, even when it's not. It is all more fun than you even knew you could have. We promise you this.

In Love,
XoTheJOGs

YOUR RELATIONSHIPS ARE HERE FOR YOU

Today we want to talk to you about an aspect of your Spirit in a body lives that you cannot escape, nor would you want to. It is an aspect that when aligned and when connected to Source every area of your life begins to flow with more ease. And when it is not in your Highest alignment, the bumps and potholes it creates on your road of life are immense.

This is the area of personal relationships. Whether with family, friends or romantic partners or even the checker at the grocery store, you cannot avoid this meaningful and important aspect of your life experience. And yet there can be much struggle for you as you seek to find the ways to best align with who you really are and Love these blessed ones around you.

And so our intention today is to support you in being able to interact, intersect and dance this life dance with these ones with more ease and certainly more joy. And it is our intention that through your powerful knowing of this information and your powerful connection to who you really are, you can soar far beyond your current realm of personal relating.

The first piece we must make clear here is that no one on this planet is here solely for you. True, the Love of your Life came specifically to meet up with you as you did for them. Even so, they are not here to solely make you happy nor are you here for solely their happiness. Your children also chose to specifically come in through you but again, they are not here for you – you are a vehicle, a conduit, a guide on their path – you are not the path or the only way for them to have all that they desire. It is ultimately their connection to their Highest Self and Source that provides the gateway to all they truly are here for and truly desire.

And so, no one came just for you. No one is here solely to make you happy and to serve your needs. And this is a very good thing because it is solely *your* responsibility, all Spirits in a body's responsibility to make their happiness their primary focus. When this is done everything in life can smooth out with more ease. So now you know the basis you are here for – you – and the others in your life are all here for them. You all agreed to meet up because you had specific gifts and messages and support and fun and joy and bliss to offer one another in this lifetime that would not be available otherwise.

Then what is your responsibility, as it were, to the others around you? What is your role in their life unfolding? And of course it is different depending on the relationship, but always for every single one it's to bring more joy and Love into their life. To, from your connected to Source place, let your own joy and Love shine to them. Now, let us be clear here because there of those of you who have a proclivity to over-do it. Over-give. You suffer from what Heather and her Soul Alignment sessions would call Over-responsibility syndrome. You do not *do this for them*, you *be* it, you radiate it. You are it. You are so fully emanating your own connection to Love and joy that everyone who comes into contact with you has this experience of Love and joy.

So that's the first bit with others and yourself. But what happens when they are not connected to their Love & joy (and perhaps you are not either at that time) and they annoy you, when they push your buttons so to speak, when they are goading you or have an agenda and you are not certain how to stand shining your beauteous Light around them?

And we say in all cases, walk away. When someone is not in their full Light and in fact they are angry at you for being in yours, there is nothing more to do than walk away. Walk away and maybe come back at another time. Say a blessing – call on your Guides and Angels of the Highest Light to bless the person and yourself and the situation and then walk away. There is no need to engage in anything that is not of the Highest Light.

So let's say you walk away but you are angry or hurt or vengeful or filled with grief. You can feel the emotion within you and you know that you don't want to do anything to hurt or harm another yet there is still that intense, not good feeling emotion right there.

And we say that is a very good thing. Because your emotion has a message for you. So we want you to sit with your emotion. Feel it boiling in your body and begin to breathe into it. Begin with an inhale through the nose – we have guided Heather to teach this to others in her sessions and we are sharing it here now – your inhale is gathering up that emotion, and as you feel it you exhale out your mouth to release it. Just keep sitting with that emotion and work with it in this way – feeling, inhaling it up and exhaling it out.

Some of you are going to want to write out your emotions to fully release them. You are going to want to write the expletives and anger and rage and grief and whatever else is there. Do it, get it out. But before you do this set your intention. Be clear that this energy that is emanating from you is yours and yours alone, and that you are not sending it to anyone, it is not meant to be an attack, it is not to hurt anyone, it is simply stymied within you and it needs to be released because it cannot stay in your body-mind. If it stays in your body-mind it hurts you, it harms your body, it breaks down your systems and delivers to you what you would call dis-ease.

So set your boundaries and intentions so that no form of attack or harm is done to another. When you do this releasing without setting those boundaries, you send energy to another that bounces back to you and hurts you 100-fold. It is not worth it dear ones, we assure you. You may, when in a more unconscious vibration, think that speaking words of venom about another or harboring thoughts of hurt and venom towards another felt like release, but really what that was doing all along was poisoning you, poisoning those you were speaking to and sending ill intent to another. And any time you harbor ill will towards another you bring on the ill intent on yourself in greater quantities. This is how the Universe is set up and it's set up as such so that you are supported, so that you can truly remember what is most important – you are here for you. And your connection to the non-physical energy around you and your ability to "work" with it is what can deliver to you the utmost of life happiness and fulfilment.

So use this process when you get angry or sad or hurt or any intense life emotions. Do not engage with the other until you can come back in a more solid, grounded, aligned place. Take the time and space you need to process your intense emotions and then come back to the situation. Sometimes you will return to the situation – depending on the relationship – and the response will be, "I Love you, I bless you and I can no longer stay intimately connected with you."

Other times you will be gifted with seeing fully that there is a path to harmony in that relationship. But you will get to neither if you do not first let yourself feel the emotions and then release it. We know this is uncomfortable for many of you. It is extremely uncomfortable for Heather. Anger is an emotion she does not like to feel or let herself feel. She does not want to feel hate in her heart, she does not want to know that it is even possible for it to be there.

But dear ones, it is there in some form or another for all of you. It is from the collective lack of Love that has built up over time, it is from previous lifetimes when you have journeyed with that other and resentments have built, it's from this lifetime and resentments have built. And all that anger or hatred or sadness or grief is simply where Light has not been shined on it. The feelings have not been allowed to be felt in a way that allows them to release. And what those feelings need is room to breathe and release.

And dear ones, when you allow yourself to do this, there you find the truth of it all, of all things. And in that truth you realize your One-ness and you realize the perfection of all that is. And even when the answer is to distance yourself from the other, or to leave the other, or to end the relationship, you are flying Higher than you've ever done because you are setting yourself free by truly feeling and releasing

Enjoy this practice. Use it as often as you need to and let us know in your prayers, in your letters, in your comments, in your emails to Heather what is unfolding for you as you set yourself free and bring more Light in.

In Love,
XoTheJOGs

SPIRIT TRUMPS EVERYTHING

The timing of your Love relationships is unique to each one of you and very profound. It is never chance although it may feel like it. When you come together with a Love it is always a Divinely timed, Divinely orchestrated event. As both parties must be ready for one another and the relational trajectory that is ahead of them. Some of these trajectories are long, some are eternal and others are for what you would call shorter periods of time as the rememberings or lessons as you might call them do not need much time to be learned.

So many of you who are desiring Love will consult psychics and intuitives and astrologers all looking to know the exact perfect timing of when you may meet your Love. For those in partnership you may be asking all of the above for the exact timing when the partnership will reach a new state of commitment or will expand in some way that you desire. And while the above may be able to access very accurate, very detailed and very right-in-that-moment information there is something you should know about Divine Timing that supersedes all matters of magic.

And that is us. Heather often says, "Spirit trumps everything." And she is correct. For when you align with the core of who you really are in concert with your non-physical team you can shift the entire trajectory of timing when it comes to Love and when it comes to anything in your life.

So let's say it is Divinely timed that you will meet your Beloved, or if you are with your Beloved already in this here and now reality, something you are desiring to have happen is set to happen in your vibrational trajectory. You see, the reason why we call it a vibrational trajectory is because when you uplevel your vibration, that trajectory will shift and adjust to meet you along your intended path. This is why the Soul Alignment work that Heather facilitates and other forms of energy work that are aligned with Source are so beneficial. They can literally support you in shifting into a whole other frequency that will match you up with your Destiny more quickly than it was originally intended. So yes, you were always going to get there, but the timing of it can and will be adjusted if you are consciously and intentionally aligning with your Spirit Team and the Source within and receiving the consistent releasing of all that no longer serves you.

So the timing is set. And you, you are aware, you know that this person or relationship or next step in your partnership is a very real possibility. You can feel it, you can practically taste it, it seems and feels so close. And perhaps the divination method you consulted said it was two years or six months from now or whatever it was in your linear time structure that you were given. And, if you accept that as fact, as truth, then that will most likely be your experience. But let's say that while you appreciated the timeline and it brought you a certain amount of relief (which is why that timeline was even allowed to be brought through – your Spirit team is there telling the astrologer or psychic or intuitive a number to provide you with relief, and that relief then allows our transmissions to reach you more clearly. We are quite clever, aren't we?!) you know, in fact you feel that this thing or person can come to you in a more accelerated timeline.

So you get to it. You use your tools, you focus in on shedding the stories and limitations that no longer serve you. You are consciously intending to ready yourself in the soonest possible alignment for this next thing. And often it will show up for you because of this. What you must do here – and what is so critical to your happiness and fulfillment and why we now say it's not so much manifesting as it is co-creating – is that you must check in with the Highest self part of you. You want to be able to tune in to the frequency of your Source self, of that true you, and see if you really are ready in this here and now moment or if the Divine Timing will serve you more fully. You do not want a half-baked manifestation as Heather calls it.

You want to be fully and completely prepared for this Love or this next expansion. And if you are intent on rushing it – you can do that, you do have the power – it's important that you are fully aligned with this intention not just in body-mind – it's quicker for you to get that alignment there – but with your Highest Self as well. This requires being honest with yourself, truly and fully honest. Not allowing yourself to fall into delusion or make excuses for yourself that do not serve you.

Perhaps the timeline given was six months and you want it now – we know, you so like to have it all now. But we are telling you, go within first. Sit for as long of a period of time as you can in quiet contemplative meditation. Ask to have it be made fully known to you – is every aspect of you ready to align with this thing that you desire? Or is there something else that must be attended to first? Is there something else that is requiring and in need of your care and attention?

Many times there is. And we are telling you it is so important that you take the time to do or address or understand more fully that which is still within you and desiring your attention before you can have this thing that you desire to have.

Otherwise, half-baked manifestation.

What we mean by that is that you will have a lot more bumps, a lot more potholes on your road, on your path and that is a lot less fun than when you fully line up the energy – your Highest self, your body, your mind – all on the same frequency, all knowing and feeling with every cell, every particle the yes-ness of what is in your trajectory or Destiny. We use Density and vibrational trajectory interchangeably, although Destiny has some negative connotations because it sounds far too fixed and we want you to know that your Destiny has far more flow to it. Oh there are things you intended for and agreed upon that you just cannot get out of no matter how hard you try, and then there are things that serve your Highest Good that you may spend a lifetime trying to avoid. And really you never can avoid anything that is for your Highest path and purpose, you'll just get to it in the next lifetime. And that's okay, there is some of that for everyone as you never get it done, never ever.

So back to our original example. The divination method you chose told you six months until your Love or until some expansion you desire would come. You check in and feel that yes, there is more work you need to do so attempting to manifest it at this time would be premature and would not yield to you the fullest and Highest expansion you desire. So, you work with someone you have a strong Soul resonance with that can hold the vibration High for you to evolve forward whatever this piece is. And in addition, you work with your Spirit Team and with your mind to shift what needs to be shifted and to step into the mind set of one who is thriving in the way you desire when it comes to Love or this expansion you desire in partnership.

Then perhaps it's four months or three months or two months and then what you desire occurs. So in this way, Divine Timing is really about full alignment which entails the releasing of what no longer serves you – otherwise known as resistance. The specific timeline is not pin-down-able and most divination methods are not accurate in this way because there are too many factors that will affect it – namely how soon you choose or not choose to line up the energy for what you desire to occur.

In Love,
XoTheJOGs

LET GO OF YOUR BAD-FEELING STORIES

When someone tells you something that feels awful to you, it affects you. It short circuits parts of your brain and activates other parts. It puts you in a response that is not of your Highest Light. And depending on your level of respect and trust for the other it can take you some time to work yourself out of whatever it is they have created in the dynamic between you.

This is why we encourage you to keep your awful feeling stories to yourselves. This is why we have guided Heather in her groups that only the Highest Light is to be shared. Because when not-aligned energy is shared, it proliferates. It simply creates more of that out into the world. And you have to ask yourself – is that what I want to put out into the world? Is that the contribution that I want to make to the planet?

Social media has been an interesting unfolding to witness. Some use it for the Highest Light – we admonished Heather from the very beginning that anything she posted had to have that frequency. And there are times when she would Love to put a sarcastic comment out into the stratosphere because that's the – we must share with you here, sarcasm is not of the Highest Light although we know many enjoy it – place that she was in, but we would not let her. She is very clear as we have told her that what you put out into the world matters.

We talk about this ripple effect of positive alignment and the same is true with out-of-alignment-ness.

When you tell your awful feeling story to your friends or to your therapist or to anyone – you are putting that story out into the world to ripple on. Healers that want to deal with not aligned energy can support you in diversifying that energy and re-appropriating it, but we still would not encourage it. And of course we would not encourage you to keep things inside of you for all of eternity because that will in turn only then harm your body. This is why the news is so damaging to so many – it's in print, it's in audio, it's in video and it's filled with a frequency of mis-alignment. Your Highest Self does not want to watch others proliferate the ripples of non-aligned actions and occurrences. And when it happens and when you do, the whole of the world is impacted by the mis-alignment.

So, we will bring it back to you – what is the solution /what do you do when you feel awful? Well, really there are so many wonderful things you can do, but we will give you our Highest recommendations so you can convert mis-aligned energy into an aligned vibration, into the vibration of Divine Love – the most beneficial vibration to the planet.

If you feel awful, that is your first indicator that you have gotten out of alignment with who you really are. Maybe you know how this happened, maybe you don't. No need to go back and try to figure it out or rehash anything. Just notice where you are at and acknowledge it. Then, get out whatever those feelings are that need to be released from within you. The best way we can say to do this is: write it out. Use your body to get rid of what is inside. Write a letter to the person who has harmed/wronged or made you angry or write a letter to no one in particular to tell the story and get it out. Go into all of the details and get it out. You'll notice you feel awful-er still because you are bringing up, drudging up the non-alignment. Then, stop when you are finished and affirm that this is now fully out of you and you are ready to move on. Burn the sheet of paper – in a safe place, Heather wants us to admonish, she does not want to be responsible for any out of alignment burnings.

Tap Cortices, she would add, to re-align your vibration. Yes, that's all fine.

Then move your body. You've got to shake off what you purged. It can be any form of exercise you are drawn to; and as you do it, imagine that you are shaking off this vibration that does not serve you as you move your body. Saging is always a very helpful practice in clearing the energy that has been brought up and needs to be fully released. We recommend doing this after you've burned the paper and after you've moved your body.

Then, when you talk to your Loved ones you can let them know about what happened from a non-charged place and you can keep the details to the very minimum so that you are not polluting them or re-polluting yourself. And you never, ever, ever, ever email about it or post about it on social media because then you are embedding forever more into consciousness this pollution. Can you see how over time there are layers of built-up non-alignment energy? Can you see how homes and offices and communities – online or in-person – can become weighted down by non-aligned energy?

And what is it? It is merely sloppy emotions. Emotions that were not healthily processed, that were instead projected and are getting stuck in environments. And it's completely unnecessary. Sage your homes, open your windows, sage your offices and cars, open your windows, bring in High vibrating quartz crystals. Sage after every argument and disagreement. Take sea salt baths. All of these are ways to keep yourself re-aligned after misalignment.

Feel your emotions and release. Feel your emotions and release and then clean up where the mess had taken place. It's like if you are cooking and make a mess, or paint and make a mess – you clean it up.

It's the same energetically and with your emotions. Over time, when these emotions build up they create energy fields of non-aligned energy and you can feel it when you walk into a room or a home or an office or a restaurant or any place of business, or when you talk to someone who has not allowed themselves to feel and release their non-aligned energy. You intuitively will know and feel it. And you are not feeling anything "bad" – what you are feeling is non-aligned energy that is stuck.

All Spirits in a body will have moments of non-alignment. There is nothing to be ashamed of or worried about. However, what you do with it is everything. If you are having non-aligned dreams or day dreams or you don't feel good most of the time – that is simply your indicator that you are in need of some alignment "work". And your alignment work is your personal "job" so to speak. No one can do this for you.

This is why healing works for some and not others. Not everyone is receptive. Not everyone truly is ready to release their non-aligned states even though they may pay for sessions or ask for sessions. This is why Heather will be offering less and less "healing" sessions, and more and more of these transmissions of upliftment.

She is concerned and worried about how all of this will work of course, and yet she cannot deny what she has seen over the years of operating a healing practice, and what we have shown her. It is always up to the individual. And these transmissions and the future offerings that we are guiding her to begin sharing will be the best path for those in greater and greater quantities to choose their alignment and to watch as they are able to shift for themselves through the practices they are given and the transmissions we provide.

The role of upliftment is really at the root of what it is needed, and it is really at the heart of what Heather's Highest path and Purpose is. It is not for her to do for you what you can do for yourself; in fact, what she "does" for you will not last long if you are not willing to fully accept and align to your Highest Self. And so, there are simpler ways to go about it. And there are ways that will lift you up and so many more Higher in the offering of it.

We want you to know and accept and rejoice in the knowing that you are the key to your happiness. That you can choose to read these transmissions and tap in to these practices, and you can receive alignment in ways that are so much more empowering to the core of who you really are. You all need one another to remind each other of who you really are, and no doubt mentors and the like are important, but no one can nor ever will do it for you. And in this way we want you to embrace and accept this so that you can experience a grander version of your life than you have ever known.

And so it is.
XoTheJOGs

THE PATH OF LOVING RELATIONSHIP

When it comes to Loving another it can feel tricky at times, can't it? How do I get my needs met *and* show up fully for the other we hear you ask. And we know that while it seems tricky there is a strong desire deep within you to do the one thing that you can do better than all others – take care of you. And while we hear you wonder and worry how a relationship can possibly work when there are two people focused on themselves as individuals as the main priority while also together in Loving partnership – we are wanting to expand your understanding of how this truly works and what it looks like for you in your life experience.

So you have two people – two people who know, through their close relationship with their Source Self, Higher Self, True Self who they really are and because of this relationship they recognized their partner almost immediately. They felt it, they knew it, they saw it and they allowed it in. So now they are together and navigating this wondrous life with one another. Which is one of the richest life experiences a Spirit in a body can have. To be consciously with their intended Beloved (or with anyone really but we are keeping our focus on Divine Love unions for this transmission) and to honor the relationship for the Divinity it is and live from a Divinely aligned place.

And now we are saying – from this conscious knowing, both will make their individual, personal happiness their main priority.

Now, we do not mean this in the way that many take it. Many hear and see this as a call for separateness or an over-focus on individuality. It is not. What we are saying is that the greatest key to success in all relationships is making one's relationship with Source and with one's Source Self the first priority. And from there all other things can expand. When you are deeply connected in this way, before you take a criticism or a complaint or a worry to your Beloved, you will first anchor into your connection with your number one relationship to gain clarity about whatever is going on for you. Then when you go to your Beloved, you have insights, aha's, clarity that you did not have before. You can say to your Beloved that you have had this incredible life experience of being triggered – often or sometimes by them specifically – and that that trigger led you to a fantastical realization that caused you to know yourself in a new and expanded way.

We gave Heather in her Spirit-Led Love course a Divine Love Manifesto – a whole outline for how to deal with triggers in Loving partnership and how to show up for one another, we gave her the components, the primary components of what makes a Loving union thrive. And we will expand on that here.

We have encouraged you that when you come together with the Love of your Life – you treat them as such, you honor them as such, that you are in gratitude for them as such. We would like to see you as couples working together as a team, as two allies, rather than two enemies, two separate beings. Now you may think we are giving you opposing information here but we are not.

Step One in a Loving partnership is to make your own connection to Source and your Source self your number one priority; this could otherwise be simplified, and what Heather is getting from this here and what she would say is, "Do your work first." Don't look to the other to make life better for you – you make life amazing for you. Don't look to the other to solve your "problems" – you, through your connection to Source, solve your "problems", sharing with your partner as it feels fit to along the way about your insights and for support and for him/her to cheer you on. This doesn't mean you cannot ask your Beloved for help, of course you can, but it's important to emphasize here for you to release expectation that another outside of you can fix or solve anything for you. You trust your connection with all that is, with Divinity to support you in the core of shifting anything in your life experience. And then you flow with the people, and sometimes it is your Beloved, who come in lovingly with the responses & support that will allow your life to flow in the way you most desire.

Step Two in Loving partnership is to have clear shared time, space, intentions, visions for the life you are creating together with one another. Don't leave one another out of this very important part of life. Plan trips together and adventures and what Heather calls date nights and what we would call non-negotiable quality time together. Have a common trajectory that you are sharing on and working towards. And when any triggers arise, take time to go within and clear out and clean up your portion of whatever is occurring.

Because you see, you are in this together – you and the Love of your Life. There is not this huge divide of separation. So many of your experts are telling you how different men and women are and how you are different animals and you are from different planets even. And we say well, in how you were conditioned to be yes. But at the core – at the core of who you really are – you are not that different at all.

All humans desire to be Loved deeply, fully and completely for who they truly are. All desire to be understood. All desire to experience deep Loving – both being Loved and giving Love. All desire a true partner to share all of life's moments with. All desire to have fun and joy and sexiness in a Loving partnership.

These are the areas we would like you to focus. We would like you to focus on the commonalities. We would like you to focus on what really allows a Loving partnership to thrive. Shared interests, shared Souls, shared heart, shared adventures.

The Love of your Life is the Love of your Life for a reason. And while it can feel easy to take the one by your side day after day for granted, we do not encourage this one bit. This leads to all sorts of hiccups that do not serve you. Make gratitude a daily part of your Loving partnership experience. Daily express your appreciation for the other and the gifts he or she brings to you. Daily look upon your Beloved with kind eyes. With loving eyes and with a full heart. Bless them every day for being in your life and gracing you with their presence. Show them in the ways they most desire to receive and that you most desire to give (you will notice it is set it up so those are pretty much one and the same) – so that they know and feel daily your Love and appreciation for them.

Do not play games. Waiting this length of time or that length of time. Experts telling you to let him/her miss you – don't give away too much – the advice goes on and on and unless the "expert" is sharing from their own deep connection to Source and to their Source self, very little of it serves you.

We say – give it all away after you've filled yourself up. For when you are totally connected to Source there is no well running dry, there is no end to the Love you can give another. It is when you do it at the expense of yourself, when you have not made your connection to who you really are your number one priority that you feel that feeling of over-giving, that depletion, that resentment. And as you well know, none of those things ever got anyone anywhere worth visiting or being.

We'll close this transmission with telling you what Step Three is in Loving partnership. Step Three is knowing beyond a shadow of a doubt that you are with this other because they are the best, the only, the most skilled, the most qualified at showing you everything you need to see to be the full you. They are the mirror – the best kind of mirror – that beams right back to you how bright and beautiful you are. They are the one who shows you how to Love deeper than you ever thought you could Love. They were hand-selected by you, by your Highest Self, by your Spirit Team as the one you wished to Love more than all others and they you. And that is one of the most pleasurable, rewarding experiences you can have as a Spirit in a body. Because take away the body and it's all Love, add the body and you have new layers to work with (what fun – really that is why you chose it!) – the wounds of the heart, the wounds of the Soul, the quirks of the personality. But when you come together with the Love of your Life, you know – they are the one to do any and all of that with.

Enjoy this and allow your Loving partnership to unfold in the ever expanding Highest Light.

Love,
XoTheJOGs

LIGHT IS ALL THAT TRULY EXISTS

We Love you very much. And it is with great compassion that we share with you our transmission today. We see many of you suffering unnecessarily and suffering at the hands of your own thoughts, and we wish to set you free from this affliction. For it is only in your deepest connection with who you really are that you discover the truth of all. The truth of the Light of all, the truth that there is no thing on this planet than can ever harm or hurt you.

Now we can hear many of you protesting that you have been hurt or harmed or you feel hurt and harm and we know. We acknowledge that that has been your experience that you have observed and interacted with aspects of this life experience that have caused you great pain. We understand. And we want to expand your framework, expand the lens with which you are viewing this world so as to call forth what is most aligned with the Highest frequency of who you really are, the Highest frequency that is available to all of you on this planet and in this time and space.

You may have felt like or thought that "bad" things or people existed. And those beliefs about "badness" may be directly related to having experiences that felt what you may call "bad" or "dark" or "wrong". But we want you to lean in and listen carefully here as we tell you that those aspects were simply thought forms that were created by others. That as they were fed more and more energy they began to take on a life of their own and perpetuate what was uncomfortable or unwanted. So imagine if the thought forms that you give energy to are thought forms that expand you, that bring light into you and that – despite what might be near or around you – you do not allow your thoughts to go anywhere else but to the Light. Imagine what happens then? What happens then is that those once seen as bad or untoward aspects no longer exist.

It is the focus that creates and summons what you do not desire to come into your experience. Now this is not meant in any way to create a means with which you can blame yourself. We will explain further. As young children, you did not conjure or dwell on harmful aspects. Yet the adults around you might have. And where you are currently, you may not have conjured up harmful aspects, but those around you might have. And there are all various levels of this. Heather is asking us repeatedly about this right now. Because she came from a background that believed in God (good) and Satan (bad). And then she finds herself in a spiritual framework with healers and teachers that are saying something similar – that there must be dark if there is Light. And we say not true. Duality is simply another creation of the mind. Why ever would you think there has to be something bad or wrong to validate or justify what is good?

And it is all perspective and perception anyway. One of you may view something as "good" and the other feels it is "bad". The husband gets a big promotion and pay increase which he feels is "good" while the wife feels it's "bad" because she views it as more stress and less time at home. Who is "right" here? Who is "wrong"? Who is to say what is "good" and what is "bad"? Really there is only that which feels aligned to the whole of who you are and that which does not. We would rather you threw out those "good" and "bad" labels altogether.

Yes, there can be all Light or what you would call "good" all of the time, but it is up to you if that is where you choose to focus. It is up to you where you focus. And if you are having seemingly "not good" or "dark" or "bad" things coming into your experience, you get to ask yourself – do I choose to see this through the lens of "bad" or "wrong" or "dark"? Or can I view it as aligned or not aligned? And if someone is bringing me something "bad" or "dark" and they are wanting me to take it, like, "here, here is this thing that I do not want and you need to take it" – and you know they do this by telling you in significant detail all about it. You can simply say, "No thank you." You can simply say, "Please do not bring that into my experience." You can simply say, "I am a beacon and a believer of the Light and I will not for one minute allow anything that does not feel aligned to me to enter my experience. And if such thing does, I know that it is simply an opportunity to choose a more aligned to who I really am path."

And in this way the whole world can be transformed. In this way, if all practiced this, you would realize that there is nothing, not one thing to fear and that in any moment you can choose whatever perception you desire and you can allow yourself to feel the alignment of it or not. It is not up to you to sort it all out. There are all sorts of thought projections out there that people have given enough credence to that has made it into something much larger than it ever needed to be. Just turn on your television and you'll see it.

And all of that only exists because enough people gave their attention to it. We are wanting you to give your attention to what is true, to what is truly you. To what your Higher Self, your Source Self, your God Self knows to be true. It is all Light and you can choose to be aligned with that or not – the choice is up to you. But trying to figure out what went wrong and how to shift the "dark/bad" or whatever you call it is unnecessary. Stay focused on the Highest Light, and only the Highest Light will come to you. Allow every not Light opportunity to be a further clarifying point, a clarification on your alignment and what is truly aligned for you and what is not. You can transmute all that you do not enjoy by connecting to the Light essence that is available to you in any moment. How do you access the Light you may ask – you simply feel Love, you take a deep breath and inhale the sweetness of a flower, you place your bare feet in the grass, you stand before your glorious ocean. You connect to the Love, to the Light that surrounds you in any given moment. The Light that many are not seeing simply because their focus is elsewhere. We are encouraging you to come back to that which you intended to be. To return back to the wholeness that is naturally you. And it is not natural to be focused on "bad/dark/non-aligned" energy. We are using those terms because they are terms we know you will understand. And we will further clarify that really the filter needs to be "aligned with me energy" and "not aligned with me energy". And the answers to that question will be different for every person because every person is interacting with the path and the world that they intended to. So bonus for you – you do not have to figure out if so and so is on the "right" path, you only have to concern yourself with your path which is the only path you ever need to know anything about.

So do not fear. Do not worry. Do not beat yourself up trying to figure it all out. Surrender to the knowing that it is all so much simpler than you could have ever imagined and that you can engage whatever thought forms feel aligned to you and say, "No thank you," to those that do not. And that in doing so you cleanse your vibration, you cleanse your mind, you release yourself from your restrictions. Because you are free. Life is Light. All is always working in your favor.

The only component that we cannot control is You. You must be willing to allow this to be your reality and get out of the conversations that say to the contrary. Stop talking about things that do not feel aligned. Stop watching things that do not feel aligned. Stop reading things that do not feel aligned. Stop trying to convince people who are not aligned to be aligned. Let it all go. Give it all up. And enjoy the splendor of who you really are which is Light. Every single one of you. The degree of the Light is different for each but you are all Light and the best way we could ever see you spending any of your time is nurturing that Light.

And so it is.
XoTheJOGs

YOUR PATH IS DIVINE

We are here with an important transmission for you. A transmission to inspire hope and to remind you of what you already know is true. You are Divine beings on a Divine journey. And yet so many of you wonder if you have somehow gotten it wrong or if you are off track or have done something that has inadvertently resulted in you not getting what you think it is you should want.

And we have to tell you that although you may take scenic routes on your path, there is never any need to fear that you are somehow ruining your life or not living it correctly. What we want to see more of you doing is being able to really enjoy each step along the way. And so few are doing this. So many are looking at what is wrong or what they perceive as wrong and they are sure that something terrible is happening because of this perceived wrong-ness.

How can my path be being sick they ask?

How can my path be being in this awful relationship?

How can my path be not loving what I'm doing?

And we say – this is your path. And if there is something about it you do not enjoy then we want you to tune in more clearly to the Highest frequency of who you are and see what inspiration comes. But sitting in those situations and focusing on why it isn't working for you or what makes it not a good fit for you only keeps and perpetuates this cycle of non-alignment. It keeps you stuck. It keeps you locked in a place you do not want to be.

So many of you are analyzing your path looking for where it went wrong. Or trying to figure out how you can somehow do it better and differently.

And that is the wrong question.

The question to be asking is – how do I enjoy this now moment? How do I fully show up for what is happening for me right now? And how do I take the parts of this now moment that really light me up and expand them and really see what that Light is and create actively and intentionally more of that?

Well, that's more than one question, but we intend that you understand

145

what we are saying here. You are seeking answers from every direction; and yes there are many answers that you can find, but you are best to stop first and be in the now moment and see what you are loving about it. And perhaps your only joy in this now moment is being alive. That's a good place to start. Start there. Start there in knowing and owning your appreciation for being alive. How can you bring more of that to more aspects of your life? Presence brings you alive. Really being engaged in whatever is happening before you is really being alive.

Heather used to think being alive was going 100 mph. She thought it was traveling every chance she could get and doing and having as many experiences as one could have. And well, that is one way to live, but it does not fill you up. Because what she was seeking was the fullness of being alive. And she thought, as many do, that if she could do more or be more things to more people or have more experiences that then she would feel whole. That then she would feel full of life. And what she got were some great experiences and some good memories. But she was tired and she was not full. She was not so filled up with life which was at the core her Higher Self's truest desire. She was so filled with wanting. She was so filled with seeking out the next opportunity or person or trip that could possibly allow her to feel alive. When her aliveness was in this moment. When her aliveness and all of your aliveness is right here, right now. It's in that person and conversation in front of you. It's in the smell of that coffee, in the taste of that delicious food, in the pleasure and joy of an embrace.

That is where you get full. It's in being fully present for your clients, for your co-workers, for your boss, for your work – whatever it is. That is the fullness of life.

And yet you forget. You forget and so you go about racing to fill those parts of you that are demanding your attention. But what those parts of you really desire is your presence. To sit with those emotions, to sit with the need, with the void, with the longing. And just be with it. Cradle it. Sit with your body pain, sit with it and talk to it and soothe it and nurture it like you would a small child.

Sit with your partner, with your Lover, with your friend and be present. See their beauty. Love them even in their most unlovable states and you loving you in yours.

Presence. It sounds cliché to Heather – someone who has been a spiritual seeker for some time – and yet she cannot deny the power of its truth. That she has never done so little in her life and yet had more experiences of true aliveness. That shedding tears of joy and appreciation and of sadness all feel so intensely and so intensely different. That her food tastes differently. That her nose is lit up by smells she has not noticed before. That she can feel the sweetness of another when before she could not.

You can expand and enliven your life 10-fold by practicing this. And this is just one part of living the fullness of your experience. But it is from this place that all other places expand from. Because when you are already living so full —when you are already so present to what is occurring in your life experience – the magic that is available to you is unlike anything you have experienced before. It is richer, you are richer. It is sweeter, you are sweeter. Is life affirming, you are more alive.

So right here, right now, bring your presence to your surroundings, to where you are and the feel of the clothes on your skin and of your feet on the ground. Notice the beauty all around you. Notice your own beauty. Let yourself feel *you* and feel life. It is pulsing for you. It is desiring you to notice it, to really notice it. Notice what happens when you focus in on the leaf of a tree or a flower – it moves, it brightens. Notice what happens when you pause and notice your partner or someone across from you. Just notice what happens. We promise you it will light up your entire life.

And so it is.
XoTheJOGs

FALL IN LOVE WITH YOU

We are increasingly falling more and more in Love with you. Can you believe it? We almost cannot either. We feel as though the Love cannot expand any further for you all and yet it does every day.

We would like the same for you when it comes to You and your life. We would like you to fall deeper and deeper into Love with yourself. We would like for you to witness yourself as the magnificent being that you are, the being that Source sees and Loves and appreciates and holds in the Highest regard. We desire for you to know yourself at the deepest levels, because in that knowing you cannot help but be dutifully, everlastingly, eternally, rapturously in Love with all that you are and all that you are becoming.

But most of you do not view yourselves in this way. You are always looking for what is wrong, what might need to be "fixed" – which is humorous to us as you are not broken – or worse yet, many of you are forever-more standing in comparison between who you are and who others are. And it serves you in only the most unhelpful of ways.

We long for you to feel the peace and admiration that Source feels for you. Can you feel even some of that right now? Look at you. Go, we are not kidding you, go to a mirror right now. Look into your gorgeous eyes, see that beautiful face and say something. What do you want to say to your beautiful self? There is so much Love all around you. Do you see or feel or know that all around you as you stand looking in that mirror are Angels and non-physical supports that are lovingly and adoringly peering back at you, and they are holding their breath (if they had any of course) in the hopes that you will see what they see as well?

Don't you know how perfect you are in all that you bring to this life? The quirks, the personality, the longing – all of it is so glorious, all of heaven and earth is in wondrous adornment of you. Really, it is so very true. Now perhaps you wonder as Heather is wondering right now how that can be – that every person has this team of admirers, supporters and cheerleaders. But it is set up exactly that way because again, we are all one. Because no one does this alone. And we know, you need your physical supports. We know. You like having that tangible, affirmative, in your hands acknowledgement, or validation or clarity that there are these supports. And yet, and yet we wish you could just for one minute feel the legions of Angels around you and know that you are never alone and that there is never any need or reason to need more than you are or more than what you are currently experiencing because you have a wealth of support right all around you. And when you work with us and acknowledge us as such and talk to us and let yourself just be with non-physical energy without judgment or worry about what others will think – then you are able to more fully relax into your life.

There are those that have what you would call spiritual experiences at various points in their life. They hear a voice or have a specific synchronicity that is meaningful to them or they see an Angel; and some – and many really, because we show ourselves to all of you at one point or the other – will squash that right down – they don't want to see it, they don't want to know it, it's too much. And then they are missing out on the very best that life has to offer them. And you are like that with seeing your own magnificence and feeling that deep Love that we have for you that we desire for you to have for you.

Imagine it – what if *no matter what* – no matter the loss, no matter the gain, no matter who Loved you or didn't Love you – every morning when you woke up and every evening when you went to bed when you looked in that mirror you knew this with absolute certainty. You knew that you were enough. And that you were Divine. And that no one could be more beautiful or talented or smart as you are. That including your own Love and respect, you had legions of Angels and non-physical supporters also beaming back that Love to you and arranging and supporting and facilitating all manner of things to guide you on your Divine path. What if you just knew that?

Then, there would never be any reason to feel lonely or ashamed or guilty or any of those terrible emotions that can result from not fully knowing your magnificence and loving yourself all the way through.

Some of you have been trained from early age to look for what is wrong. To be prepared for something that could go wrong. To look for what might not be okay in the hopes of protecting yourself. And we say – you don't need to do that. We are on it. We are adjusting and shifting and organizing things to work out for you so there is never any need for you to try to get out ahead of anything. We've got your back as the saying goes. And you are just depleting your energy and leaking your energy when you worry, when you try to play it safe, when you are waiting for the other shoe to drop. It's just not worth it and it is entirely too taxing on your physical body.

So, we want to make a deal with you, we want to inspire you to a new way of being. We want you to do more than just look in the mirror and say I Love you. We want you to feel the Love, we want you to tune your subtle sense to the legions of Angels and non-physical supporters all around you as you stand looking in that mirror and feel their Love beaming back to you. We want you to close your eyes and allow this Love to envelop you, allow yourself to absorb this Love that is so pure and so true for the true you. And then re-open your eyes and see if you can also allow yourself to feel that Love for your magnificence and amazingness. We know you can. We feel it and we are ready for you to have this experience more of the time.

With a Love like this, there is nothing you cannot be, do or have. There is no blessing that will not grace your presence. There is nothing but great, deep, big and profound Love for you.

Ever in Love with all that you are and are becoming,
XoTheJOGs

DEBUNKING "WHAT IS WRONG WITH ME?"

"What is wrong with me?" This is a question the majority of you ask on a regular basis. And many of you do not even know that this is the question you are asking. For some it has become such a constant – like a program running on your computer without you even recognizing that it's there – that you do not realize that 99% of your actions and thoughts and next steps are being fueled by this insidious belief that does not serve one single one of you.

We would say that this, "What is wrong with me?" limitation is responsible for most of the mis-aligned choices and experiences that most of you are experiencing. The belief that this question hints at is this: "I am flawed. I am wrong. I am bad. I cannot trust myself." And none of these statements are even remotely true. Not even remotely.

The opposite is actually true.

You are perfect.

You are Divine.

You are the epitome of goodness.

You can trust yourself above all.

Now imagine if the above beliefs were running in the background for you full-time? Imagine how different your life would truly be. When, "What is wrong with me?" is running it leads you to second-guess, over-think, worry and in general not have the life experience you were meant for. When the true truth above is operating you know you cannot get it wrong, that everything is always working out for you, that your core desires are there because they are your path, that the way is always being revealed to you.

When you are experiencing a life like that, you are living in what Heather calls Magic or Spirit-led living and what we call how life is meant to be for you.

We are eager for those of you bringing children into the world, or who have children, to begin to share our version of beliefs with your children. As parents you have this incredible opportunity to give your children the ability to start and live this life from an expanded, Higher consciousness perspective.

And when you tell them all day every day of their goodness and perfection and their ability to trust themselves, you are setting them up for a life unlike which most have lived. Most are coming from a perspective of feeing bad or wrong, and then as they evolve are learning that their alleged "wrong-ness" is simply untrue. And then there is a need to de-program or uninstall those old programs filled with the operating system of, "There is something wrong with me."

And even so, we must tell you that there is nothing wrong with it unfolding in this manner. We would say it is how you intended and now, in your knowing of this expanded truth of your perfection and trustworthiness, as you bring your children into the world you can give them something your parents simply didn't know how to because your parents had the same programs of wrong-ness running that they gave to you.

Uninstalling these programs of being wrong or bad or not trustworthy needn't be an exhaustive process. It will be multi-layered depending on your past experience, your age in this lifetime and your trajectory. But that is no problem, as what else would you do? You did come here to enjoy the natural evolution into who you really are, so why not add this to the mix so that you can be set free more fully of your limitations?

The truth is, there has never been anything wrong with you. Ever. You may not be like everyone else – but we have a secret for you, masses of individuals who appear to be like everyone else are only wearing masks that allow them to appear that way. No one is like everyone else. Each of you is incredibly unique and diverse and profound in your offering of who you really are. There are those of you that flock together and resonate with one another because you have similar paths or similar trajectories or similar desires for this lifetime. Those you resonate with so strongly are usually those your Soul chose to resonate with for the expanded evolution of you all. But never ever are any of you just like the other. You all have your individual quirks and bits and aspects that make you so unabashedly, breathtakingly you. And we would not change it for one minute. And those who want you to change – either as a child or in your now state – are missing out on appreciating all that you are.

This does not mean there is nothing for you to expand into. Quite the contrary. There is everything to expand into – not from a place of being flawed or broken, but rather from a place of great desire to see what is possible for you in this lifetime, to see where you can Soar to when you are fully aligned and fully loving yourself.

We would like each of you to take our above words and memorize them and to raise your level of awareness so that whenever a story of wrong-ness or different-ness or flawed-ness comes in you can remind yourself of what is true.

Imagine what you will do knowing this about yourself. Knowing that it's okay for you to be whatever it is you are at your core. It will allow you let go of masks and limitations with more ease because you are then able to fully stand in the power of your magnificence. And when you do that there is only the knowing of your perfection.

To the perfect-ness that you are and are becoming more of,
XoTheJOGs

YOU ARE YOUR HOME

We want to address you on the topic of home today. Of what it means to be truly at home, to know your home and to root into your home in a way that will serve you tremendously in your life experience. Of course many of you may think or say, "Well, I have a home, I live in it," and we are wanting to expand your concept or understanding of home here and its essential-ness to you.

Often when people come together with a Soul partner they will say, "It felt like coming home." Or when they are looking for a house to live in they will say, "It felt like home." Or when they are in a group or in a community – as Heather's Spirit School participants regularly say, "I feel like I'm home," in this program/tribe/experience.

Recently Heather realized that what her Soul was most longing for was a home. And yet she has two, and so what we were conveying to her is that this is beyond the physical structures. We are drilling down deeper here.

What is your truth when it comes to the concept of home and what does it mean anyway?

Typically when you all are using this term it's to describe a feeling of core alignment. "It felt like coming home, it felt like home, he/she felt like home." It's a familiarity that nurtures you, it's a familiarity that feels safe and secure, like a small child would feel at home with their parents knowing they are safe and protected from the outside world.

As adults, though, this concept of home is important for you, too. It is important because it gives you a core stability, a core knowing, a core foundation from which to move from and center your life around.

But with ever-changing circumstances and environments, how do you know and where do you find home? And we want to present to you the possibility that home does not lie outside of you or in anything in the physical. That in fact it is a feeling within yourself. A feeling of worthiness, a feeling of Love, a feeling of knowing at your core that who you are is so inherently blessed and perfect just as it is.

We would like to see more of you walking around and in your lives knowing this perfection for yourself. Knowing with solidarity that you are so truly and purely perfect just as you are in this right now moment. That you find the feeling of home when you are sitting with yourself, when you are sitting anywhere, no matter where it is. That when you are with yourself you are home. And how you are with yourself is shown through your presence and honoring of the uniqueness, of the giftedness that is you.

We are not attempting to discount the warm and delicious feelings that you have when you come together with a Soul partner or Soul friend or Soul opportunity or Soul tribe or even your Soul home. What we are encouraging is that no matter those outer circumstances that you can always feel your at-home-ness within yourself.

You see, many are running from themselves, from truly knowing themselves. They are keeping themselves busy and overbooked and focused on others' "problems" all in an unconscious attempt to avoid themselves because they fear that what they will find will not be to their liking. In fact, they fear they would discover that they were not a "good" person or, more accurately, a "lovable" person in any way.

Of course this fear is unfounded but based and steeped in previous trauma – whether in this lifetime or a previous one. In truth you are always whole and always worthy and there is never anything to fear about your ability to know and own and believe in your inherent goodness and rightness in the world. But so many do and again, this is mostly unconscious.

If you've ever put your hope in something outside of yourself and then when it did not turn out the way you wanted it to be you felt a sense of loss and sense of de-stabilization, you have experienced this feeling of not-at-home-ness. And we are encouraging you to remember that things will change. External circumstances will adjust – whatever they are. They will move in favor of your desires and sometimes not in favor of your desires (although always still in your Highest good). And when you can sit with yourself wherever you are and feel at peace in the midst of those circumstances, you are home. When you can feel your worthiness and of your home-ness in yourself then you are unshakable by outside forces.

Even placing your stability in us – in your Spirit team – does not allow you to feel the full truth of who you really are. Allow yourself to feel your worthiness just as you are – a Spirit in a body who has power beyond measure. Who is so powerful he/she can choose any emotion, any circumstance to summon forth. So powerful he/she can consciously and co-creatively come together with non-physical energy and experience even more magic in the body experience.

It all starts with you. You are the most powerful when you Love yourself wholly and fully. When you know that no other outside circumstances or person(s) can fill you up like what happens when you come home to yourself.

When you recharge from spending quiet time with yourself. Appreciating yourself and your quirks and your personality, and your preferences, and how you look – all of it. That when you can do this you are transforming not only your own self but those who come into contact with you. To truly Love yourself is the greatest gift anyone can give to themselves. And it is only a gift you can give to you.

Much is made about what it means to Love yourself and we – always the prefer-ers of keeping things as simple as possible – say that this is when you can appreciate all aspects of yourself, especially those aspects others would deem "strange" or "weird" or not likable. When you can look at yourself honestly and see it all and say, "I Love you – and especially for those things, too," you are truly home.

How this Love of self is best expressed is through making choices that most uplift and nurture you, by always honoring and trusting your intuitive sense no matter who or what anyone else says and always choosing the most loving way to express yourself about yourself and about others.

You are so powerful you can choose to not choose all of this, but it is our desire that you will choose this coming home to yourself, to your true nature, to loving who you are in ways that you have only thought of conceptually but which can now be fully integrated by you.

And so it is.
XoTheJOGs

TRIGGERS IN LOVE & LIFE, REFRAMED

When we talk about Love, we hear you all hold your breath in eager anticipation for whatever we will say. And we know this is an area that matters so much to you because it is an area that not only maters so much but it is an area that you all are evolving forward for the collective consciousness. What does it truly mean to Love another? What does it mean to dance this dance of deeply loving and growing together?

It has been said so many times that relationship is the place where true growth occurs. And it is true. With the other you grow, you expand. And in that growth and expansion, something interesting often happens. You begin to get on each other's nerves. You begin to anger or irritate each other. You begin to pull back. These aspects that you call triggers – those pesky bits you all are trying to get away from – are simply opportunities for growth, and not just any growth – growth into the core of who you really are.

And did you know you can transform triggers by simply putting new focus on them? You can transform anything in this way. So, imagine – what if you stopped looking at the things that aggravated you about your current partner or someone in your life as triggers and instead called them what they truly are – an opportunity to connect with my Highest Self and connect with the other from that place?

Now we don't mean to say – live in a minefield of triggers because that will develop you. That is hard on you. That is wearing on your physical and emotional and mental body. We are not saying to be in environments that constantly trigger you. But we are saying that environments that constantly trigger you can be transformed, and in their transformation you can easily release them or step in further to them – depending on what serves your Highest good.

So many are wanting the one answer – the answer that will solve it all, the answer that will bring them everything they need to know. And we want you know it doesn't work like that. There are great truths and there is an important distinction here between great truths and your truth. At the core of it all – at the core of everything – you must run everything we speak or anyone speaks through the filter of your own connection with your Higher Self and with your Higher Consciousness.

It doesn't matter what anyone speaks; if it feels off to you then it will not be a vehicle to serve you well. And of course there are things that others share that really inspire you and then there are things that really aggravate you. And both are worth addressing. It is like this in your relationships – the partner that triggers you the most is worth giving your attention to because therein lies so many great truths for you to discover. But you are incapable of discovering those truths if you are caught up in it, if you are taking the bait and believing that it's truly about the thing is that you are triggered about.

You see, dear ones, it is always about *you*. In this way, this life is a selfish endeavor because you are the only one you are ever going to develop or grow. And hear this – in your developing and growing you clear the space for the ones you Love to do the same. You cannot ever, ever, ever get another to change or shift or grow through force or coercion or trying to convince them. The way they shift is by you getting out of their field, out of their way and focusing on your growth. When you do that it clears up the energetic space which allows them to step into their growth and alignment if that is what they are meant to do with you. If they are not meant to do that with you, they will simply fall away.

All of the gnashing of teeth about do I stay or go in relationship is unnecessary. Stay with *you*. Focus on you, make your alignment number one – your partner will join you or fall away but either way a solution will emerge. Too many are wanting to get the other to do something differently than they are.. Heather received an email recently advertising some program about what men need to do to "get" their woman and "keep" her – using tactics or techniques or quite seemingly logical ideas. But none of that truly works dear ones. Because at the core of it all is your ability to make your connection with yourself and your Higher Self and your Spirit Team number one, and the relationships that you attract from that place will serve your Highest alignment. And when triggers come up – which we now are asking you to call Higher Self expansion points – you can roll through them knowing it is not personally about what you think or assume it's about. It is occurring for your Highest good. And how you get or keep anyone is by getting and keeping yourself. By respecting and loving yourself so much you will not allow anyone else's misalignment or anger or drama to tear you out of yours. And we get that this seems "hard" but we shrug our figurative shoulders here because it is the path of being a Spirit in a body in relationship.

Your dear one, your Lovely, your Beloved will always support you in your evolution. They can do so gently or roughly – it depends on what you expect, what's in your trajectory and the path for both of you. But one way or the other you will get what you need to become more fully who you are. And you do not have to keep dragging it out lifetime after lifetime. You can make a commitment in the here and now to allow that to occur for you now so that no one, no Love, no Beloved, no person, no-thing pulls you out of your expansion into the totality of bliss that you are.

Feels far reaching? Feels too big? That is only information showing you that you are really good at limiting you. And if you were not good at limiting you – imagine what would be possible.

Higher Self expansion points – we want you to write that down. Anytime you feel charged, stand and note that what you are experiencing is an expansion point and sink into the deliciousness of that. Then, every person who shows up is a gift. Every person a blessing. Every person an opportunity to Love and know yourself more deeply. And when that happens, you can open your heart to them and Love them more fully than you've ever Loved another because you get it. You get that you all are One. You get that they are Divine. You get that they are perfect just as you are perfect. You get that none of it matters in the way that you think and that everything matters in ways you cannot imagine.

And so it is.
XoTheJOGs

YOU NEED NOT EVER SETTLE

There is something all of you need to know. It is something you often forget but of which serves you at the Highest possible level. It is this core truth – you did not come here for anything less than your fullest desires. You see, many of you forget this and so you work as best as you can to make things, situations, and people work for you and acclimate to them when they are not actually the most aligned experiences of your life experience. You are trying to force, you are trying to make work that which really in its fullest expression is not even close to being aligned for you. You may make excuses for the person or opportunities or whatever it is – but at the core of you, you know you can do better.

And we are here to tell you, you *can* do better.

If there is anything in your life experience that is not matching up for you – that does not on all levels or cylinders feel like a big, fat yes – then there are some adjustments to be made.

Now typically, you would then say or feel that you must discard said opportunity, person or aspect and we say even taking that step is too premature. You are not even ready to go there yet. What you must first do is what Heather would call the alchemical process and what we would call only the "work" ever worth doing – preparing your vibration, your mindset, your body, your energies for the fullness of your desire.

Good enough will never do for any of you. "Almost" what you desire won't work either. But you get impatient, you get antsy and so you dive in because well, some of you figure, "It's close enough." And we're telling you "close enough" will never fully satisfy you, it will always leave you longing for more.

It will always feel like something is missing, because something *is* missing. And not necessarily in the other person or in the opportunity – but in you.

Because you forgot the most important piece of information you could ever hope to know, and that is that you are a Divine being and you do not have to ever receive less than your full desire. Nowhere in your life contract does it say, "Settle for less than what you fully desire." You forgot that you, you alone have the ability to shift yourself into circumstances and events and relationships that will yield to you your utmost desires. You and you alone have the ability to co-create a life that truly lights you up on all levels. And unless you're doing that, you are not living the fullest of this life experience.

Not settling does not mean adjusting your desires. It means aligning to your desires. And then holding to them so firmly that no matter who shows him/herself to you, no matter what opportunities arise, you hold steady in that knowing of what you truly desire and what is fully yours to experience. And this can be what you would describe as challenging especially if the person or situation or circumstance or relationship is not behaving in the way you fully desire it to in its current form.

But that is always going to be the case – there will always be something that needs some fine-tuning or adjustment but the fine-tuning or adjustment isn't the person/place or thing – it's you. It's you consciously reconnecting back to what you truly desire and from that place re-aligning to what is truly you.

For example: In the midst of something not unfolding in the way you truly desire:

Go into meditation, journal, utilize whatever self-care tools put you into a good feeling place, an aligned place. Then, ask your Guides & Angels of the Highest Light (otherwise known as your Spirit Team) to make known to you what you desire in this particular area that is "up" for you. Allow whatever comes through or pops in to come in. And let us be clear here, you are not just awaiting someone (i.e. your Spirit Team/Source) to pop in the information for you, you are a cooperative, co-creative component here. You allow yourself to tune in and imagine what would be better than where you are at right now.

Then, once you lock into what that would be, you say with firmness and clarity and conviction, "I now call this into my experience. I now allow this to be my true reality." And then you spend any time you would normally go into ruminating on the situation as it currently is and place that focused time and energy on what you aligned with in your more relaxed and open state.

When you have to interact with person/place/thing that is currently not in a state you desire, you call in your Spirit Team, you tap, you breathe deep breaths, you ask to see them through the eyes of Source and you walk into every encounter with them from that perspective, from that place. And you let what needs to occur to occur without your reactivity or interference or desire to control. Just try it out and see what happens.

And if it still doesn't quite meet what you are intending, you just keep coming back to what would fill you up more. You come back to your truth and you never ever, ever allow yourself to settle for anything less than what feels most joyful to you.

What does it really mean, that term settle, anyway? It implies that it stops, that you stop and that when you stop it shouldn't be on something that is just "okay". Well, we're here to tell you that you are on an eternal journey whether you are currently in the physical or non-physical, and so what is most important is for you to have daily connection to what would light you up the most and spend conscious time with it, reflecting on it. And then as you make this a regular habit, fewer and fewer aspects of your life have to be off or out of balance or out of alignment as you would call them.

You do have the ability and support to discern what will fit your course first in your thought, first in your daydreams and then allow what wants to adjust and align from there to do so.

But you never ever have to sit in any situation or relationship or whatever it is and say, "This is mine, I just have to suck it up and deal with it." No, you do not. In every moment and in every situation you have the opportunity to choose something that feels better to you. And sometimes that is going to be taking a nap or going for a walk or it's going to be getting a mentor or taking a class or reading a book – but in every moment you can do something to shift the frequency of wherever you are at if it is not feeling good to you. And the harder it feels to do this is just information to let you know that you've got a lot of stories going on that are not letting you feel as magnificent as you truly are. And that's okay. From that place you can decide how you want to proceed, you can decide what tools you need to engage to allow yourself a greater leap, a greater shift, a bigger vantage point to jump into.

We know you must think that we think that you are struggling too much, as we highlight these areas. But we know this is simply par for the course. This is part of being a Spirit in a body. It's what you signed up for. And it's what we signed up for to support you in this way, with these transmissions so that you need not go at it alone. So that you know with certainty that you are supported and Loved and have a myriad of resources to living a life that truly serves you.

And so it is.
XoTheJOGs

YOUR LIFE MATTERS

There are beliefs of thought out in your world that say this – everything is fleeting, nothing really matters, it's better to be detached. And we say nonsense. We say, everything is permanent in this sense – everything you experience matters. Many of these experiences are imprinted on your Soul. Many of those experiences will shift consciousness forward or keep it stuck. What you do matters.

We are not suggesting you cling to life or try to make it something it's not. But we would never advise to act as though it doesn't matter, that it is fleeting and it's not worth it. That is absolutely in direct opposition to what your Soul knows to be true.

Now, when you are having a hard time of it this may be helpful. Let's say a Spirit in a body has a lot of momentum that is not serving them, they are in what you would describe as a heavy feeling place – then sometimes saying, "Oh, it's fleeting or impermanent," will bring them relief out of a place of despair. But once they are out of despair it is clear that that statement is no longer beneficial for them.

Your life matters. Every moment of your life matters.

What we wish to see of you is your ability to sink into every moment and be fully present to it so that you can soak up the wonderfulness that it is. And in that soaking up of wonderfulness you can experience true bliss, you can experience the eternalness of you, you can experience the permanence of you. So it's true, that moment will not last – technically by your created time standards – for an eternity. But in the imprint of your Soul and in the imprint of consciousness it just might. And so we want you to treat all that occurs for you with how we see it, which is that it all matters. And how you choose to show up in any given moment matters. And sometimes you will show up fully aligned in your brilliance and you will support your own self in feeling joy, and your own Soul in expanding further forward and the collective consciousness in evolving forward as well. And in other moments you may not show up in all of your brilliance, you may be having a Higher Self expansion point, or what you might call triggers. And in those moments you are being clarified; your Soul is allowing a wound to be looked at and have the opportunity to evolve it forward, and all of the collective consciousness has an opportunity to evolve forward from this experience.

This is how it works. So you can see that in every moment it is happening *for* you, and *for* all. And in that happening for you and for all, the world is becoming a more beautiful place, and life has the opportunity to flourish in ways it had not before you came to this moment in your life.

Some say this impermanence is true because your Loved ones won't live forever, you won't live forever, the moment won't live forever. And we say – untrue. Not true at all. Your Loved ones do live forever, you do live forever – the eternal nature of your Soul goes on and on forever. There will be a transition out of this physical body into another, but you are going with your Loved ones and they are going with you. It is not goodbye – it is see you on the flip side! It is not over forevermore, it is simply an eternal moment transitioning into a moment that is even more aligned. It does not have to be drama or awfulness ever. It can be that you get to know this and know it well and make your transition and bid, "See you soon!" to those you Love and vice versa.

And this moment, the impermanence of this moment – as we stated before – is simply not true. This moment has the ability to be imprinted upon your Soul forevermore. It has the ability to be a moment that you cherish for all of eternity. Or it has the ability to be a moment that allows you to become more of who you really are at the most aligned level. But either way there is nothing impermanent about it.

Where things get off for you all is this belief in time scarcity. This belief that if I cannot stretch this out forevermore in my now reality then it doesn't matter or something has gone wrong or I am wrong or something is wrong. And that is simply not true and not serving you. The power of presence allows you to sink into and feel more fully the eternal nature of every moment. Because a lifetime can exist in each moment and in each opportunity and in each relationship. Can you feel this? Can you feel the Light in this?

We are wanting you to know this so powerfully and to really let yourself feel it. We guided Heather to watch a talk where the author and teacher was saying, "Why does life even matter? It's so fleeting and impermanent." And Heather saw the heaviness on the faces of those talking and we just could not wait to get her to this moment to share this with you. That story may serve those in a place of despair as we mentioned before, but it is not the Highest Truth accessible to and by you. And our intention with these transmissions is to bring you the Highest Light accessible to you so that you can live your lives with more joy, more bliss, more abundance and more *yes*.

Can you hear us? Can you feel us?

If so, your life will go very well for you.

XoTheJOGs.

WHY LOVE LEAVING HURTS

So, you want to know why Love hurts? Why you just can't be fine after a Love ends or goes away or completes? Heather was asking us this very question today. *Why is there so much grieving if we know everything is working out for us? Why is it so devastating when it doesn't work out even when we know there is simply a completion happening and nothing to be upset about?*

And we say – one, because you're in a body and the body allows you to experience a variety of emotions. And two, if there is a deep sense of loss and grief it is linked to not being able to fully and clearly with every cell in your body understand this deep truth – Love never truly leaves. Love is eternal. You will Love one another for millennia when it is a deep, true Love and it is only the relationship that shifts or changes from a physical manifestation into a non-physical manifestation that you are experiencing this sense of loss.

In this way it is like what you call death where there is this transitioning out of a physical energy into a non-physical energy.

That is how it is with Love. And just like when you grieve those who you deem as dead – you also grieve the "loss" of Love.

However, both could be healed with relative ease when you recognize that while yes the physical manifestation of that Love or person is no longer present, the eternalness in the nonphysical realm remains.

Here's the thing – you are going to reunite with your Loved ones in every lifetime. You are going to see each other and dance together again and do it up in a whole new way next time. So there is no genuine loss. We understand that from your place of being in a body it is harder to access this knowing and it feels more commonplace to stay in the zone of the illusion which is – if I cannot see it, it does not exist.

This of course is not true. There is so much that is unseen by you that is more real than that table in front of you. You know this inherently and at a deep level.

Also the body makes contracts. Every person you are sexually intimate with – there is a forming or bonding of energy there and that energy carries on whether you can see the physical manifestation of it or not. This is why we do not encourage sex with every person you are attracted to. Of course, it is your body and you have the free will ability to choose whatever you desire, but from a Higher Consciousness perspective, it does not serve you to be sexually intimate with anyone who is not a great Love. It simply creates more of what you might call interference in your body-mind and energy field. Now of course over time you can clear that up – but why make a mess, we ask, when it is unnecessary to do so?

This bonding through sexual intimacy can serve as the reason why you may also feel a sense of deep loss and grief even if the other was not a Great Love. We encourage you to follow the clearing practices we have given Heather and that Heather has laid out in her energetic toolkit. This will clear you and allow you to feel more fully your truest truth on this topic of Love and it's alleged "leaving".

And so, yes, we acknowledge that you may feel loss or sorrow about what seems to be the ending of a relationship. And yet, there is no need for this. It is alright for you to feel this way and if the emotions are there, let yourself feel them and release them. And then in a quieter moment when you are feeling more relaxed and out of that feeling of loss, sit with yourself on the topic of this person and sit with the true you. Your true self. And from that connection to who you really are you will know and see and be able to honor that – they have not gone anywhere. Maybe physically they are no longer present, but you can feel the Love and you can also feel that they had their path to go tend to that you were not meant to follow them on and vice versa. Then from that place you can bless them and wish them well.

You are not getting this wrong, dear ones, you could just be more aligned on this subject matter. We will relish the day when death is treated the same way by you. When you, yes, let yourself feel it if the grief is there, but for the most part you let yourself know the truth – the energy and Soul of the other is still there and still accessible by you but it is time for them to go on a part of their journey that you cannot go with them, because it would not serve your or their Highest Good to do so. If it would serve your Highest Good to do so, you would have gone with them and there would not have been a separation of the energy.

And so, take heart. By all means, feel what you need to feel but do not use someone else "leaving" as your excuse to not have the most glorious life possible. They left so that you could flourish in new ways; they left so they could flourish in new ways. They had to go on their journey to have the most glorious experience they could have and now it is up to you to do the same.

And so it is.
XoTheJOGs

FOLLOW YOUR TRUE DESIRES

When you are desiring something, it feels good to you doesn't it? It feels good to marinate in the abundance of what it would be like to have that thing that you desire. It feels good to imagine the possibilities and the adventures that could be before you with this desire manifesting fully into your 3D experience. And we say any level of enjoying your desires is for your benefit. Some may call this visualization or day dreaming, we say it's part of being a conscious co-creator with Spirit.

Letting yourself sink into and simmer in the activities and joy of having what you desire activates within you a vibrational offering, a vibrational field, a vibrational projection of what you desire. And when you begin to dance on a regular basis with this – we would suggest daily with that desire and how good it feels and sink into the specifics of it – then you begin to radiate this desire in your field. You begin putting out a beacon beckoning it to come to you.

At the same time when you are talking about or worrying about or imagining something that scares you or you do not want, the same thing is true and like a beacon you begin to call it forth.

Now your scientists and athletes have known about this power for some time, as they have found that the athletes that visualize their winning plays experience more winning plays. And the, what you would call, New Age community has talked about this and of course it is mentioned in almost any conversation around quantum physics.

And yet some are resistant to using the power of the mind in this way. You get too worried you are not doing it right or enough or that you'll create something you don't really want. And we say it needn't be that complicated. Just go in your mind to a scene that feels good to you. Some say they can't visualize and of course we say that's impossible – every single one of you has the ability to imagine what you do want in your life. And if you feel or say that you cannot visualize then one, of course that will be your experience; and two, we say that is just letting you know how much of a blockage you have

168

created to allowing yourself to have what is truly yours to experience in this lifetime.

And why does it matter anyway having or experiencing these desires? Some of your teachers would say desires do not serve you or are not good for you and others say – follow every desire.

We would like to present a balanced approach to desires. We would like you to tune in to what truly serves you and use that as your guiding Light.

Desires that come from others – from your media or culture or family – do not serve you, that is true. But desires that do not go away despite your best efforts or desires that are there whether you want them or not, desires that pop in at moments you wouldn't expect or desires that you dream about – those are what we call aligned desires. Those are Soul desires. They are part of your path, your Destiny, your trajectory. And when you allow yourself to marinate in and sink into what it would be like to experience these desires, you will have greater Love, joy and abundance than you have ever known.

These Soul desires are a big part of why you incarnated in this lifetime. And they not only make life more fun and more enjoyable for you, they raise the vibration of your planet. They raise the frequency of possibility and vitality for all around you and all that may be touched by you. You are literally soothing the collective consciousness when you choose in the direction of your Highest Soul desires. When you allow yourself to go after and experience what you know deep within you will be the only thing to ever fill you up in the ways you are really meant to experience.

Desires are not frivolous as some might say. They are a necessity. They are the driving force behind why you are here. You did not come here to toil or suffer or pay penance as some of your religions and new thoughts systems would have you believe. You are not here to prove anything or win back something lost.

You are here to have a life experience unlike any you have had prior. To experience how wonderful it is to line up with your desires and watch them come into being and have the impact on the world that you are here for. Yes, the world. When you are thriving, you create a vibrational field around you of thriving, and then everywhere you go and every person you meet – they get a drop or something more of your thriving.

The other day Heather was at a gas station – no biggie, just taking care of things – and she was in her optimistic, loving life mode and chatting up the nice lady gracious enough to fill her gas tank. And the lady said, "You are so nice, you are so sweet. Most people aren't nice like you are. I really appreciate you. Thank you." And by the end of the exchange they were exchanging honey's and sweetie's and just oozing Love at each other. That woman went Higher in her day and in her Light because of that interaction. And Heather went Higher in her day and in her life because of that interaction. And then from there, she interacted with more people and spread the vibration and the woman did the same thing.

And those two may never see one another ever again but it does not matter. The work has been done, the action sequence of vibration that Source desires for all had been integrated.

And this is how it is when you are living your core Soul desires. When Heather was following the beat of another's drum, when she was doing work she disliked because she thought she had to, or in a relationship because she was in weak place and chose a partner that mirrored that to her, or when she was in scarcity – she did not have that sort of impact on the world. She had the opposite.

And the same is true for you. This is why following and experiencing your true desires matters. Because when you are experiencing them, the whole of you benefits. So many more of you go Higher because you are following the call of your Soul. Heather calls this Magic and we call this the way your life is meant to be.

We are complete.
XoTheJOGs

LET GO OF CONTROL

To some, Love feels like a game that they cannot win, that they cannot conquer and we wish so very much that you could see this whole Love bit in a new Light. We wish and intend for you that you can see Love through the eyes of Source. For when you do, you know there is nothing to conquer nor win.

You recognize that Love is a part of life, just like food is a part of life, just like your car or bike or whatever you use for transport is a part of your life. And we are not saying this to diminish the impact of your Love relationships. We know, they are more valuable and important to you than your transport and you might even say more important than food.

What we are saying is this – Love relationships are a Divine part of your life experience. They are here to support you in your ever expanding unfolding of becoming more of who you really are. And some of them, as we have shared, will last for the rest of your life in this lifetime and then carry on into the next as it is an eternal Love. And some of them – even if there is that deep Love – will have to move on and all will be perfectly fine and aligned. So yes, we've explained this to you – you understand this.

And yet you fret and worry and try to control the outcomes of those you Love. You try to figure out who is the perfect partner for you, or the Love of your Life if you follow our transmissions. You try to nudge your current partner into more alignment with who you think he or she should be. If you are single you do everything in your power at times to bring this Love to you, or on the flip side you hole up and hide away – all in a means to control the outcomes of your life experience.

And we say – this will never serve you. And you know this because it does not feel like the Highest and best use of your time. But some of you are so used to controlling every aspect – or shall we say, think you're controlling every aspect – of your life you don't even realize that you are trying to treat your Love relationships like another item on your to-do list or you're avoiding it like you do other things in your life experience.

We want you to see all of this through the eyes of Source and recognize that no person would or could be before you or be in your experience without a tremendous gift to present to you. And so it is not about controlling or trying to get to a perceived known outcome, it is about surrendering and opening up yourself to receive the gift that this one is bringing to you.

It is not about trying to be the perfect person for another or be perfect in general in the hopes that then, that finally then you'll receive all of the bounties of the Universe. It doesn't work like that. You are not being rewarded or punished – you are living a Life. You are living. You are alive.

All of it is here for you. All of the emotions you wanted to feel because that's the beauty of being alive. And all of these people or just the one person you Love are exactly whom you wanted to be with, because they are the best one suited to remind you of so much that your Higher Self and Spirit Team wish for you to be reminded of.

Who you are with them tells you everything you need to know.

So, who are you with this one or that one? How do you feel in your body when you are with this one or that one?

Heather will notice that after she spends time with some people she goes straight to her head to try to figure it out. And we have shown her that she does that in an attempt to protect her heart, to shield herself from feeling something that wants to be felt by her very deeply.

So if you notice yourself going into a spin cycle in your mind, just know that's you protecting yourself from feeling something – something that wants your attention and wants to be felt by you.

And when you can let yourself feel whatever that is, you are setting yourself up for surrender into your true path. You are setting yourself up for more conscious awareness of who you really are, with the core of you.

And isn't that what you wanted? We will tell you – it is what you wanted and want. It is the truest and best alignment of your desire in this body – to really feel and know and be present for that excitement, that sadness, that "pain", that bliss, that joy. And to realize that the emotions that feel horrible to you are only there because they need you to know that something greater is calling you. And often that greater-ness is allowing yourself to feel the true bliss that is within you.

We know you are in a body, and with an emotional body it creates a unique system with which to navigate life through. But, you're in a body and that is just as you intended it and it is Divine!

Allow yourself to feel the fullness of your heart – and that is what many are avoiding or trying to avoid when it comes to Love and relationships. So they will analyze and try to figure out and criticize and make decisions. Heather Loves to make decisions. She Loves to meet someone and just claim that she knows and she is done or going all in. And we applaud her desire to be so sure and yet we say, "Easy now. Easy. Let Spirit show you the way."

In every moment you have a choice to co-create with Spirit, with your team, with non-physical energy – however you want to frame it up. You get to choose – do I want to let this be revealed or do I want to control this into what I want or make a decision about what this is and then project all over it what I think it is? Or do I want to take a breath, sip my tea, be fully in the moment and ask Spirit to show me everything I need to know in this here and now moment.

Now notice, we didn't say, "Show me everything that I need to know about this individual forevermore." How could that be? You are shifting and evolving and expanding at such a beautiful pace. How could we show you everything you would ever need to know about another all in one moment? And trust us, us showing you everything would cause more ungroundedness in your body than you want to experience. You are shown what you need to know and see in that moment to lead you to the next moment which leads you to the next moment. And you glimpse possibilities of projections of thought with another, but we urge and encourage you to notice these, bless them and come back to your here and now moment. What am I feeling now? How do I feel in the presence of this person?

Do I feel good? Do I feel uplifted? Do I feel more like myself? Do I feel happy? What is happening in my body when I'm with this person? You can use this for new people you are meeting or your current partner. Just notice. And let the noticing lead you to the next noticing and ask and set your intentions for what you want or desire and then go back to your breath.

You are not in control. You are not in control. You are not in control.

We gave this to Heather after her first introduction, what she is calling her first psychic surgery with us. And she was mortified by this statement. She was in disbelief. And she promptly decided that was incorrect information or she was hearing it incorrectly.

And no, she wasn't hearing it incorrectly but she was translating it incorrectly as some of you may be right now.

You are not fully in control of how your life unfolds. You are not from your personality and conscious mind fully in control of who you Love or who you spend your life with or not spend your life with. Your Higher Self created your Destiny or vibrational trajectory or path and chose your personality. All of it was so very intentionally, so very masterfully chosen for you so that you could come here and live a life that you would talk about for eons to come.

You really did. And yes, to us, you are all superstars on the cover of magazines and the way you use your life and the way you align with us or the way you show up for the situations in your life and the Loves in your life – they make you superstars to us. We are beaming in awe and gratitude. We know, in a body – it is a whole other ballgame as you would say. And you are a rockstar in your ballgame. You truly are.

You are not in control of everything and certainly not in control of who you Love. You know this, don't you? You can't explain it, you just Love the person. And it's your "job" then, where you can use your choice is to do as we describe – be present, pay attention to your body sensations, to your energy, ask for support, set your intentions and sink back into breath. And trust and know that the one before you is a gift. And it is not up to you to make this gift stay or go or stay for eternity or for one year or two. It is your job and your choice to allow the gift to be given and to follow the signs that lead you to its grandest unfolding. We wish this for you, for all of you.

With our copious magnitude of Love for you,
XoTheJOGs

YOU CAN RELEASE YOUR PAIN

When your body is in pain, we often hear you ask, "What does it mean?" And for some, they translate it to mean they must fix it or do something to end the pain. For others, they translate it as a punishment for wrongdoing. And yet others will avoid their pain at all costs, doing whatever is necessary to numb or block or hinder it.

Heather is asking, as many of you are – what is the Highest path in relation to this? And that is the question that has birthed these transmissions. The strong desire by Heather to live her Highest Path & Purpose as she recognized that her own will was not taking her to the depths of or the great heights that are truly possibly as a Spirit in a body. And others of you are wanting to know as well.

And so when there is pain in your body of any kind it is always communication from the unconscious via the body to your conscious self. It may be a message to take a new action or to let go or release something. It may be a message that there are old stories operating that are ready to be seen by you and then released. It may be letting you know there are emotions inside of you that you have either taken on from others or are your own that need to be felt and released.

Every time, without exception, it is a message from You to you. It is one of the best communication systems your Higher Self has in communicating and bringing the unconscious to Light.

And so the body and "pain" or "dis-ease" are one of the clearest ways your Higher Self will allow what is unseen within to come into the seen. And when there are chronic conditions at play it's generally due to the fact that the full message has not yet been fully and consciously received by you, which includes the action that is being asked for has not yet been taken.

How you pain yourself emotionally and mentally over these occurrences! How many are avoiding knowing this and treating their body in this Divine way! The very thing the illness or pain is "forcing" you to do is the very thing your Higher Self desires for you to do but could not get you to do any other way.

And we understand that this can feel annoying or frustrating to you. You have things you want and the way you want things to be and you do not like it when your body sidelines you. But we are telling you your body must "sideline" you if it is to get the message through as crystal clear as it needs to.

Your body is always giving you a gift. If you have to slow down or stop something or totally change your diet or change what you're talking about or spend more time taking naps or dancing or limit who you spend time with – those are all things your Higher Self is wanting for you that it was not able to get through to you in any other way.

So in this, your body is always, every time helping you, supporting you, giving you exactly what you need. And when you push through anyway and tough it out, when you numb out, when you focus on fixing rather than listening – every time it simply delays the message in being fully communicated and therefore delays the full beauty of your life experience that is here for you.

In this way there is nothing to fear with pain or dis-ease – rather they are messages redirecting you, nudging you, supporting you in becoming more fully and wholly that which you truly are. And if you find yourself to a be a sensitive person, all that means is that there much that you agreed to evolve forward in this lifetime and so you chose experiences that would allow for this.

Anytime you are in pain, you can allow yourself to drill down to the emotions at play. Let yourself feel them. Many times that alone will shift you out of the pain. There are many ways to manage pain and dis-ease, we agree, and you must always follow the guidance you receive from yourself about what modalities or practices or tools to use to support you. We are not saying that any one way is correct or incorrect, but we are saying that you will be served in the Highest Light when you allow your pain or dis-ease to be the transformative tool it is meant to be. When you stop seeking outside of you the answers to what ails you, but when you use the pain or dis-ease as an opportunity to steep yourself in meditation and journaling and loving and knowing yourself on the most intimate levels. When you allow the path of dis-ease to be what it is meant to be – a tool for becoming more of who you really are – then you can transcend some of the biggest fears and limitations that Spirits in a body have put on themselves for eons.

We see you out there and you are doing it all beautifully. And our intention is that these transmissions continue to support and nudge you into greater alignment with the whole of you are so that you can have the most magnificent life you could have ever imagined.

And so it is.
XoTheJOGs

THE ANSWER YOU SEEK IS RIGHT HERE

When you are looking for answers to your most pressing questions that is when the answers will most evade you. We know, this is frustrating for you and may seem counter-intuitive, yet we assure you it is exactly as it is meant to be, for it "teaches" you one of the most important tools to living a life that is most in alignment with your Highest Self.

Let's imagine that you are a bee, and you are desperately in search of sweet nectar, for it is your primary purpose and aim to capture this nectar and support the community and collective with which you care so much about and are so apart of. And so you go out in search for the nectar, but everywhere you look it is not. Or when you arrive, other bees have already done what you so desperately intended to do. And so you continue on, growing increasingly more frustrated with your inability to capture that which is your purpose, to capture that which you know is the one thing that will make you feel most like you have done your "job" in your life experience.

Finally you give up – every flower stop has been void of any real bounty. Sure a little here or there, but not enough to fill you up or make the progress that your community needs. You decide to head back to your home or community and call it a day as the sun is getting close to setting. You are disheartened but you feel certain – dejectedly so – that there is nothing more to be done. Then, as you buzz back home, a flower bed of untold colors lays before you. You know you took the same route out today but somehow you did not see this bounteous beautiful bed of flowers that is beckoning to you. You catch yourself experiencing heightened excitement, a moment of fierce happiness washes over you, "Yes, I will accomplish my purpose today and support my community and myself and it will feel oh so good!" But you quickly quiet that response for fear this flower bed will only be more of the same – already taken care of by other bees.

Only, upon your arrival, you find just the opposite. There is so much sweetness here, there's enough goodness in this flower bed alone for the whole of your community. You quickly send out communication to those closest to you in your community so that you all can do what you are here to do and support the flowers and your community in flourishing.

Perhaps some of you have discovered something similar. When you are seeking that which you feel you must find, it occurs that it cannot come to you. But when you give up so to speak, when you surrender, when you let go of the belief that you have to find the answer, you open yourself up to finding the most abundance you've ever come upon before. You find yourself lapping up in the luxury of your desire. It is often that which you discount that has the Highest potential to fill you up.

Why is this? When you are so desiring the answer to your question, when you so wish to know the answer to your questions you are emitting – and we have mentioned this before to you – you are literally emitting such a strong vibration of wanting that it delays your ability to align with the answer.

And so we want you to be in the best state you can ever be in for knowing anything or doing anything or having anything – relaxed, joyful and ready to receive. Many times you are like that bee and it's out of sheer frustration that you give up, that you stop searching, and it is in those moments that the alignment of the manifestation can occur.

And you often find that that option or route or person or opportunity that you discounted, that you thought nothing of – you gave little if any thought to – ends up being the exact solution and answer that is most aligned for you.

It is a funny thing about being a Spirit in a body in that you have the beauty of your five senses, the power of your mind, the power of your energy fields, and it is as though you get distracted by all of it and you forget that the truest truth for you will always be in the simplest of unfoldings. It needn't be an arduous journey to your truth and to your alignment. Unless you want it to be. Unless you believe it has to be. We are encouraging you to practice a new belief – a belief that reminds you that all that you desire is right under your nose. It's the option you hadn't even noticed.

Be mindful here to not now, with this knowledge, go looking for the little known discounted option sure that now *that* will be your answer. Remember that energy of pressing in, of making happen only energetically delays what you most desire. Instead practice relaxation – let go of attachment to the outcome you "think" is the best or that which you are desperately seeking. We find this to be the best way to shift anything and everything for you. Bring your senses and your body-mind and energy fields into a state of relaxation, which is simply another word for the state of allowing.

Right now for Heather this is foot massages in a decadent setting, sitting in the sun, driving long drives and listening to us or her favorite music or daydreaming about what would most light her up.

Find a way to soften into your relaxation. No matter what you face, if and when you do this more of what you desire can come to you.

Relaxation is your key to finding the answers you seek. When you do this, you realize there is nothing to find, only that which to allow. And that in doing so what you desire will and can come to you effortlessly, it will just pop in – in your thoughts, into your email box, into your mail box, onto your door step, right in front of you.

And in your relaxation new truths and insights and aha's can come.

Find what puts you in the most easeful state. Create the environment of relaxation and watch and enjoy as you begin to not only savor and enjoy your life experience more fully but that which you are seeking to know can come to you with greater ease than you ever imagined possible.

In Love,
XoTheJOGs

YOU CAN NAVIGATE ANY DIFFICULTY WITH EASE

One of things many of you ask both unconsciously and consciously is how you can navigate personal difficulties more gracefully, more easefully, more abundantly. We watch as some fight and struggle, while others avoid and repress, and still others allow themselves to be confused and locked in confusion. And we know and understand and acknowledge that while you may logically be able to see that these behaviors do not serve you in the moment or at the time they seem to be or feel to be the best, you can follow in those moments that call for your expansion at such a High degree.

The fullest and Highest expansion and expression of you is one that is connected to who you really are, to your Highest Self, and to the part of you that can respond from that aligned place.

And all of you, we would say, desire at a core level to respond from that aligned, who you truly are place. And we do not suggest or recommend beating up on yourself if that does not occur, but we do advise that you take action today, right here, right now to begin to plant the seeds for this so that aligned responses are your regular experience.

Here is what we want to share with you as directly and clearly as possible. Take a deep breath, tap Cortices if you need to, and open yourself up to receiving this truth:

- Things in your life will occur that do not feel like they are in the Highest Light for you.
- The reason for their occurrence is multi-layered at times and for a variety of reasons, but we can tell you that if it is occurring, it is meant to be – whether from your practiced vibration in this life or from something you agreed to evolve forward in this lifetime. You truly don't need to know more than this. If it's happening in your experience it's supposed to be there. So, let's get to shifting it into a

Higher frequency and let go of the analysis of why it's even there in the first place.

- Your "job" is to ask, "How can I allow this to situation, person, experience to allow me to go deeper into Loving and Higher into who I really am?" That is the question that will most serve your attention and focus.

We are not asking you to stifle your emotions. No, your emotions must be felt and released, and we have given you many tools to do this, namely writing out these emotions in all of their passion and vigor and then burning the sheets of paper with the focused intention of fully releasing them as you do.

We are asking you to step into a Higher frequency with how you react and show up for things going "wrong" in your life experience. Because they are not wrong. They are yours to experience and your rejection of them only makes them grow in their severity or intensity or pain for you. And so we say, ask how this – whatever this is – can allow you to go deeper into Loving, and Higher into who you really are?

What if this experience is the catalyst for your greatest unfolding? What if this experience leads you to billions of dollars or to the Love of your Life or to the most happy, peace-filled emotional state you have ever desired?

You do not know, you do not truly know – even those of you that think you do – of what is possible from every experience in your life experience. We promise you that every bit of it has the potential to land you into a far more aligned place than you were beforehand. And if you could just see this and look at this and honor this about your life, you would find yourself skipping down the street more, laughing more, smiling more, hugging more, being thrilled more of the time. Really and truly you would and you will.

So what does going deeper in Love mean? It means quite simply that you will understand more fully the nature of Love. Not from your mind or from cerebral analysis, but from your heart, from your body, from the energy all within and around you. To feel the depths of Love that you can and do and are here to feel.

Higher into who you really are? That is your ability to transcend previous limitations, previous pieces of your story and of your life experience that are not and were never the true you, but only conditioned, practiced reactions and responses that are no longer necessary for you to engage in. When you become more of who you really are you feel more peace, you experience more flow in life, there is clarity more of the time. And you emanate from you an energy that few could put into fully expressed words but which makes you a magnet for all that your Soul desires.

And so, we ask you to stop before your reactions occur from your physical and emotional body and to remember our three points above, asking yourself the most important question – "How can this take me deeper into Loving and Higher into who I really am?" This question can be carried with you into every and all situations. Because every and all situations give you an opportunity for this. The real question here is – and this is the co-creative part of this journey – will you take it? Will you choose to use these tools to empower and expand your life into something beyond your current comprehension?

We are holding that vision for you, we see you there with us.

In Love,
XoTheJOGs

YOUR DREAMS HAVE MESSAGES FOR YOU

Dreams are often an interesting part of your Spirit in a body experience. All of you have different experiences at different times in the dream state. And we want to clear up some possible misinformation on this important topic, because in doing so it will support you in understanding more clearly your dreams, how they work and function and the best way to allow this area of your life experience to stay in the Highest Light.

We know there are many who delve deeply into their dreams, who feel that within the context of their dreams are all number of revelations about themselves and their lives and some even presume there exists information about others. So we will clear this all up here to support you in flowing with more ease in your dream state and taking from it what is meant to serve you in the Highest Light.

One – The majority of your dreams are coming from the ability of your deep unconscious to process through, work out or "heal" aspects that are now ready to release or are trying to release. Your ability to release these aspects is tied to and often linked to your own ability to adjust your focus in your waking state. For instance, if you have gone through a what feels to you like a painful break-up of any sort of relationship or job or opportunity and talk about it daily or think about it daily then your dreams that feature this person or opportunity or relationship are trying to "work" out or resolve those painful emotions. However, if you keep your focus in your wake state with a negative perspective on this topic, you will not be able to fully heal in the way your Higher Self wishes you to.

You see, your body-mind-Spirit is set up to serve you. It is set up to support you. We've thought of everything. Negative focuses stuck in the body-mind will attempt to release through your dream state. But unless it has your cooperation in shifting your focus, it will be far more challenging to do. Which is why some report having similar dreams or dreams on the same topic for years and years at a time. For over 15 years Heather repeatedly had the same dream scenario over and over again featuring her sisters. It boggled her, as she was not yet on this Spirit-led path. Now she can see that her Higher Self was working feverishly to heal this aspect of her over-care-giving/worrying self but because it was so active in her day-to-day life it took a lot of time for it to fully release.

If you are having dreams that upset you or disturb you or scare you – just know and acknowledge that heavier aspects locked within are trying to be healed and released by your Higher Self through this connection to your unconscious. What you can do to work with this is to acknowledge upon waking that the dream is your body-mind-Spirit's response to healing this for you. And then make a commitment to no longer focus on that area in your life so that it can be fully released with ease.

Two – Some of you feel you have received predictions or future event information or information for another in your dream state. We do not deny that for some of you this is a way you receive guidance. However, we ask you to – if you feel you are one of these – own your power in this co-creative process and ask that the information that comes to you is for the Highest Light and Highest benefit. And that anything that does not meet within these boundaries be made unavailable to you. When you are a Spirit in a body and your focus is on living your Highest Path & Purpose nothing less will do. If you feel you are blessed with the ability to receive premonitions via the dream state, ensure that you are cooperating with these premonitions in being and coming through only in the Highest Light state. And be mindful to check in with that deepest part of yourself before you share them. Often, these are dreams just like what we described above (You healing you) but have been confused with being a premonition or a message for others.

Three – Conversations you have with Loved ones in your dream state are often real. When there is not the ability for the two bodies to meet face to face and have the vulnerable and deep conversations needed to evolve forward, it is not uncommon that your Souls will meet up during your dream state to "work" things out and process what has been left undone. Acknowledge and honor these dreams as such, blessing them. There is nothing you need to do, only bless the occurrences and trust that all is being taken care of in the Highest Light.

It is not uncommon for you to dream of someone or something and then experience it or hear from that person in the physical. This is because our dear ones – it is all working together. Your dream state is a benefit to you, it is here to serve you and support you. Any of the above listed aspects may be at play and so 3D manifestations may result. This is just one aspect of the magic that is available to you in this life experience.

What we want to ask of you is to release the feeling or the need that you have to "do" something after these dreams occur. Simply acknowledge them, trust that you'll be led if there is anything to do and enjoy the brilliance and magnificence of this life experience that allows you, as you sleep, to also experience deep healing and alignment.

We are not joking when we tell you really and truly everything is always working out *for* you. Everything is always leading you to the next piece of your magnificent life experience. And so, we want to soothe and encourage you here to remember this so that your dream state – no matter how it comes through – can be another Divine unfolding and delight for you on this path.

And so it is.
XoTheJOGs

RELEASE ENERGY LEAKS

In your day-to-day life you come across all sorts of distractions and ways to keep yourselves occupied. We watch as you spend countless hours on social media or searching for something you may never actually purchase or use or maybe you engage in lengthy email exchanges or phone conversations that go seemingly nowhere. Or text messages or kitten videos or interviews or TV shows or any number of ways you can connect with the outside world.

Now none of these things are negative for you in the most general of senses. They are not hurting you, but they are pulling at your energy, they are pulling at your attention, they are often not allowing you to focus in the one area that serves you the most greatly to focus. And that area of focus is on your body and on this present moment.

So often these technological aspects or interactions are splitting your energy – part of you is in your body, part of you is floating off elsewhere. Part of you is engaged in what is, and part of you is not aware that you're sitting with your toes curled or your hands in fists or that there is a pulsing pain in your lower back that needs your care and Love.

It seems as we watch you that sometimes it seems easier for you to not be present in your body. That's why so many over caffeinate or over drink or overeat or take herbs or pharmaceuticals that you would call drugs. It seems as though you tell yourself that it would just be easier if you were not right here right now. Or as the case often is, you told yourself that a long time ago when something unpleasant happened and so it has become a habit for you, a habit of not being fully present in your body and instead being half-in or half-out, not fully committed to the expansive bliss that is waiting for you when you are fully anchored into your body and into the present moment.

One of things we have shifted for Heather has been with her food intake – many changes there but the primary ones that relate to our transmission today is – no caffeine, no sugar, no alcohol. And this – the no sugar part in particular – has been difficult for her and challenging at times. She fought us the first few weeks and then slowly slid into surrender. But she has wondered, why, why does it matter? Sure she's enjoying the way her body feels and looks, how she sleeps better than she's ever slept, how her digestion and elimination is so much healthier. She is feeling physically better than ever. Her skin is glowing in new places. She is surprised by all of this and yet those are simply side benefits to her following these dietary changes.

They support her above all in being more fully present in her body. She has found it fascinating how much clearer she feels – not having previously noticed that caffeine or sugar or alcohol could cloud her in the way that it now does if she takes part in it.

When you are fully anchored into your body – and you are not escaping it through food or drink or "drugs" or technology or drama – you are able to feel yourself in a new way. You are able to feel and be present to what is before you. You are aware of the subtle nuances that you were not aware of before. You are able to enjoy more fully the moment in front of you, whether it's a beautiful sunset or a beautiful conversation with someone you Love or a beautiful meal. You are able to feel the sensations in every area of your body. When you are heavily engaged in technology – splitting your energy between something you're listening to and an email or any number of other distractions – you are not aware of these sensations. You are fully present to the moment. When you are eating while listening or watching something, you are not able to fully enjoy either aspect.

And when you are able to enjoy the fullness of your life experience, life takes on a new quality to it. Heather talks a lot about and has experienced this for herself and watched this occur for her clients – when one begins to work with money as energy it seems to have a stretchy quality to it. It stretches, it lasts longer, it goes farther.

The same is true with time here. When you begin to let go of aspects of your life experience that take you out of the present moment, time stretches, the laughter is richer and sweeter, the conversations are more enjoyable, the food tastes better, the insights are clearer – everything is suddenly brighter and more sharp and crisp. And when you finally do look at the time, the day feels so much longer. You're no longer being pulled in two different directions or scattering your mind working on several things all at one time. You are able to slow down, be present to what is before you and enjoy it. To laugh at the joke or shed tears of gratitude at that compliment. Or really enjoy every morsel of food in that bite. Or appreciate at a level you never had before the person in front of you.

And we say – this is the richness of life. This is the richness that you came here for. Your time and your experiences can stretch just as your money does. But it requires you slowing down, turning off the devices, not overindulging in the food that pulls you out of your body. Allowing yourself to feel your toes on the earth and your hands on your body or clasped with someone you Love. It requires you to care about your life in an extraordinary way. It requires you to want to get the most out of this life.

We know, there are so many things pulling at your attention. So many things to watch and listen to and see and do. We know. And there are so many delightful caffeinated beverages and sugary goodies and alcoholic yumminess. And none of these are "bad" per se. But if you find they pull you out of your body and out of your now moment, then you are just not getting the fullness of your life experience. You are not able to experience the bliss that you were meant to and intended to experience being right here right now, hearing those birds and so appreciating their songs or taking time to admire and smell your flowers and appreciate the beauty they bring to you.

We ask that all of you slow down. Take more deep breaths. Less is more for you. And in this less-ness you will uncover the magnificence of life in a new way. You will discover all of the hidden beauty and Love and richness that is available to you in every moment. And as you are able to really feel it and be present to it, you open yourself into a state of receiving that allows more of what you are appreciating – in all different forms – to come to you.

And so it is.
XoTheJOGs

YOU ARE SPIRIT

We are wanting to talk with you about something today that will allow you to live your life more freely. Because at the root of everything that is what you desire. That's why you desire money and this person or that person or this opportunity or that opportunity. You want to feel free, you want to feel as though you are unencumbered, unrestricted from living the life that makes you feel the most joyful, that feels the best to you.

In truth you are always free. In truth no matter where you are or what you are doing you are free. Because again, we must remind you – *You.Are.A.Spirit*. You are a Spirit. Do you get that? Do you understand that? So often humans assign us – Spirit, God, etc. – all of the power. They say, "Oh someone else is running the show, someone else made these choices and someone else is in charge of my life." Whether they give that to us or to another person in their life.

But whichever way they assign the responsibility, it's not true.

You are *Spirit*. You are a Spirit, just as we are. Only you have a body. That's it! You have a body. And so in that body-being-ness of yours there is a personality and conditioning and an eighth chakra – many charkas actually. And there are programs and past life memories and all sorts of things that come with having a body. But having this body is like a pantsuit you put on – you are still Spirit. And you put on the suit because you wanted to put the suit on. In fact, you couldn't wait to put it on. Because in your body with all of these programs and past life pieces and experiences are all of the things you set out to experience and evolve forward and align to or release. You chose this. And you set it up just perfectly for yourself.

You even added the piece where, for some time, you would "forget" this, you would assign the power elsewhere, along with blame. But neither are needed because you have it all. You do!

You know why humans desire to have it all and that saying is popular in many areas? Because you *do* have it all. You have it all right at your fingertips. Every single human being / Spirit in a body on this planet has it all right at their fingertips. Every one of you.

You are Spirit which means you have the ability and wherewithal to connect to the Highest Light of Source/God/Universe – whatever you want to call it – at any time. You have the power and ability to choose the Highest Light path for yourself in any and every moment. You have the ability to heal yourself from and of what ails you. You have the ability to transcend any limitations that are put before you.

You just forgot. You forgot because well, that's part of the deal too. And there are those that are here to remind you. These transmissions are here to remind you. These transmissions serve as a basis for what can be remembered that is already activated and known by the core you.

You are Spirit which means all that you desire is within your reach. And your body is just the added bonus that you chose to make this journey ever more interesting.

We told Heather last night to look at her life like a scavenger hunt. She used to Love *Where in the World is Carmen Sandiego* when she was younger, so we told her – pretend like that's what your life is. Just ask for the next clue, the next piece of the puzzle. Treat everyone you meet and everyone who comes into your life has another clue to the magic that is your life's journey. Just let them be that for you. Let yourself enjoy the journey with this magnificent body that you have and all of the fun players in your life.

Never forgetting or at the very least allowing yourself to be reminded that you are a Spirit and so you can break out of the illusion at any time. You can allow this journey to be a fun game you are playing, and if you ever get to taking it way too seriously bringing yourself misery and pain you can bring yourself back into your full Spirit knowing – which is – this is just the suit that you have on. And you'll wear this for 80-100 or however many years you are called to or desire to wear it.

It really can be that simple. It really can be that light. So many stories get created about this human experience you are having and so many of them don't serve you. But you all are powerful. You're so powerful that if you want to believe in negativity or heaviness or darkness, then you can. You can choose to spend your life that way if that's what feels best to you. But we know – it doesn't feel best to anyone to choose to live their life that way. It's just that they forgot that life was much Lighter and freer and more joyous than anyone had ever told them. And that it can be a fun game, a choosing from one clue to the next. And you can work with your Spirit Team and ask for new clues and ask for expanded clues and, if you are open to receiving them, they will come to you. And even those who are not reading these transmissions – yet – their Spirit team is still there, throwing in nudges of Light whenever they can, hoping to catch their attention, hoping to awaken them from the illusion that anything more or different from what we've shared here is happening.

Your freedom is innate within you because you are *Spirit*. Have we mentioned that yet? You are. And in this Spirit-ness of you, you have the ability to tune in to another frequency/vibration outside of the body and connect to your truest truth and let that path lead you forward. And it can and will lead you to all that feels good to you, and will allow all that does not to be released from you with ease.

So we ask of you – wake up to this truth. Wake up to this knowing. Embrace your Divinity and choose your Highest Light unfolding. Ask to be shown the path. Ask to be shown the way, for in doing so, your life experience as a Spirit in a body in this lifetime will transcend what your mind can even begin to imagine.

And so it is.
XoxTheJOGs

LIVE YOUR HIGHEST PATH

So, how do you know if you're living the best life available for you? How do you know if you are aligned and fully on your Highest Path? It's far easier than you may think. A going within to the core of who you are through meditation will yield to you the truth that is imperative for you to know to flourish in all of the ways that you are meant to flourish in this lifetime.

You know you are on the Highest Path for you when you cannot imagine anything other than where you are right now. In this here and now moment you can feel the "yes" of wherever you are. You can feel how it is exactly where you intended to be. You feel a peace in you, a full alignment in your yes. Heather has talked about this before, about how she thought she knew what alignment was. She thought it was that giddy, "Weeeeeee!" that she would feel when an opportunity or person or situation came before her. But now, now she knows differently. She knows that that, "Weeeee!" may or may not have indicated full alignment and that full alignment does not feel buzzy but rather feels like a deep yes. A deep yes that goes from the crown to the root. A yes, that is solid and stable and peaceful and delightful and so affirming. That buzzy, "Weeeeee!"-ness is actually letting you know that something is afoot, although usually that something is a wound that has been activated in some way. And so when you feel the buzzy, "Weeeeee!" stop and take a few deep breaths, quiet yourself as best you can and ask what wants to be known about this situation and where you are at in that here and now moment.

Remember too, dear ones that it is all information; there is nothing to worry about when the buzzy comes up. We simply want to encourage you to dig deeper when it shows up, to further investigate why the buzzing is there. There is information and messages for you underneath. It is a form of alignment but it – the buzzy "yes" – will most likely lead you to mis-aligned manifestations that, in the long-run, will not support you. This is something Heather might call half-baked manifestations. And again nothing is wrong with this, but certainly if you can align with your Highest Path and Purpose –

we know you are wanting to as we are also desiring this level of alignment for you. Because when you experience the sweet Divinity of your full alignment with your Highest Path and Purpose there is simply no comparison. There is nothing else that will ever do for you. Your life then becomes this blissful, easeful, joyful, smooth experience more of the time that allows you to flow with all of life in a joyous, harmonious way. That's when you know you are on your Highest Path.

But some of you have become overly dependent on drama as your primary way to feel alive. To highs and lows. To buzzy "yes's" and painful lows. And we know – that can feel exhilarating at times, but you will be better served when you experience the flow and the alignment of full alignment of that crown to root solidarity and yes-ness. It is from that place that you will truly feel more deeply. And of course in the drama of it all you think that's what's happening – you're feeling. But so many of you are not even fully present in your body during these dramatic times because the intensity is so great, and so you are not fully feeling your life in the way you intended.

When you are in that fully aligned place, you feel everything in an expansive way that is beyond what you could have imagined. You feel fully the sensations in your body. You feel fully the joy. You feel fully the laughter, the Love, the harmony. And that is what we are wanting for you.

Heather used to think this kind of life was boring. She used to feel sorry for people who just seemed to easily and effortlessly glide through various aspects of life. She thought they were missing out on all of what she had become programmed to believe was "fun". Specifically she laughs and jokes now about her judgment of Eckhart Tolle. She would sort of roll her eyes and think, "How boring," when he would talk about the present moment and the birds singling and the joyous harmony of life.

And now, she finds herself talking about the very same things – encouraging others to align with *that*.

She finds herself reveling in how good it feels to be alive, listening to the birds and looking at the sparkling water and sipping a tea and laughing with those she Loves.

How boring she used to think. How truly magnificent she now thinks!

And we say – how aligned. We say – how peaceful. We say – you are experiencing a full alignment in those sweet moments and it is more of those that you inevitably crave. It is those moments you will reflect on as you look back and reflect on your Spirit in a body journey. It is those moments that will fill you with the tenderness and joy of the life you have lived.

It is more of those moments that your Soul craves. Those connected, in the moment, living your Highest Path moments.

We are not suggesting that every moment will be this way for you. There will always be variety and life will give you plenty of opportunities to stretch and grow into the core of who you really are. And some of those experiences may be bumpy, they may contain some potholes as we like to say. And that's okay. But we are providing you here with what will serve you above all else.

This Highest Path is a fully aligned, solid from crown to root feeling of "yes-ness". It is filled with the peace and gentleness that is your Soul, that is your Highest Self, that is Source. And we recommend aligning with and reveling in that alignment as often as you can, while letting go of any disbelief that you could and will and deserve to have more of that more of the time. We want you to know that life, in all of its glory doesn't need to be a roller coaster in order to truly be the life you intended. Rather, the life you intended allows you to fully feel and fully expand and fully be present to what is before you. It is filled with delicious foods that are pure in their manifestation, with people that our heart opens to in greater quantities just by being with them, with environments that nourish you and elevate you, with all manner of things that uplift you and remind you of the beauty and brilliance and magnificence of who you are.

Imagine if you only chose the above, imagine if you let only what nourished and uplifted and elevated you into your life? Well, yes, then you would find yourself living your Highest Path and Purpose. It needn't be grandiose in its external manifestation, only grandiose in its feeling and expansion in your heart.

Watch for this, choose this, align to this and just watch. Just watch what happens next when you do.

Until next time,
XoTheJOGs

BALANCE YOUR LIFE LIKE THIS

In your world, you are seemingly fighting against so much. An onslaught of advertising messages, emails, familial duties as a wife/husband, mother/father, sister/daughter, friend, Lover and then as your own individual Spirit in a body. How does one navigate these "obligations" – many of which you have much Love for but which also seem to deplete and weigh you down in the totality of their requirements.

For certainly you know that your relationships need time and attention and Love and support. You know that your living your Highest Path & Purpose also asks the same of you. So, "How," you might ask, "can I balance all of these 'responsibilities' and take the much needed care of myself that is necessary for me to live the most magnificent life that is available to me?"

And we say that it is far easier than you can imagine or is made out to be. It does however require you to set up a sacred container for your life. It asks that you set the boundaries and desires of your most magnificent life and that you stray from them not one iota. It asks that you step into your magnificence, allowing yourself to be seen in the radiant way that you are meant to be seen and bow in honor to your Highest Path. And when you do this, all of these seeming obligations are no longer that.

We are going to give you an exact formula for this. Here is the magic that you are desiring and wanting and that in the heart of who you really are you know without doubt that is, above all else, where your magnificence lies.

At the core of it all, it lies within you. Creating an environment for fulfillment, joy, Love and abundance is the key for you. How can you create an environment that brings you ease, joy, abundance, Love? Start by looking at your typical day, your morning/afternoon/evening. Segment it like this if that feels good to you. Write it out on a piece of paper if you must or sit with it in meditation. Scan through your average day (even for those of you that do not feel any day is average – just call it forth and see what shows up).

Where are the energy leaks?

Perhaps in the emails you are signed up for? Or the social media that you scroll through? Cut out what feels heavy and not like a full body YES. Immediately cut anything from your experience that is not uplifting. This may be a workout class or a tea date with a friend or an email newsletter you've been subscribed to for eons. Whatever it is, let go of what is heavy and lacks the ability to fully uplift you and remind you of your beauty and magnificence.

What conversations are you having that are not allowing you to be the fullness of who you are? What are you talking about the majority of the time? Cut out those conversations. Direct your energy to those areas that lift you up. Now many of you may not even fully recognize what lifts you up because you have become so used to focusing your energies on obligations and things that do not take you Higher.

But know this, it starts with you above all else. It starts with you. You are the hub of your environment and life experience which means making these adjustments is imperative to allowing your life and all of your relationships to flow with ease.

Your clothes – what clothes are you wearing? Choose clothing and accessories and – for the Divine Feminine among you – the hair and make-up support that allows you to feel your most gorgeous and radiant. In fact, view all of your life from this lens from your décor to your practitioners to your transportation to your beverages. What makes you feel beautiful and radiant? Make that your priority.

The releasing of the old feels so liberating *and* it opens you up to receive what is in a Higher alignment for you. It allows you to receive what truly serves your Highest and best *and* take an expanded step forward into what serves you. We are not suggested that you throw out anything old or that has been with you for a long time. We are talking about releasing anything from your day-to-day that does not nourish, uplift and expand you. That does not speak to the radiance of who you really are.

So once that has been done you should and will find yourself with more spaciousness in your life experience. More opportunities open to bring in what you really want to be doing or being or spending your time with.

Now, look at your key relationships. Who are the people that are the most important to you? Who uplifts you? Who do you feel most at ease and like yourself with? Who do you feel nourished by and in the presence of?

Write out who these individuals are for you. Make your relationships with these glorious ones a priority above all others. If for any reason your romantic partner is not included in this list – make it a priority to delve into that relationship dynamic further to see if you can reconnect to the aspects of that relationship that need attention or what needs to be done to attract in a partner who can be a source of upliftment and nourishment.

Make these relationships a regular priority in the ways that feel most beneficial to you. We are not instructing you on how this should play out in your individual life – allow yourself to be guided here. You will know; and if you do not know, the way it unfolds will tell you everything you need to know. If for instance you are trying to set up a weekly connection date with one of the nourishers in your life, but it's just not happening – that's a redirection from Spirit – perhaps try for a monthly connection or spontaneous time together. Trust the unfolding of the path as guidance!

Make a list of your most nourishing activities. What is it that you do that makes you feel most supported? Most at ease? Most nourished? Most you? Commit to regular integration of these activities in your life. Allow yourself to see and experience the wonder that this life has to offer you. You know this by what feels good to you. By what feels peaceful and fun and easy and light.

And there are those that would say, "Oh no, that's just living the easy life – you can't do that! You have to push yourself, you have to try harder, you have to go and go."

And while we understand the motivation behind that mode of thought, we do not support it. In the pushing you create an energetic vibrational field that acts as a repellant and a drain on your physical body. It is far, far better to be in a place of relaxation and ease and then, from that place, be inspired to take action. And you will be inspired to take action. It will happen. When you are following the process of making nourishing yourself, your environment, and your relationships a priority, you are being nourished from so many angles that inspired action cannot *not* be part of your experience. It is going to be yours and it is going to be yours with ease.

We've given you here a beautiful step by step process to allow your life to feel less obligated and more like the life you came here to live – a life of living your truest path and purpose, while also filled with abundance and joy and Love.

Enjoy!

In Love,
XoTheJOGs

CLAIM YOUR GREATNESS (WITH AN EGO EXPLANATION/EXPANSION TOO!)

To claim your greatness is an exaltation that we recently gave Heather's Spirit School participants and it is something that we want to expand on in this expanded community setting.

What does it mean to claim one's greatness? And why is it so important you do so?

We encourage this because it is truly the key to receiving and experiencing all that you desire at a core level of your life's unfolding. It is in claiming how truly great you are that you align with your Highest Light expression, it's how you align with Source in the fullest sense possible.

Now there are many misnomers in your world about what it means to claim your greatness and how this manifests, and we are here to debunk these now so that you can more fully understand the true nature of what we are sharing with you here.

Claiming one's greatness is about standing fully in one's power. In one's power as a Spirit with a body that is here for a Divine purpose, that is to serve the larger good and the larger capacity or collective of Spirits in a body around you. In doing so, you support the Spirit in a body consciousness as a whole in evolving forward, which allows more of the whole to have life experiences that fill them up and provide much joy and expansion.

Claiming your greatness allows you to Love yourself more fully than you've ever Loved yourself before. It's about accepting yourself as you are and saying that, "Who I am is truly great and in this greatness I will shine forth my Light so that others may also claim their greatness." It is not about claiming your greatness so someone else is not great. This is not how the world works. We would Love it if you all could suspend your belief of duality. This belief that there has to be the polar opposite to anything that exists in the framework of the world. Perhaps when we you were at other levels of consciousness this was important to believe, but that is no longer the case. It truly will serve you better to see that only the Highest Light is here for you and no one needs to suffer if you thrive.

And so, in claiming your greatness you are really serving the greater good, because in doing so and in shining your Light in this regard others are inspired to the same, and then you have a ripple effect of myriads of individuals who Love themselves wholly and fully, who are committed to living their Highest Path and Purpose and who will not accept less than their fullest alignment for their life unfolding. And imagine if you will that more of you were living in that way and you would have a planet full of beaming, thriving, interdependent, happy people.

Which is inevitably where you are all headed, we must tell you. Your movies and religions and naysayers and political correspondents would like to tell you otherwise. They would like you to think you're headed towards some kind of eternal damnation but of course that is all fiction. Fiction you can choose to believe in, but fiction that will not serve you or give you the life that your Higher Self truly desires.

So claiming your greatness matters because it is in this way that you are of the Highest service. It's in this way that you have the biggest impact on the planet, on your family, on your community, on the world. We are not kidding you. Just one of you standing in your greatness and shining that Light, impacts so many who may not even be able to consciously acknowledge that's what put the kick in their step on that day or lightened their load, but it was it.

And what we are asking of you, of those of you who are drawn to these transmissions, who recognize the truth emanating from them, we are asking that all of you begin to claim your greatness. Honor yourself. Celebrate yourself. Ask to be shown and to be made known to you your Highest Purpose. Ask to be able to fully embody that and give your gifts with the most Light. Some want to put this just into the box of career. You Spirits in a body still like to compartmentalize your lives in this way, but it is unnecessary. Every bit of your life can be your purpose, it can be about bringing the Light and being in service to the whole. It can be about sharing your gifts with your clients or coworkers or the gas station attendant (if you live in Oregon like Heather). It can be anywhere at anytime. It is not just relegated to what you do for work or career.

Ask where and how you can give your Highest gift. Ask to be shown the path that will allow you to have the impact you are here to have with and for the people and beings (as they may be animals or plants or nature that you are here to serve) you are most here to support and serve.

Claim your greatness. Claim it and do not apologize for it. Know that in doing so you are supporting so many more in also being able to do this as well. Some may call this arrogant or egotistical and we promise you we will address this misnomer around ego as well. It is so important for you all to be able to evolve forward these concepts, these concepts that are used by you and by others to keep you locked out of the fullness of your expansion.

Ego is a concept that served some at one time but is no longer a concept that supports you. You use it – and we are watching you when you do – as your excuse to not claim your greatness.

There is nothing more great than claiming your greatness. There is nothing more transformative than this. Did Jesus hold back? In the accounts you read about him – whether you are a believer or not – did he hold back from walking into the tax officers' quarters and giving them a piece of his greatness? Did he hold back from walking the streets sharing what was coming through him to all whom he met? Did he hold back from proclaiming that he was the Son of God? Now, this has led many on a whole other interpretation of what he meant but for now, let's just focus on the fact that this man claimed his greatness. And whether or not you believe in the stories surrounding this man, you all are still talking about him a couple thousand years later.

Claim your greatness and do it through your connection to your Higher Self, to your Source self, to your connection with Spirit. Ask each day to be shown how you can more greatly own your greatness and step into the magnificent power of who you are and how you came to be of service. This is the way you were meant to live. And you need not do it as Jesus did, please do not misunderstand us. We give the illustration to support you in further understanding what we are talking about here. You must do it in the way that is most authentically you and that will be different for everyone but nonetheless, it is needed and necessary for you to do so. It will allow your life to expand and you will feel even more deeply in Love with yourself and this magnificent planet and all of the beings on it when you do.

And so it is.
XoTheJOGs

CO-CREATE WITH MORE EASE

When you are in the place of receiving you are in the most powerful state of being that a Spirit in a body can be in. For in that state of receiving you open yourself up to – without resistance – receiving what is yours to experience, what has been desiring you and has been wanting to come into alignment with you.

So as much as you can allow yourself into a state of receiving, more and more of what you truly desire can come to you. But often, often you are in a place of pushing forward. You are in a place of wanting and leaning into your desires. You are sticking your necks out trying to see if it's coming yet or if it is here yet or where it is. And from that vantage point, it is very tricky for what you desire to come to you in the most easeful way.

And so in an attempt to push forward in making what you desire come to you, you will often throw money at it. You will often push in more, thinking that if you just dedicated more time to the having of what you want – the house, the car, the relationship, the business – that then, then it would come. And we say, maybe, maybe not. Because you must be able to see what vibration you are in when you are throwing money at what you desire, trying to get what you want and where you are throwing your money and what frame of alignment are you in or not when you are doing so.

We would like to see you all more empowered to your own greatness. We would like to see you standing fully in your knowing that you could not desire something from the core of your being unless it was destined to be yours. And then from that place we would like you to open your arms to receive. And if there is anything you are throwing your money at, have it be something that reminds you of the above. Have it be something that empowers you to your greatness and aligns you to the fullest receiving of what you deserve to receive. Filling yourself up with more information, with more of what we would call static, does not help you and it does not serve you.

Heather has had this experience. She is wanting to learn more on a certain subject and so she, in a flurry, signed up for a newsletter from someone she felt would provide her with valuable information to support her in her learning. However, she notices that every time she reads the newsletter she feels very intense energy – it's so overwhelming it's almost like her eyes cannot take in the information that is intended for her.

And we said to her – not the path. Not the clearest way to receive. Go meditate. Go sage yourself. Go tap. Go for a walk in nature, but do not read anymore from that individual.

And it's not because there is anything wrong with what is being offered or that the information isn't correct. It's just that it is not the exact, Highest aligned information for where Heather is at on her journey. And there are other things that she reads and receives or purchase that are exactly the opposite. When she reads them she feels light and at peace and clear and we say – that's what you're looking for. If taking in information or connecting to a person or someone or something feels overwhelming or makes you feel bad or is so intense your eyes cross – it's not for you. It's not that you have to do something to make it for you – it's just not for you.

Do you see how you push? How so often you feel you must get what you desire and so you lean in with an attempt to make it happen, in an attempt to understand it and make it work for you? And we are wanting you to soften that into receiving. And the way to be in receiving is to follow only what feels good to you, what feels clear, what feels like a full yes – you can apply this to anything, not just the co-creation of that which you desire.

And we want you to investigate these desires of yours. Sit with them in your body. Where are they vibrating in your body? What do you notice about how they feel when you think of them? We want you aiming for full body alignment. We want from your crown to your root for it to feel like a yes. If it's buzzy in the upper parts of your body – not there yet – close, it's close in being a "yes" – but not quite. If it feels heavy, definitely not aligned for you. If it spaces you out or makes you feel stuck in your head – guess what – the energy is stuck in your head and not serving you.

It can feel tough, we know, to slow down enough to feel this, but doing so will save you more discomfort than you can imagine. It is actually more difficult to keep pushing forward, to keep trying to figure things out, to keep trying to make things work the way you think they should work. It is far more Highly serving of you and who you are when you allow yourself to receive. When you allow yourself to follow that which feels most light and clear.

So, feel into why you desire that money or romantic partner or house or car or whatever it is. Why is this important to you? Feel deeply into it. And if you feel the full body alignment of it you can move on to the next step – what feels like the clearest, most light, most fun way to allow yourself to receive it into your life.

If this involves getting more information or a nudge to take action that will bring you a step closer to receiving it into your life, make sure that whatever that step is feels like a full body yes again. If it's a person you need to hire or a class to take, make sure you feel a full Soul resonance, make sure they feel like one of your people, make sure it feels so very right to you in its alignment. Then, move forward.

When you can do so from an aligned perspective, then you are in receiving mode. Then things can begin to move and work for you in a way that you could not have imagined.

It's so important when you are co-creating with your Spirit Team – and with all of the Universe really – that you slow it down to understand why things are important to you, where those desires reside in your body, to – before taking action – slow down to feel the full Soul resonance with whatever action it is. And from that place, from that expanded place you are now aligned. You are now in a place of receiving that allows what you utmostly desire to flow to you with more ease and grace and abundance than you could have ever seen coming for you.

We are desiring for you to allow yourself this spaciousness. We are desiring for you to allow yourself to live in this kind of richness. A life that is so expansive, so rich, so filled to the brim with goodness that you will not sacrifice a moment of your bliss for a rushed result or answer or seeming solution. You will instead expand yourself into full alignment and then, only then, move forward into your most aligned point of bliss.

We know you can do this and we know you can do this with ease. We believe in you and we are there with you, applauding you, cheering you on and so grateful for your ability to show up for your life in this leading-edge manner.

And so it is.
XoTheJOGs

GIVE IT UP TO YOUR SPIRIT TEAM

In your seeking and in your searching you will find within you a powerhouse. A powerhouse, a wealth of knowledge. A wealth of eternal knowledge that is here at your disposal, that is readily available to you. All of you have access to this knowledge but many do not realize it. For within your grasp is the ability to connect with all that you desire, to know about all of life and your path and what lies before you. And we promise you that if you will open yourselves up to receiving this wealth of knowledge you will live a life far surpassing your dreams and far past any life you have ever lived before.

This powerhouse of knowledge is like your own personal Google and it is merely a question away. You don't even have to type your question or submit it anywhere, you can simply call in your Spirit Team, ask your question out loud and await the answer. Wait to be shown with specific clarity what the answer is.

You no longer need to fret or worry over what decision to make and when. You can simply offer it up as Heather would say. Ask out loud to your Spirit team to take care of it. Ask that your Highest Good be made known to you and that all unfolds in your Highest good and thus, when that happens, the Highest good of all.

Heather is finding that she used to waste an inordinate amount of time worrying about how or when or where something might happen. Now, she simply calls us in and offers it up and asks that the Highest good for her be done. And then, she goes about her business. And when the time comes for whatever the decision was or next step she is in awe of how the person or opportunity or whatever it is, just shifts to match what feels the best for everyone. It's uncanny, she says. And we say – it is the way it is meant to be for all of you. It needn't be that complicated and life needn't be that difficult or demanding or hard. You really can work with the Universal forces all around you and ask that your needs be met. Whether it's a dollar amount or a Love, or new car or job or whatever it is – you can ask. And then open your arms to receive. The key to this is that you must be willing to trust. You must be willing to let go to allow what your truth is to come to you. And this is not sitting around all day waiting for the answers, this is meditating, asking, meditating a little more, then following any guidance or nudges about what to do next. Often Heather finds it works best when she doesn't again let herself think about the thing that she has offered up. She simply moves forward in her day.

And we are in favor of this – go distract yourself, go have fun, go do the laundry or take care of business in some way. Let the answer come to you. And the answer may not arrive in the time you think it should, but it will arrive. Heather marvels as it seems that right in the 11th hour the answer will appear, and we say that was finally when all of her resistance to receiving it had evaporated and then the outcome could come to her.

We want you to know that this is what we mean when we talk about co-creation. You don't even have to know for sure if what you're asking for is aligned. We will show you, we will respond. So, take whatever it is that is bothering you or coming up for you and offer it up to us. Ask that the Highest good be done and that whatever is meant to occur will with ease and grace. And then meditate a bit more and off you go. It is the most beautiful practice and it leads to the most peaceful life you could ever imagine.

Heather had spent just about a full day with this thing in her life popping in as a worry. And she was working her practice and tapping and breathing and walking and talking to us, but she didn't give it to us. She was working with it trying to figure it out and get to ease. Finally, after her last meditation she realized she had not offered it to us to take and work out for her.

Instantly she felt lighter, brighter and more at peace. And wouldn't you know it but several minutes later, what she desired and had been working over in her mind all day came in with ease.

This is co-creation. This is how you were supposed to live. This is how you will most enjoy living. This is your birthright. That the ease of the Universe is upon you and everything you desire can flow to you with ease. And that which you desire that is not in alignment can release with ease – if you ask for this. Yes, we cannot insert ourselves into your experience, so it is important to give us the full range of permission to adjust on the behalf of your Highest good. That is why with every offering up that Heather makes to us she includes, "And if this thing that I am asking about is not in my Highest good, please allow it to release – with ease and grace." And in that, she opens the way for all possibilities that serve her Highest good to come in, and we say that is the best way you can allow what is meant to come to you to come to you and to keep mis-aligned manifestations from having their place in your life.

Enjoy this practice and enjoy the bounty that comes from working with your Spirit Team in this way.

In Love,
XoTheJOGs

CONNECT TO THE VISION OF YOUR LIFE

Your vision for your life may be big. It may be in a state of indecision, but whether or not you actively or consciously tune in to it, there is a vision in place for your life. This vision was developed and designed before you incarnated into this physical body that you are now in. You carefully crafted many of the key aspects of your life experience. You were considerate in setting the vibrational frequency with specific details, aspects of who you are in your personality and circumstances of your life experience that would allow you to remember, recognize and be/do/have all that you desired to in this lifetime. You had an aim, a clear vision, things you wanted to accomplish, experiences you desired to experience, and people that were an integral part of your unfolding.

This vision is with you now; this vision is all around you now vibrationally and can be accessed by you to the degree that it serves your Highest Good to have access to this information. Some, depending on your personality type may find that having greater information about their life's vision doesn't feel good while others, the more they know, the more they soar. It really is up to your Spirit Team and your personality that indicates how much of your vision is made available to you.

But know this – there is a vision that you created for this lifetime for yourself and all that you experience is either directly pointing to it or nudging you into alignment with it. Some ask if they can get this vision wrong or miss it or mess it up. And we say – of course, as we have said many times before – there is no such thing as messing anything up. You may not get to it in this lifetime if you do not consciously decide to allow it to be made known to you. But so what – you'll get to it in the next lifetime. Some Souls are very focused on their vision and have a strong desire to live it out in the finest of details.

Your vision is a vision that has been built upon for many, many lifetimes. Each lifetime brought you one step closer to this vision. And what is magnificent about this is that, for many aspects of your life vision, once it is reached in physical form, then a new aspect of your vision is birthed as you are on an eternal journey that allows you to expand and experience life in new ways. Your vision is the guiding force of your life. It's why certain – what you would call – "goals" just won't go away as much as you desire them to. It's why, no matter what, you cannot get that person or thing or job or project out of heart and mind. Whatever it is that continues to show up again and again is a key component of your vision.

There are some who feel they are unable to align with this vision, and we say that there is not one of you that cannot align with your vision. If you desire to know more about the path that has been created for you by that Higher Self part of you, you can know it. You may not get the entire end all be all vision, but you will get what you need to take the next steps needed.

What we notice is that so few are asking their Spirit Team this question. So few are celebrating that the vision is there and known by the deeper part of them, and that their life has been specifically created so that they would go down this path and they would know these answers, and that new pieces of their vision could be born into the world.

Others feel they know pieces of their visions but it still feels incomplete as though something were missing. And we say – follow that feeling. What is missing? Ask to be shown what is missing. Ask to be shown where you need to go or what you need to do to align with the deeper, more expanded understanding of the vision that you are here for.

Why does this matter?

As consciousness shifts more and more, and more and more of you are opening up to these transmissions and to what is possible for you in this lifetime, you have the opportunity to more consciously and actively co-create with your vision and with your Spirit Team while in the body. Long ago the vision was set, but not as many were coming to a fuller understanding of life and what was possible for them while in the body. So of course they were still on their path and experiencing some of what they desired to, but it was not being done so by them as consciously while in the body. And so those around them while they were in the body would describe these ones as simply "lucky", as neither the Spirit in a body who was experiencing the flow or those around them knew consciously what was happening. That they have a non-physical part of them, that they have lived many lifetimes, and many of the other aspects of this Spirit in a body experience we have shared with you. Now that consciousness is where it's at currently, more of you can work with your Spirit Team and adjust and accelerate your vision while in the body.

Yes, you heard us correctly – as Heather is asking for clarification here – you *can* shift the frequency of your vision and path while you are in the body and through conscious co-creation with your Spirit Team and Higher Self. We will continue to give you more on this in the transmissions to come, but first we wanted to plant this seed. That your vision is set into motion the moment you incarnate and your Higher Self is aware of it, and as you increase your awareness you can "jump forward", as it were, to accelerate the expansion of your vision. Perhaps at what you all might call a "regular" lifetime pace it would take a couple of lifetimes to experience something or get to a certain piece of our vision. But when you are a conscious and deliberate co-creator with your Spirit Team and Higher Self, you may be able to accelerate this path and experience many aspects of your vision that may not have been accessible initially in this lifetime. As you expand and grow, and as your awareness is raised, you have the ability to align with even more than you may have intended for this lifetime.

It's an incredible experience to witness for us, and we are so celebrating with you when you achieve this level of alignment. And by achieve we do not mean this is something to strive for. We would never encourage that. But we do encourage opening to and bringing in the receptivity and willingness to experience the Highest expansions of the vision for your eternal life unfolding – in this here and now lifetime. Knowing that there is more goodness and acceleration of what is possible for you in this lifetime – even beyond what you may have originally intended. That is just another beautiful aspect of living at this time in consciousness and why we are now able to bring through transmissions of this magnitude to those who are ready and willing for this level of living in the world.

We are so eager for what is to come for all of you as this expansion in your understanding comes in. Enjoy the integration of this knowledge and we promise, there will be a widening of your understanding about this in the future, when the time is just right.

XoTheJOGs

CLAIM YOUR GREATNESS & WATCH YOUR LIFE EXPAND

When we are talking about claiming your greatness, many nod as if they understand this, and we want to expand it for you further as there are places here to go deeper into that will allow you to more fully claim your greatness in a way that has never been done before – although it is certainly what Source and your Higher Self most desire for you.

What is it about claiming your greatness that matters? When you are empowered in the fullness of who you really are, you shine brighter. And when you shine brighter you are more easily and effortlessly able to have the impact on the world that you are meant to have. And when you are more able to have the impact on the world that you are here to have, the world is a better place, your life is better, the people around you are happier, because you also are happier. It's a domino effect with more and more individuals benefitting as you claim and live your Highest Path & Purpose or your greatness. And that's probably the most simple way for us to explain this path of claiming your greatness.

But it goes deeper than that still. Because when you claim your greatness, first to yourself and then perhaps publically – either in verbal form or through your intentional actions of living your Highest Path & Purpose – you may notice something new emerge. You may notice fear. Some would describe it as extreme fear or even terror. And when you go deeper into this fear you find a ripple of sensations of fear and unworthiness and doubt that cause some to become paralyzed in moving forward with ease in living their Highest Path & Purpose, and therefore the life of their truest, realest dreams.

What is this fear? Why is it there? Heather really wants to understand this as she was so surprised by the fear that came up for her and for many she serves when it comes to living their Highest unfolding. The fear, the fear is of course a message to you. The fear wants you to understand the level with which you have hidden from yourself your magnificence, your greatness and the importance of this in your lifetime. But why is it important? Why couldn't you all just go about your lives, hiding out in situations, relationships, "drugs", food, alcohol – flying under the radar if you will? Well, plenty have done this for many, many generations; however, it does not serve the whole of you nor Source for more of you to be living in this manner. There is a call deep within every Spirit in a body – whether they know it or not – to experience the magnificence of their Light. To experience the magnificence of their power. To know and be in a body and choose the Highest Light. To know and be in a body and choose the path that will impact the most in the most powerful way possible as it also most powerfully impacts the self.

And you know what is coming next don't you? Heather can feel it and she feels the excitement and the overwhelming whoa-ness of this. You know what happens when you're in a body and claim the above don't you? You are then an Ascended Master. You are then a Spirit walking the planet freely and truly. There is nothing that can touch or hurt you. You have now realized fully the true nature of you and thus of all. And when you are in that place, when you are in that Divine place – oh, how delicious it is – when you are there you have then transcended every limitation. Every obstacle, every story that says otherwise. Every story that says you are not that, when you are in fact that.

The fear – if you will let yourself feel into it further – is really massive, unexplainable excitement. And you translate it as fear because it is not just your excitement you are feeling, it is the excitement of the whole – of Source itself, of your Spirit Team, of every Guide and Angel of the Highest Light in the proximity of the Universe. Because this, our dear ones, is what you came to realize. And it is magnificent. It is large. It is otherworldly while rooted in the core of your planet. You inaccurately translate it as massive fear because your filters, or what we could call programs – and this is information your body-mind is giving to you – are still in great quantity and running with a stream of thought that says your magnificence is to be feared. These are stories given to you but they are not accurate in any way.

And so, this is why we want all of you claiming your greatness. This is why we want every single Spirit in a body claiming their greatness. Because then, no limitations exist. Because then you know with absolute certainty what this existence is about.

It's about you, it's about Love. It's about Source energy. It's about creating the most beautiful painting on the planet because it is you creating it and you living it and you beaming it to all who have eyes to see it. It's about laughing with another and that laugher radiating joy into every cell of your being and every cell of every being in any nearby radius around you. It's about remembering your birthright. It's about coming to the end of the game, only it's not an end – it's a new beginning with untold possibilities on the other side of it.

What if – we want you to play with us here – what if this were really all just a game? It is alluded to again and again. What if it was all an illusion – set up specifically for you to get here? To get to the moment when you let go of all the stories and instead claim your grandness, claim your worthiness and claim your greatness. And then poof! Up goes the curtain, out comes the balloons and confetti, the crowd cheers and roars with delight. And you, mildly stunned, in that instant remember – you remember that you signed up for this game and that you co-created this elaborate journey with "obstacles" and "wins" and with "successes" and "failures" all aimed at getting you here – to the place where you decided you could not and would not spend another minute of your time and energy worrying or changing who you were. That you had to – no matter how terrifying – you had to go for it as the saying goes, and claim your magnificence and commit to living your Highest Path and then take action in doing so.

Perhaps this is not just something we are having you imagine. Perhaps this is true. Perhaps that is why we are consistently telling you not to stress or worry or fear so much that which is not anything at all to fear. Perhaps that's why we tell you death is not anything to worry about – it's part of the game, it's part of the unfolding. It's just changing out of costumes.

We know you have heard ideas like this float around before, we know you have. And we are coming through to tell you that those ideas are true. That it is true.

And so, "Why?" Heather asks, "What's the point of the game?" She is on the edge of her seat here as we share this.

Well, for starters, it's fun. For starters, it's a really fun game to play. It's why you play board games right? Why do you all Love that game Cards Against Humanity so much? Oh, yes, we see you playing that game and having the best time. Or Heather, she used to Love Monopoly and Clue. Why? Because it was fun to try on a different persona and play with new rules and see what you could navigate through. It's what your actors and actresses know – it's fun to pretend. It's fun to play. And then imagine that you could just focus your powerful mind on a new scenario and over time you would play that new version of your game.

So for starters, it's fun and you, btws – as Heather would say – Love to have fun.

Second, you are evolving, as you play this game, what it means to be a Spirit in a body forward. We have told you this many times before. And Heather is asking us here, sort of exasperated in wanting to understand this more fully – so we just end up right back where we started as full on Spirit? So it's like a circle? What's the point of that? Why do we have to or need to do that? And we are saying – that's where you are wrong, Heather – because we don't know yet. We don't know what will happen when all of consciousness is synched up in this way. We know what happens when more and more of you do. We know that as you align with your Highest Path that many of you will know and honor and fully claim your Ascended Master-ship – right here while in a body. We have, we did this very thing and here we are now supporting others who were like us. We have been through the journey we are now supporting you through. And you will do the same for others when the time comes.

But we do not know what lies on the other side of all of you claiming your greatness and embodying your Spirit-ness while in a body. Can you imagine? Can you imagine – everyone fully aware of One-ness consciousness? Everyone fully aware that they can create, play, align to their heart's content and that it takes from no one? Can you imagine all of you standing side by side, so equally in Love with yourselves as you are grateful for the others around you? Can you imagine?

Can you imagine how different the world would look?

Can you imagine the untold joy and abundance that your planet would benefit from as you, all do, as all planets would? Can you imagine?

We know your minds may have trouble imagining this, and we are in eager anticipation as to the manifestation of this unfolding. It will happen, we are certain of that. And you are part of this. If you are reading this transmission, if you have been brought to this transmission, you are part of this. You will experience this and you will be part of the leading change. You will be part of the Highest Light enveloping your entire planet – your leading edge – never before like this planet. And what that will give birth to, we can hardly wait to see and experience and know.

And so it is.

In Love,
XoTheJOGs

SHIFT YOUR SHIT

We are loving and appreciating you even when you are unable to Love and appreciate you. We are Loving and appreciating you even when you are in reaction. We are Loving and appreciating you even when you are in resistance. We are Loving and appreciating you no matter what place or space you are in.

Your ability to feel this Love and appreciation from us and to receive the wisdom from us is inaccessible to you from your place of resistance or reaction. You can feel it inside of you can't you – that prickliness? That discomfort? You don't want to feel that way but you just can't help it, we hear you say.

"So-and-so did this or so-and-so did that or this is not going my way or this is not happening as I Intended it too." And we want to remind you of what we have reminded you of before – things will not always go the way you desire, things will sometimes feel like they are going "wrong" to you. You will get triggered. Things will happen. But that is not any indication that anything is actually "wrong". It is only an indication of information, of a call for re-alignment or a call for release of what no longer is in alignment yet still remains within you.

You have an opportunity in each moment to choose a new thought, to choose a new action sequence for yourself, to choose a thought form or response that will take you Higher as opposed to continuing on a vibration of discord of dis-ease.

You can stop that train of thought right here, right now by simply choosing to. We know you do not believe it can be that simple, but it is.

Here's how it works:

First, identify the resistance in your body, where does this resistance live in your body. Place one or both of your hands there. Breathe into this resistance. Imagine that your inhale through your nose is gathering it up and your exhale is releasing it through your mouth.

Do that three to seven times – as many as feels right for you.

As you are using your breath, imagine the exhale of release is then scooped up by Source energy and, whatever that not good feeling emotion is, is transmuted into Divine Love by Source.

Then say, as you tap Cortices, "I now actively choose to feel happy (joyful, good, elated – whatever emotion feels most like a yes to you)." Imagine as you are tapping Cortices you are literally tapping in that newly chosen emotion. Imagine as you tap that any remaining not good feeling thoughts are being surrendered to Source for transmutation to Divine Love energy.

Now some might argue that that is hardly taking care of "your problems". That this is hardly a solution.

And we will say – we are not finished yet.

Once you actively choose a greater, more aligned state, you can begin to make choices and take action that perpetuates that new state. And as you do, you open up the opportunity for your truth to come into you. Now you have raised your vibration to a level that will allow you to hear and feel and know the wisdom from your Highest Self and from your Spirit team. Now, in this moment of feeling more of who you are, you can make a new choice from a place of connection, rather than a place of disconnection.

When you do this, you are opening yourself up to a whole new trajectory of what is possible for you. New solutions and possibilities and opportunities have the ability to flow to you from this newly, more aligned state.

We understand that when you are triggered or in reaction this is not possible for you. And we believe that letting yourself acknowledge this, and then consciously and intentionally using your breath to release it while then actively choosing a new feeling state, gives you an opportunity to push reset and to realign with your true nature.

Depending on how triggered or hooked you are by whatever is happening, you may have to do this a few times, so you must let your intuition guide you. Afterwards you may want to dance or go for a walk or do something to shake off this movement of energy.

We want you to remember that you are empowered to shift and release what no longer serves you. You have the capacity to work with the, what you call, triggers and release them. You have the capacity to witness a stream of thought and say, "This does not work for me," and then make a new choice from that place.

You do not have to stay in not food feeling places. You do not have to stay in reaction. You can do better, you can choose better. Those thought forms that have had hold of you for many, many years – perhaps even your whole lifetime – can be released, and you do have the ability to release them. You do have the ability to create a new reality for yourself. All that is needed is your openness, willingness and ability to believe, even if just a smidge, that anything is possible for you.

Because anything is possible for you.

All manner of impediments can be released when you allow them to. All stories, no matter how long they have been with you, have the ability to be set free and transmuted into Divine Love by Source. All that does not serve you can be transformed, and instead your life can be surrounded by all that does serve you. You do have the ability to shift it all. You do, truly and surely you do.

And we are right here, cheering you on, watching you as you do.

And so it is.
XoTheJOGs

DEATH & THE AGING PROCESS...NEW REVELATIONS

We are wanting you to know the seemingly unknowable. We know that when you are armed with this "unknowable" information your life as a Spirit in a body takes on a new form that exceeds your wildest dreams. We want this for you and not only do we want it, as wanting implies not having it, we know it is your ultimate intention that you will know the "unknowable". As consciousness elevates you have access to information that previously was not available to you, this information – especially when applied – allows you to take your life experience into uncharted territory. Territory you intended you would be able to discover and uncover and illuminate in your life journey.

We are wanting you to take a deep breath here and allow your body to soften and relax, to allow your body to open up to the information that is being presented to you. We want you to be fully present in your body, for when you are fully present in your body you have access to the here and now illumination for your life experience. In fact it is that tendency to go back into the past or forward into the future that keeps you from receiving and accessing all that desires to be delivered to you in your here and now. It is when you are in your here and now that you are able to receive – with ease and grace – the Highest Light available to you. We are wanting you to open up in this way to receive the Highest Light that is available to you, and we know you too so desire this.

It is in this way that we are coming before you to tell you these innumerable truths. These are truths that at a deep, core level you will feel a knowing and a yes to. These deep core truths light the path for you to be the best and most and Highest that you are here to be and will be.

So here is one of these truths now, a truth unlike any other. A truth that will light you up and set you free into the wholeness of who you really are.

You did not come here to die.

You did not come here to live to die.

You did not come here to experience death and then that was the end of the story.

You came here to live.

There are many adages in your cultures and in your shared stories that talk about a cycle of life. That you must age, die, grow old and then that is it, the cycle is complete.

We want you to know that this is not true. We want you to know that while this may have been true in the past and in previous consciousness, it is not true now. There is an opportunity for you to break this expectation of your life experience and step into your truest and Highest unfolding.

Imagine, if you will, that you could be here in your body and live and live and live and live and grow happier and more joyful, as opposed to your cultural story that says you must age, become weaker, get old, life becomes less vibrant and then you die.

Imagine, if you will, if you were to live a joyful life, and then at some point along the way you realized you had completed what you came to complete, that a new desire was calling you and it was a desire to try on a new or different way of being in the world. And so you closed your eyes one day or night, and when you opened them you were then in another time and place, ready to see what your next adventure would be in your next Spirit in a body life experience.

For some, they will open their eyes and choose to stay in the Spirit experience to support other Spirits in a body. Others will choose to come back into another body and have a new experience – bringing forward what wanted to be brought forward from the previous lifetime.

But imagine if even that was unnecessary. Imagine that there was nothing to bring forward because everything had been completed that needed to be completed in your lifetime. So you were waking up in your new lifetime with a whole fresh slate of fun opportunities and possibilities and variety that you wanted to bring into your Spirit in a body experience. You would see your "old" friends and Loved ones, and they are those you have chosen to travel with again and again, lifetime after lifetime. In this way you would not feel alone as they would be your home base touch points. Those people that feel like home that remind you that you are not alone as a Spirit in a body and that all is working out for you.

You would have your non-physical team, although depending on your level of consciousness and the variety you choose to surround yourself with in that lifetime you would remember this at various points along the way.

Imagine, if you will, that this is how life goes. Imagine that you do not have to go into an aging or death process that is depleting and exhausting and not – in the simplest way we can say it – fun. Imagine that you get to maintain your youthful vigor and splendor and then when the time feels right you will transition out of this lifetime. You would be conscious about it, so if you chose to, you could let those closest to you know about your decision and your knowing that it was time to make your transition.

You also wouldn't have to fill your faces and bodies with fillers and injections all in the hopes of maintaining some semblance of what your cultures teach is most attractive – youth. You would know that you could think your way and focus your way and intend your way into more vitality and youthfulness. You would know that it is not about maintaining a standard of aesthetics from your past, but in developing into an outward expression of your Soul's truth –and you could choose what that would look like at any age on your timeline.

What we are saying to you here is that you have more choice than you know. That so much of what happens in your life experience happens from a place of auto-pilot, of, "This is how people believe, so this is how I believe," instead of stopping to check in with your Highest Self and stopping to check in with your deepest truth. We want you to do that now, we want you to check in with your deepest truth, with your truest truth, with your Highest Path. And see – is this possible for me? Could I choose the way I desire my aging process and "death" process to go? Could I really just decide or rather know when the time is to make my transition and go to sleep and then awake in a new reality? Is that possible?

Be with this and let this information wash over you. Allow yourself to know your Highest Truth on this matter.

We are wanting to say – do not take our word for it, allow your deeper connection to who you are guide you. Deep within you will hear and know the answers. Deep within you will hear and know that all is truly well and you have the ability to consciously choose so much more than you realize.

And so it is.
XoTheJOGs

YOU HAVE THE POWER

In your world, you often struggle and strain to find your peace, to find equilibrium. There is usually a predictable process that your world collectively will go through when faced with an area that must be evolved forward. First is usually a great amount of resistance and gnashing of teeth, of strife and struggle and pain. Then on the other side of it, sometimes an agreement will be found and a new level of balance will be enacted. If not though, you will often continue to fight for decades over aspects and items that could be easily solved with a win-win for all had there been the presence and acceptance of Divine Will and Spirit involved.

And so, we bring you this transmission not to commentate on the dysfunction of your world – because there is much more wonderful about it than not – but to bring you guidance and understanding on how you in your here and now reality can begin to turn the tide for the masses. How you, one of seven billion Spirits in a body, has the power and the ability to shift outcomes for the whole. How when aligned fully with the core of who you really are – thus Source or God-force energy – all is possible in the Highest realms and for all.

We talk much to you about your power and many of you read or hear these words and somehow discard the relevance of this information for yourselves personally. We want to illustrate this power to you now. Heather was recently at an event where she did not enjoy or like what was happening in the outcomes. People were getting hurt and she wished for that to change. Next to her sat her nephew who is what you all would call a Crystal Child and which we would call a Beloved One. And Heather said to herself and to him that they needed to change their focus. They needed to stop getting upset about those getting hurt at this – we'll call it – sporting event. And so they did. She began to say out loud, "Only good things are happening for everyone involved here, only good things." And her nephew began to say it too. And wouldn't you know it, for the rest of the event, no one else was hurt. The opposing parties both got what they wanted and all was well.

And Heather thought – surely I do not have that kind of power and yet it felt that we were able to change the tide. And we say to you – it is true. You *do* have the power and the ability to shift the frequency of whatever is before you into a Higher frequency if you are aligned with your Source self. This is an event Heather would typically, in the past, have had an alcoholic beverage at, which would have diminished her ability to be as powerful as alcohol or anything that alters your system and awareness weakens the ability to be a clear channel for Divine Will. And since she does this "work" in the world she is attuned and aligned with her Highest Self and has the ability to radically impact the positive outcomes she desires.

We share this because you all have this ability. You have this ability to look at something that is happening in your world, whether it is a sporting event or the news or some kind of situation that you come upon or whatever it is and you have the ability to – from your aligned state – call forth the Highest Good. Not from a pushing or forcing perspective. You can simply chant, "Only good things are happening for all involved," and you can hold that intention that only good will come to all those involved.

And in doing so – when you are aligned – you produce a vibrational frequency that is able to elevate far beyond the vibration of those around you. And in doing this you are able to elevate what is occurring to a Higher frequency. You are that powerful. You are able to shift, in whatever ways you are called, what is happening into a Higher frequency when you are in a Higher frequency. And when you come together with other aligned ones and you all put your focused intention on only good things are happening – watch out – the acceptation of the vibration is more than a million times what it would be individually and then radical, radical change will and can occur.

The key component here is your aligned state. That is why we are talking to you all day – well, not all day, but everyday – just about regarding how you can be in an aligned state. Because yes, it brings good things to you, yes it is the path to your ultimate Wealth and everything else you desire and it also brings magnificent things to all when you focus your energy in a Highest Light way.

And you may wonder or question how you could create in someone else's experience and we are not saying you have the power for that. But you do – through your focused intention – have the power to raise the vibrational frequency of what is happening around you, and when you do – those personally involved have access to this Higher frequency when they may not have realized it before and this allows the shifting to occur with more ease.

In the example we shared about Heather, animals were part of this event. And your animals do not have the same levels of resistance that humans often do, so it was even easier for the animals to feel the vibrational shift and saunter right into it, and when they did, all went well for everyone.

You can do this for anything that is before you in your life, and you can experience radical change and expansion of your wealth when you do. Imagine if many aligned beings placed this kind of focus on the financial markets or their investments or any number of aspects that impact your world or that you are a part of. It will take alignment above all, it will take being aligned to your Highest Self above all. And when you are aligned with your Highest Self above all and you place your focus on whatever is before you as only being in the Highest Good, that will be your experience.

We are not ones to encourage you to seek out bad news or situations filled with discord to practice this. But we are encouraging that if you ever find yourself in a situation or in front of or hearing about something that is not in the Highest Alignment, that you can – through your aligned state – call forth the Highest Good for all involved.

Practice this, notice what happens as you begin to bring your powerful focused intention into whatever is before you. Watch in awe as you recognize the power of your focused thought and of your vibration. Watch in amazement as your life continues to yield to you greater and greater abundance from your intention of the Highest Good for all before you. Heather often talks about the ripple effect from alignment and yes, that is true, *and* you can be even more conscious in how you impact the world and this is one powerful way to do so.

XoTheJOGs

YOU ARE HERE TO LIVE RICH

In these times of great expansion many of you are hearing the Call. You are hearing the Call of that deeper part of you that is inviting you to experience life in new ways and at new levels. Gone are the days that you expect or days that do not fill you up in the way that you most deserve to feel filled. We are intending for all of you a truly Rich life. A life filled with the joy and expansion that you most Love to experience in your life experience.

Much is said about your word Rich and much is thought about it, too. That somehow this word has become tainted by stories about what it means for one to be Rich in their Spirit in a body experience. We want to talk about the richness, the true richness that all are genuinely seeking for and how you can bring that into your experience with much ease and grace.

Rich living is not merely about money. This is the message we will give to you over and over again. Far too much is made out of money and its place in your life. Yes, it is the form of exchange that you use to experience more freedom in your life. Yes, that is true. But if you were to place your focus on the other areas that truly make a life rich, then the money would flow to you with ease and there would be nothing for you to worry about. It is your focus on money and its lack or not-enough-ness that repels it from your experience, just as we have described happens with anything that you put an intense, "must have" focus on.

So when we are talking about living a rich life we are talking about your opportunity to live the fullest, richest life experience. A life that contains all of the aspects and elements that most light you up. And so you are here at this point in time on your journey with an opportunity to live in the fullness of *You*. That's where we desire for you to start. Starting with the fullness of You. Starting with getting clear about what fills you up. What does a rich life look like for you?

Heather has written about and talked about her own journey with this. She thought prior to our direct involvement in her life experience that the words rich and wealth were focused solely on cash-money as she calls it. And what she has learned through her connection with us is that that is not the case at all. That is one aspect, and a tiny aspect we will say of what it truly means to live a wealthy, rich life. Do not misunderstand as we can feel many of you are bristling to this – cash-money as Heather calls it will be with you in wondrous amounts, but only when you follow the principles outlined, meaning you release your intent focus on having to have the money and needing it and aching for it. It is just like anything you desire in your life experience, it will flow to you when you can relax into the knowing that it is yours to have already and all you need do is allow it in.

But again, we want your focus to be on what fills you up. Make a list, take time to reflect on it. Take yourself out in nature and ask yourself – what fills me up? What lights up my path? What makes me most come alive? Who are the people I most desire to experience this life with? Get clear about these areas. Get clear about what a Rich life looks like for you. Let it flow to you. Write it down, feel it throughout your body and then consciously and intentionally begin to take action to bring this into your life.

One thing Heather was surprised to uncover about herself is that Rich living for her meant having nicer things. She has never been one to like or desire things. In fact, she had been pretty proud of this fact. She has always been one who spent her money on experiences and things were just things to her of little or no matter. Over time she is feeling called to upgrade her things. To bring in higher quality and more aligned representations of what feels good to her. Her home, she carefully crafted as an oasis and recently she has felt the pull to make that even more true. Noticing that the vibration of the things she had before – either purchased on discount or gifted to her – no longer felt aligned to her. That what made her feel rich was being in environments that reflected that back to her and that included her home. This was not something she ever imagined would be true for her. But it is and she is having a lot of fun feeling the vibrational alignment with things, when this had been an area she had disregarded all of her life.

Now this may not be the case for you, as all of you are unique, beautiful beings on your own beautiful and inspiring path. But we share this example to allow you to really go to new places here with this. What does Rich living look like to you? What does it feel like? And how can you bring that into your experience now?

Heather is laughing about this latest expansion for her and saying that she blames the flowers. She tuned in to the fact that she felt rich when she had fresh cut flowers in every room in her home. And then after months of that, she realized she needed to then upgrade the vibration of the things in her home. So you see, it all is always expanding and evolving and when you take action in the direction of this Rich life that you are here for, sometimes just as simple – we are not joking here – as simple as bringing in fresh cut flowers or as big as buying a new car or changing the nature of your investments –

taking the action to bring this into manifestation will make all of the difference.

We want and we are always advocating for you to be clear first and foremost about who you are and what is most important to you at a Soul, core You level. You know what is most important to you by the way it feels. By how "yes" it feels above all. And then, in that "yes" place action must be taken. And that action will elevate you to new heights in embodying and living a life of more and greater wealth.

We will continue to work with you here on this as we expand your understanding and all of consciousness's understanding of what true wealth is and what it means to truly live rich. Start here, begin to get a clearer picture on what Rich living is to you and yes, we hear some of you asking this, yes you can include the numbers in your bank account. Just release the need to perseverate on any of these aspects. Notice them and take the easiest actions you can take to bring them into being. Then notice the next piece and take actions to bring those in and so on.

And from there, once you are in this expanded place, we will share more with you in the transmissions to come.

In Love,
XoTheJOGs

A CHECKLIST OF HIGHEST ALIGNMENT

In this Divine time that you are living, there are many opportunities available to you to shine your Light more brightly, to embrace and claim your Highest Path and Soul's Purpose and to live at a level of wealth consciousness that far exceeds what you've been culturally or religiously or in any other way conditioned with. You are standing on a precipice of huge expansion and huge possibility. And this is not meant to overwhelm or frighten you, this is meant to enliven you, to activate that deep Soul call within that is yearning to step forward and be leading the charge.

Yet some feel overwhelmed or paralyzed by the possibilities that stand before them. They desire to push on with the way things are, afraid of what may come from what is calling to them. And so often they dig their heels in and shy away from their true path and purpose. And we understand and acknowledge that it may not feel "easy" to take the actions needed to line your life up in all ways with your Highest Path. But we will tell you that this fear is unnecessary. Because what you will find is that yes, if you are way, way, way far out of alignment with your Highest Path, the steps you sometimes need to take to be brought back into alignment can create the need for some significant clean-up in your life. However, once you are in greater alignment with your Highest Path and Purpose your life feels better than it's ever felt. Your days are more easeful, your relationships more joyous, the money just flows to you – in fact, all manner of things just flow to you. And this is the way that you originally intended to live.

Yet nowhere in your conditioning set you up for this. But one of the reasons why this time in the world is so exciting is that more and more of you are coming to know this, and so you are raising your children with these knowings and giving them this wisdom, and then a whole new wave of impact is being put into place so that more and more than ever than even now will live more fully their experience as a Spirit in a body. More and more will live lives that look like Magic and miracles and yet are the product of a Soul aligned life.

226

It is not a stretch to think or imagine that this will one day be the experience for all.

But in the meantime you may ask, what are we to do when that fear and the stubbornness seems to lock us up and keep us from the bounty and the truth and the beauty that awaits.

And we say – first you must see it within yourself. Sometimes it is helpful for a trusted advisor or teacher or mentor to gently point this out to you, sometimes the action must be more significant to allow you to see that you may be inadvertently stymieing up what wants to be known and experienced by and through you. If you sense that this may be the case for you – ask someone you work with as a practitioner or someone who knows you at a deep level what their take is on this. Try to ask someone who can be more objective with you.

The willingness to expand into your Highest Path and Purpose is the energy that leads you forward. When you notice unwillingness or unreadiness you have an opportunity to shift yourself into a more willing place. But this is not something that can be done for you, it is something that you must be willing to do for yourself once you see and know it, and once it has been made clear to you.

Others of you are so worried that you are sabotaging yourselves that you are constantly tracking and checking your progress which also slows you down.

It is this fine balance for you all of being aware, balanced and ease-ful, yet still taking focused action to lead you forward.

There are so many gifts available to you in this lifetime, gifts that you must claim in order to experience the fullness of them. And we do not mean specifically say, "I want this___," as we have shared with you that being overly specific can create mis-aligned manifestations. You need only be willing to receive and then, as we have shared before, be focused on creating an environment that will allow your Highest Path & Purpose to flow to you in all manner of ways.

You can checklist through your life and see – what is currently in alignment with my Highest Path & Purpose? Be sure to take a moment and celebrate yourself, celebrate your ability to bring any area of your life into alignment with your Higher Self and your Highest Path & Purpose. This is the way of all of the great Masters. This is the way of once few and now many more than ever before. After that, check in – what is not yet in alignment with my Highest Self – write that out too. Is there an action you can take today or this week that could bring you closer into alignment on these areas of your life? The more aligned aspects of your life with your Highest Path & Purpose, the more ease and joy and relaxation and abundance you will experience in your life.

These are relatively simple processes that we give to you time and again, and yet they have big impact in your ability to live a life of your dreams. To live the life you most desired to live when you first came here to live the life that only you can live because there is only one of you in all of the Universe.

We are so desiring for you to experience the fullness of having more and more and soon every area of your life in the Highest alignment. And then passing on these tools and skills to your children while showcasing what a Soul aligned life looks like has the capacity to support the ripple effect of future and future generations in living the wealthy, rich, Soul aligned life that all are here for.

Enjoy this reveal as you "checklist" the various areas of your life and watch as your focused intention on bringing specific aspects into alignment will shift the energy and experience of it – almost immediately.

And so it is.
XoTheJOGs

ACKNOWLEDGEMENTS

First and foremost I have to thank the JOGs. These five non-physical energies whom I "met" at the John of God Casa in Brazil in 2013 have saved me. They have made me a better woman, a better human being, a better Spirit in a body than I could have ever imagined myself to be. I Love you JOGs more than words and I seriously thank Source for the gift that you are in my life every single day. And I know you know all of this already of course, because you are right there with me through this life experience. I would not and could not be who I am without you. Thank you, thank you – eternally and forevermore.

Huge gratitude to my sister, Alison, who has been such a profound support to me as I went through all of the incredible shifts that bringing through these transmissions from the JOGs has brought in my life and into so many lives. Thank you for believing in me Ali, and being the best sister a girl could ask for.

Thank you to Rebecca and Alison E. for being my ladies to call when transmissions were coming through fast and furious and I had no idea what to do with it all, and for always being so loving and supportive as we navigate this Spirit-led journey together.

Thank you to Janet Galipo who has been supporting me with BodyTalk sessions (whenever the JOGs would allow it, that is) from day one on this journey. Your support has been instrumental during this powerfully intense time in my life.

Thank you to my amazing Magic Maker community that now spans the globe. I Love each of you and it is so incredible to see this "work" transform and uplift your lives as it does mine.

Thank you to my assistant, Audrey, who designed this beautiful cover, edited this book alongside me and who allows me to stay in my Zone of Genius so that I can do this "work" in the world. I Love you girl, and I'm so grateful to have you on my team. Thank you a million times over. The JOGs and I are blowing you kisses!

Thank you to everyone in my life who has truly supported me and believed in me as I travel this path less taken. I am so in awe of what my life has become and I am so curious where it is leading me and all of us to next...

With bounteous Love & Magic,
XoHeather

ESPECIALLY FOR YOU…

If you would like to stay in regular communication with Heather & the JOGs and receive a free energetic toolkit to support your Spirit-Led Living expansion, sign-up here: bit.ly/1C7y6CR

TELL OTHERS!

Did you Love this book? Has it transformed your life? Is it now a regular part of your daily spiritual practice? Tell the world about it with an Amazon review. Reviews make all of the difference especially with this level of leading edge work, and myself and the JOGs would so appreciate your kind words.

ADDITIONAL BOOKS BY HEATHER STRANG:

The Quest: A Tale of Desire & Magic
http://amzn.to/1Ngr4E4

Think True Love & Spirituality can't be hot?

For 30-year-old Kathryn Casey, merging the two has developed into a lifelong quest. A mind-blowing psychic prophecy sends Kathryn on a journey that melds meditation and wine, the Amazon and New Zealanders, hot sex and dark chocolate, and psychic healings complete with strappy sandals.

The Quest delves into the core of one woman's search for great love. This novel follows Kathryn throughout rainy Portland, OR, as she attempts to capture what she desires most, while avoiding the treacherous pitfalls of self-sabotage.

When Kathryn assumes she's found "The One" prophesized to enter her life, the Universe works tirelessly to bring her experiences and synchronicities that force her to think for herself. Along the way, she's visited by new and old friends alike who remind her that finding "The One" requires deeper insight into the self. Armed with this knowledge, Kathryn makes a shocking discovery that forces her to reconsider everything she thought to be true — from her lifelong quest to her desire to bypass motherhood.

Following Bliss
http://amzn.to/1QmIMWx

Get up at seven in the morning. Take shower. Go to work at Hello Portland. Pick up gluten-free cupcakes for Laney's party. Receive messages from the other side. Attempt to relay said messages to a sexy stranger. Get rejected.

This was not Shelby Hanson's typical to-do list. But it was exactly what was on the agenda for her one early fall day in Portland, Ore. Across town, Daniel Tillman was attempting his own impossible to-do list—to write a historical fiction novel with enough pizazz to win the heart of one of the nation's top literary agents, Kaley Hamilton, at the Willamette Writers Conference.

To an outsider, Shelby and Daniel's daily activities may appear ludicrous at best. In truth, they're both being led to love, romance and some wild nights in Maui.

Bet you didn't see that one coming…

Following Bliss gives readers a sneak peek into how who we love is often carefully orchestrated by the other side. Experience the fear, the excitement and the romance that causes Shelby and Daniel to collide into one another, and into the next chapter of their lives. Along the way, they lean on the support of Kathryn and Scott from *The Quest: A Tale of Desire & Magic*.

Following Bliss truly takes readers on a ride of romance and intrigue along with some sexy sightseeing. Mixing in chick-lit, visionary fiction and a side of paranormal romance—*Following Bliss* proves that there's so much more behind why we choose who we love.

And Then It Was You
http://amzn.to/1M9aG9K

31-year-old Allie Strauss thought she had found true love.

But when her husband of five years ends their marriage over breakfast one Thursday morning, Allie's world is turned upside down.

She is thrust into a dark night of the Soul and re-emerges with new highlights, a seriously up-leveled wardrobe and a new attitude that makes even her once skeptical self believe in the Law of Attraction.

In an unprecedented move, Allie gallivants down to the Gulf Coast away from the safety of her home and family in Oceanside, Oregon & winds up in the arms of a sexy stranger.

Allie's magical journey reminds her and all of us that when it comes to true love everyone wins – even when everything is on the line.

Printed in Great Britain
by Amazon